Of Seeds and the People of God

Of Seeds and the People of God

Preaching as Parable, Crucifixion, and Testimony

MICHAEL P. KNOWLES

Foreword by
Paul Scott Wilson

CASCADE *Books* • Eugene, Oregon

OF SEEDS AND THE PEOPLE OF GOD
Preaching as Parable, Crucifixion, and Testimony

Copyright © 2015 Michael P. Knowles. All rights reserved. Except for brief quotations in critical publications or reviews, no part of this book may be reproduced in any manner without prior written permission from the publisher. Write: Permissions. Wipf and Stock Publishers, 199 W. 8th Ave., Suite 3, Eugene, OR 97401.

Cascade Books
An Imprint of Wipf and Stock Publishers
199 W. 8th Ave., Suite 3
Eugene, OR 97401

www.wipfandstock.com

ISBN 13: 978-1-62564-820-4

Cataloguing-in-Publication Data

Knowles, Michael P.

Of seeds and the people of God : preaching as parable, crucifixion, and testimony / Michael P. Knowles.

xxiv + 264 p. ; 23 cm. Includes bibliographical references and indexes.

ISBN 13: 978-1-62564-820-4

1. Preaching. 2. Jesus Christ—Parables—Homiletical use. 3. Bible. Gospels—Criticsm, interpretation, etc. I. Title.

BV4211 .K55 2015

Manufactured in the USA.   03/11/2015

Contents

Foreword by Paul Scott Wilson | vii
Acknowledgments | xi
Texts and Abbreviations | xiii
Permissions | xvii
Introduction: Words, and the Word of God | xix

PART ONE: GOD'S FIELD

CHAPTER 1
Parables, and Parables of Growth:
Who Has Ploughed These Fields Before Us? | 3

CHAPTER 2
"I Will Watch over Them to Build and to Plant":
Nature and Nation in the World of Jesus' Day | 21

CHAPTER 3
"Consider the Lilies": Reading Jesus' Agricultural Parables | 40

PART TWO: GOD'S BODY, GOD'S BUILDING

CHAPTER 4
"Not with Plausible Words of Wisdom":
Preaching Shaped by the Cross | 89

PART THREE: GOD'S WORD

CHAPTER 5
"We Speak of What We Know and Testify to What We Have Seen":
Homiletics as Testimony | 135

CHAPTER 6
"God's Field, God's Laborers":
Preaching as Parabolic Testimony to the Grace of God | 178

Appendix A: Questions for Preachers | 213
Appendix B: Sermons | 215

Bibliography | 235
Ancient Document Index | 249
Name Index | 263

Foreword

In January 1996, the Hubble telescope examined a tiny spot in the night sky no bigger than a pinhead to the naked eye. The Hubble Deep Field image looks remarkably like the night sky with countless stars as seen by the naked eye. In actual fact, however, that picture is of the farthest limits of the universe, and when computers zoom in on that image, what look like individual stars are in fact hundreds of individual galaxies like our own Milky Way. The light that we currently see from them began its journey 10 billion years ago, which is how far away they are. Scientists tell us that that infinitesimally small spot in the sky is not unusual for what it discloses. In all there are hundreds of billions of galaxies in the entire universe and billions of planets that likely could, like ours, support life.

Such numbers are incomprehensible. Albert Einstein is claimed to have said, "Once you can accept the universe as matter expanding into nothing that is something, wearing stripes with plaid comes easy." It is hard for us humans to imagine that the world we see and experience each day, filled as it is with so much activity and so many people, each with their own stories, is so tiny—how small we each are and how much tinier even than a pinpoint is an individual lifespan in terms of the billions of years of creation. For some people, like myself, such contemplation can yield conflicting emotions: wonder and awe yet also a deep and primitive kind of anxiety. It is countered by wonder and awe of another sort, the knowledge that comes through faith in a God who sees the sparrow fall and counts even the hairs on our heads.

Contemplation of this sort may come close to what Michael Knowles prescribes as necessary for all preachers. Only by embracing our utter insignificance can we begin to encounter the possibility of preaching. We put aside any presumption of spiritual authority, strip ourselves of any claim to be able to speak God's word, discount the years of education and training in preparation for the preaching task—in fact we must yield to our complete human inadequacy to preach, in order to preach. The Word that we preach is not a Bible text, it is the person of Jesus Christ, who can only be known by entering his crucifixion, and receiving from him through the Spirit the life-giving power of his resurrection.

Many biblical texts support the notion of dying to self and living for Christ. It is a common New Testament theme, and many Christians identify it with baptism, not preaching. Paul says in Romans 6:4, "Therefore we have been buried with him by baptism into death, so that, just as Christ was raised from the dead by the glory of the Father, so we too might walk in newness of life." In Galatians 2:20 he says, "It is no longer I who live, but it is Christ who lives in me. And the life I now live in the flesh I live by faith in the Son of God." Jesus says in John 12:24, "Very truly, I tell you, unless a grain of wheat falls into the earth and dies, it remains just a single grain; but if it dies, it bears much fruit." First Peter 1:23 echoes this imagery and links it to rebirth: "You have been born anew, not of perishable but of imperishable seed, through the living and enduring word of God." Baptism and anointing with the Spirit lies behind Jesus' words in John 3:3, "Very truly, I tell you, no one can see the kingdom of God without being born from above" (or "born again" KJV), and 3:5–6, "Very truly, I tell you, no one can enter the kingdom of God without being born of water and Spirit. What is born of the flesh is flesh, and what is born of the Spirit is spirit."

Dying to self and living for Christ extends explicitly beyond baptism and spiritual anointing to discipleship and ministry when Jesus says in Luke 9:23, "If any want to become my followers, let them deny themselves and take up their cross daily and follow me." Perhaps the closest that the Bible comes to connecting dying to self and living for Christ with preaching is in the link to martyrdom or witness, as in Mark 8:35, "For those who want to save their life will lose it, and those who lose their life for my sake, and for the sake of the gospel, will save it."

Michael Knowles takes this idea further. In what Jesus said in his parables of seeds and wheat, vineyards and fields, Knowles finds reason to extend the notion of dying to self to the act of preaching. All Christians must pick up their crosses and follow wherever Christ leads, yet can it be that preachers encounter something of this notion each time they preach? Seeds are utterly dependent upon God. As a people of God, we are like seeds requiring God's life-giving provisions for us to produce. As preachers, we hear and receive the seed of God's Word, and yield to what Knowles calls "the life-giving prerogative of God." God alone has life-giving power. Knowles encourages preachers to cultivate "learned theological helplessness." Ministry will rely on "willing inability and loving reliance" for its success. By yielding any claim to be able to sustain our own lives, we give over our trust to God to provide what is needed.

Preachers are no different from other Christians except in being set apart for their task through call, examination, and ordination. It is a fresh thought, however, that preachers in an additional way encounter dying to self and living for Christ in a manner that is peculiar to their task. Preachers have long known that even as their task can be energizing, it can also be draining. Preachers in my grandparents' generation used to compare the energy needed to deliver a sermon to the energy needed to run a marathon (sermons tended to be longer then). In the sense that preachers give to the task "their all," preaching is a kind of dying. Preachers must also die to self in their sermons by entering the places of suffering and death, to lift up the cries of the people and minister the gospel to them. Proclamation of the words of good news at the heart of the gospel requires that preachers to a large extent give up any notions of their own identity in order to speak the costly words Christ says to the people, "in this moment, you are mine, I died for you, I forgive you, I will be with you always . . ."

Preaching involves a self-emptying *(kenosis)* in the manner of Christ in Philippians 2:5–7, "Let the same mind be in you that was in Christ Jesus, who, though he was in the form of God, did not regard equality with God as something to be exploited, but emptied himself, taking the form of a slave." In doing this we echo the words and actions of John the Baptist in relation to Jesus, "He must increase, but I must decrease" (John 3:30). The role of witness functions in service of One who is greater and in whom the power of the Word is acknowledged. The human words we offer in a sermon themselves must die in the moment of delivery; they are but dying sounds, yet by their offering faith comes to life. As Paul says, "So faith comes from what is heard, and what is heard comes through the word of Christ" (Rom 10:17). The preacher's role dies as the deliverer of that Word and is taken up by the Spirit who ushers that Word to completion in the life and work of the body of Christ, kneeling in service to the world.

This kind of death to self is the opposite of what many people, especially women, have been falsely taught about being invisible and for whom death to self is oppressive. The death to self that comes from Spirit-assisted *kenosis* is the sort that brings us all more fully to whom God intends us to be, conformed to the image of Christ. We are utterly distinct and loved for who we are, yet all that is beautiful in us is enhanced by its likeness to Christ and our willingness to witness in words and deeds on his behalf.

Alla Renée Bozarth speaks of *kenosis*, "The self-aware ego places us in a subject-object relationship not only to others but to ourselves. . . . The way out of the ego is through attention toward others, especially through intense concentration on an *Other.*"[1] *Kenosis* for her is accompanied with *plerosis*, or being filled by the Spirit, as two movements of a single process: "But the interpreter never ceases to remain a person. There is no loss of consciousness or self in interpretation, but only of self-consciousness and ego-centric self, in order to reveal the true self so that it can become engaged with the poem. Kenosis for the interpreter is a loving attitude of humility and nonresistance toward the text."[2] Bozarth implies that preaching as dying is only a part of the story in that new identity is received. If baptism is dying to the old self to be born again, sanctification is a continuing action of dying to old ways of being in order to become whom the Holy Spirit empowers us to be.

In faith, words of testimony to the central good news of the Christ event become resurrection words. The Spirit gives them new life in the listeners. As they receive them they are filled by the Spirit and begin to enact their personal and communal ministries to the world. This is the ongoing process of the Word becoming flesh, that all people may see the glory of God and share in God's generous, loving, and just provision for all. The preacher, looking ahead, entrusts the sermon to God for its life. Jesus says, "See, I am making all things new" (Rev 21:5). The preacher, looking ahead, knows that the final end is none other than Jesus Christ as the ultimate fulfillment of all the promises of God, to which each sermon contributes. Charles Bartow once commented, "We are eschatologically, not ontologically, determined. The future . . . is fixed in Christ. . . . In him God is present for us, and in him we are present for God."[3]

Knowles speaks of preachers practicing and participating in a ministry of resurrection in which preaching becomes an embodiment of God's realm. The parables evoke a theology of divine providence and encourage hearers to rely upon the power of a God who is generous beyond measure in calling life from death. In a post-Christian era such as our own, when many churches struggle and look for new ways to draw others in, Knowles's reframing of preaching is so compelling: "Every human effort to expound the things of God must recognize its own inadequacy—even fail and fall silent—before it can be authenticated by the One of whom it speaks."

Paul Scott Wilson
Emmanuel College of Victoria University in the University of Toronto
March 17, 2014

---

1. Bozarth, *The Word's Body*, 86.
2. Ibid., 90.
3. Bartow, *The Preaching Moment*, 50.

Acknowledgments

It is well to acknowledge one's debts, especially when they cannot be adequately repaid. I am grateful to President Stanley Porter and the Senate of McMaster Divinity College for granting a year of research leave that permitted sufficient time and freedom from other responsibilities for the completion of this project. By way of more specific contribution, Dustin Boreland, Adam Brown, David Courey, Aaron Gerrard, Matt Lowe, Sandra Smith, and Tommy Tsui have each offered invaluable criticisms in response to earlier drafts of the manuscript; their probing comments have challenged and clarified my thinking so as, I trust, to render this study more helpful and relevant to readers than would otherwise have been the case.

Texts and Abbreviations

Unless otherwise indicated, biblical texts in English are cited from the New Revised Standard Version. Hebrew and Greek texts are cited from Karl Elliger, et al., eds., *Biblia Hebraica Stuttgartensia*, 5th Corrected Edition (Stuttgart: Deutsche Bibelgesellschaft, 1997); Alfred Rahlfs, ed., *Septuaginta* (Stuttgart: Württembergische Bibelanstalt/Deutsche Bibelgesellschaft, 1935); and Kurt Aland, et al., eds., *The Greek New Testament*, 4th Revised Edition (Stuttgart: Deutsche Bibelgesellschaft, 1994), initially accessed via Gramcord for Windows 2.3 (Vancouver, WA: Gramcord Institute, 1998). Abbreviations for biblical books, translations, reference works, and journals follow the protocols indicated by Patrick H. Alexander, et al., eds., *The SBL Handbook of Style For Ancient Near Eastern, Biblical, and Christian Studies* (Peabody, MA: Hendrickson, 1999).

ABD   *The Anchor Bible Dictionary.* Edited by David Noel Freedman. 6 vols. New York: Doubleday, 1992.

CD   *Church Dogmatics.* Karl Barth. Translated by G. W. Bromiley. 14 vols. Edinburgh: T & T Clark, 1956–1981.

GNT   *Good News Translation.* Today's English Version, 2nd ed. New York: American Bible Society, 1992.

JB   *The Jerusalem Bible: Reader's Edition.* Garden City, NY: Doubleday, 1966, 1968, 1976.

L&N   *Greek-English Lexicon of the New Testament: Based on Semantic Domains.* Edited by J. P. Louw and E. A. Nida. 2nd ed. New York: United Bible Societies, 1989.

NASB   *The New American Standard Bible.* La Habra, CA: The Lockman Foundation, 1995.

NEB   *The New English Bible, with the Apocrypha.* New York: Oxford, 1970.

NIV *The Holy Bible: New International Version.* New York: New York International Bible Society, 1978.

NJPS *Tanakh: The Holy Scriptures. The New JPS Translation According to the Traditional Hebrew Text.* Philadelphia: Jewish Publication Society, 1985.

NRSV *New Revised Standard Version Bible.* New York: Division of Christian Education of the National Council of the Churches of Christ in the United States of America, 1989.

OTP *Old Testament Pseudepigrapha.* Edited by James H. Charlesworth. 2 vols. New York: Doubleday, 1983/1985.

RSV *Revised Standard Version Bible, Second Edition.* New York: Division of Christian Education of the National Council of the Churches of Christ in the United States of America, 1971.

TDNT *Theological Dictionary of the New Testament.* Edited by Gerhard Kittel and Gerhard Friedrich. Translated by Geoffrey W. Bromiley. 10 vols. Grand Rapids: Eerdmans, 1964–1976.

TDOT *Theological Dictionary of the Old Testament.* Edited by G. Johannes Botterweck and Helmer Ringgren. Translated by Geoffrey W. Bromiley, et al. 14 vols. Grand Rapids: Eerdmans, 1974–2004.

TNIV *The Holy Bible: Today's New International Version.* Colorado Springs: International Bible Society, 2001, 2005.

ABBREVIATIONS FOR ANCIENT SOURCES AND TEXTS

1 En.	*1 Enoch*
1 Clem.	*1 Clement*
1Q21	Aramaic Testament of Levi (Qumran)
1QH	Thanksgiving Hymns (Qumran)
1QIsa^a	Isaiah Scroll (Qumran)
11Q ApPs^a	11Q Apocryphal Psalms^a (Qumran)
2 Bar.	*2 Baruch (Syriac Apocalypse)*
4 Ezra	*Fourth Ezra*
4QMMT	Sectarian Manifesto (Qumran)
'Abot R. Nat.	*'Abot de Rabbi Nathan*

Alleg. Interp.	Philo of Alexandria, *Allegorical Interpretation*
Ant.	Josephus, *Jewish Antiquities*
Apol.	Justin Martyr, *First Apology*
b.	Babylonian Talmud
B. Meṣiʿa	*Baba Meṣiʿa*
B. Qam.	*Baba Qamma*
Ber.	*Berakot*
Cher.	Philo of Alexandria, *De cherubim* (*On the Cherubim*)
Comm. Matt.	Origen, *Commentarium in evangelium Matthaei* (*Commentary on the Gospel of Matthew*)
Deut. Rab.	*Deuteronomy Rabbah*
Fin.	Cicero, *De Finibus Bonorum et Malorum* (*On the Ends of Good and Evil*)
Flacc.	Philo of Alexandria, *In Flaccum* (*Against Flaccus*)
Gen. Rab.	*Genesis Rabbah*
Hist.	Tacitus, *Historiae* (*Histories*)
Hist. Plant.	Theophrastus, *De Historia Plantarum* (*Concerning the History of Plants*)
Jub.	*Jubilees*
Ketub.	*Ketubbot*
Kil.	*Kilʾayim*
LXX	Septuagint
m.	Mishnah
Mid.	*Middot*
Mut.	Philo of Alexandria, *De mutatione nominum* (*On the Change of Names*)

Nat.	Pliny the Elder, *Naturalis historia* (*Natural History*)
Naz.	*Nazir*
Ned.	*Nedarim*
Nid.	*Niddah*
Num. Rab.	*Numbers Rabbah*
Oct.	Minucius Felix, *Octavius*
Pr. Man.	*Prayer of Manasseh*
Pss. Sol.	*Psalms of Solomon*
QG	Philo of Alexandria, *Quaestiones et solutiones in Genesin* (*Questions and Answers on Genesis*)
Rerum Rust.	Marcus Terentius Varro, *Rerum Rusticarum Libri Tres* (*Three Books on Agriculture*)
Rust.	Columella, *De Re Rustica* (*On Agriculture*)
Sam. Tg.	*Samaritan Targum*
Sib. Or.	*Sibylline Oracles*
Spec. Leg.	Philo of Alexandria, *De Specialibus Legibus* (*On the Special Laws*)
t.	*Tosefta*
T. Ab.	*Testament of Abraham*
T. Levi	*Testament of Levi*
T. Mos.	*Testament of Moses*
Taʿan.	*Taʿanit*
Ṭehar.	*Ṭeharot*
Tg. Neof.	*Targum Neofiti*
Verr.	Cicero, *In Verrum* (*Against Verres*)
War	Josephus, *The Jewish War*

Permissions

Michael P. Knowles, "Abel, Cain, and the Judgment of Jesus," *Homily Service* 43.3 (April, 2010) 96–99, reprinted by permission of Taylor & Francis LLC, www.tandfonline.com.

Scripture quotations marked (GNT) are from the *Good News Translation* in Today's English Version—Second Edition. Copyright © 1992 by American Bible Society. Used by Permission.

Scripture quotations marked (JB) are from *The Jerusalem Bible*, copyright © 1966, 1968, 1976 by Darton, Longman & Todd, Ltd. and Doubleday, a division of Bantam Doubleday Dell Publishing Group, Inc., and used by permission of the publishers.

Tanakh: The Holy Scriptures. The New JPS Translation According to the Traditional Hebrew Text. Philadelphia: Jewish Publication Society, 1985.

Scripture quotations taken from the New American Standard Bible®, copyright © 1960, 1962, 1963, 1968, 1971, 1972, 1973, 1975, 1977, 1995 by The Lockman Foundation. Used by permission. (www.Lockman.org)

Scripture quotations taken from the New English Bible, copyright © Cambridge University Press and Oxford University Press 1961, 1970. All rights reserved.

Scripture quotations marked (NIV) are taken from the Holy Bible, New International Version®, NIV®. Copyright © 1973, 1978, 1984, 2011 by Biblica, Inc.™ Used by permission of Zondervan. All rights reserved worldwide. www.zondervan.com. The "NIV" and "New International Version" are trademarks registered in the United States Patent and Trademark Office by Biblica, Inc.™

New Revised Standard Version Bible, copyright 1989, Division of Christian Education of the National Council of the Churches of Christ in the United States of America. Used by permission. All rights reserved.

Revised Standard Version of the Bible, copyright 1952 [2nd edition, 1971] by the Division of Christian Education of the National Council of the Churches of Christ in the United States of America. Used by permission. All rights reserved.

Scripture taken from the *Holy Bible, Today's New International Version*®. TNIV®.

Copyright © 2001, 2005 by International Bible Society. Used by permission of Zondervan. All rights reserved worldwide.

Introduction
Words, and the Word of God

"How-to" books on preaching are not lacking. There are (broadly speaking) books on "How to Preach to Strangers," "How to Preach to Postmoderns," "How to Preach from Scripture," "How to Preach from Parables"—how to preach, in short, from any number of different angles. However odd or unexpected it may seem in contrast to all these other books, this one is at least partly about how *not* to preach. The argument proposed here is that preaching is, in the most important sense of all, a humanly impossible task: it is not something that we can effectively undertake on our own. Newly minted preachers set out to persuade, convince, and encourage their hearers. Yet after only a few years (although for some it takes many more, and others never quite arrive at this insight), midcareer preachers often discover that the sermons they labor so hard to produce are no longer especially persuasive, convincing, or encouraging, even to themselves. Any preacher who doubts this need only look back at their own sermon manuscripts from a year or two prior. Personal experience reveals that, with very few exceptions, sermons of which I was quite confident at the time sound bland, banal, sometimes even embarrassing in retrospect. Strangely, they did not (always!) seem so at the time I preached them, either to myself or to others. Since it is hard to imagine that hindsight alone is the consistent source of this change in perspective, there must be some other explanation. Perhaps it is the fact that effective sermons consist of far more than notes on a cue card or mere words from the pulpit. This book is about how the true source of persuasion, conviction, encouragement, and sometimes even transformation lies largely outside ourselves. The chapters that follow attempt to explain how and why this is so, both biblically and theologically, adding practical suggestions for preaching in a manner that comes to terms with the limitations of human endeavor.

The main argument of the following study concerns theology and spirituality rather than structure or form: it is that Christian preaching at its most potent simply bears witness to the life-giving power of God. Although this sounds simple enough, in practice it is made immeasurably more complex by the fact that our model for undertaking such a task is Jesus of Nazareth. We have to reckon not only with Jesus' actual teaching about God as the giver of life (that is, the life-giving reign or "kingdom of God"), but also with his personal example, his paradoxical embodiment of the manner in which God bestows the gift of life on a broken and dying creation. Even if we only want to preach *about* Jesus, but all the more so if we are to preach *like* Jesus, we will find ourselves drawn into his death before it becomes possible to proclaim the implications of his life. It is not simply that participation in Jesus' death and resurrection is a *prior* condition for effective preaching—that preachers need first to be soundly converted and alive in Christ—but that ongoing imitation of his death and resurrection is a necessary *present* condition for preaching that is faithful to him.

According to the standards by which the endeavors of church and academy are divided into strictly separate sub-disciplines, this study attempts too much by far. It contains detailed exegesis of numerous texts from both biblical testaments; it discusses ancient Jewish perspectives on the natural world, the spiritual theology of Saint Paul, Augustine's theories of meaning, Luther's *theologia crucis*, Walter Brueggemann on biblical theology, the hermeneutics of Paul Ricoeur, and Jacques Ellul on the impact of technology. Not least, it comments extensively on the practice and purpose of homiletics. By rights, proper treatment of each topic requires a book of its own (and many of these are cited in the accompanying footnotes). Yet however different, the three essential components of this study—scriptural exegesis, theological interpretation, and practical application—reflect three aspects of the weekly process out of which the Sunday sermon typically emerges. Whether consciously or not, preachers examine the biblical text within the framework of a specific theology, and from the viewpoint of a particular spiritual outlook shape any resulting insights according to a concrete and practical rhetorical strategy. This combination of theology, spirituality, exegesis, and methodology (along with much else) inspires a creative ferment that may—eventually!—produce a manuscript fit for preaching. For this reason, it seems only appropriate to address more than one aspect of the homiletical process, even if this means transgressing the boundaries of distinct academic disciplines, all the more so as these different elements cannot fail to have a powerful and mutual impact on one another.

It is fashionable to complain that preaching is in trouble these days, as I myself have done more than a few times. But despite our cultural preoccupation with such issues, I am not convinced that our main problem is one of language, structure, or technique: the renewal of preaching does not require us—at least as the first item on our agenda—to tinker with the exercise of preaching itself. No doubt the valiant members of the ship's band, playing "Nearer My God to Thee" as the RMS *Titanic* sank beneath the North Atlantic waves, had all taken care to tune their instruments, perhaps even to polish the brass until it shone. No doubt they were without exception skilled musicians, maintained the proper tempo, played the correct musical notes, and faithfully followed the flourishes of the conductor's baton. Some, apparently, enjoyed the added benefit of being devout Methodists. But none of these brave efforts kept the stricken ship afloat or prevented the players from drowning, shiny instruments and all. The analogy to preaching—at least within foundering mainline denominations of the post-Christian West—should prove instructive. Basic attention to principles of logic, structure, and the rules of grammar will, of course, aid effective communication from the pulpit. Arresting illustrations will doubtless make the preacher's message (such as it is) more memorable. But as I tell my students in their introductory homiletics course, most of them have many years left in which to discover their preferred method of sermon delivery, or to hone their skills in composition and verbal expression. In the meantime, however, theological content and godly purpose are more pressing issues. Neophyte preachers first need to discover something worth saying, something that their congregations might even be willing to heed.

In this we have much to learn from the manner in which Jesus himself testified concerning the ways of God. To indulge in an illuminating play on words, Jesus' language is consistently "parabolic," not only in the sense that he tells parables, but also because (especially for those as yet unclear about his identity) his teaching functions like a parabola, capturing light and sound and energy from a more distant yet powerful source, then focusing it to a point of intense concentration, accessibility, even revelation. That more distant source is, of course, God, from whom all light and life proceed. Viewed in this manner, parables convey their intended meaning only to the extent that they succeed in directing attention away from themselves. They serve as examples of what literary critic Stanley Fish once called "self-consuming artifacts": they are ultimately about something other than themselves, reflecting and deflecting meaning rather than fully embodying or containing it.[1]

---

1. "A self-consuming artifact signifies most successfully when it fails, when it points *away* from itself to something its forms cannot capture" (Fish, *Self-Consuming Artifacts*, 4 [emphasis original]).

In this sense, too, good preaching is "parabolic." From Jesus' individual parables we will glean much useful homiletical material about God as the source of all life. The first section of the following study concerns Jesus' agricultural parables in particular, those that speak of seeds and wheat, of farming, growth, and fruitfulness as clues to the gift of life that comes from God. Because I have taught on Jesus' parables over the course of several years, earlier stages in my thinking are reflected in previously published studies, among them treatments of the parable of the Sower—one in relation to the book of *Jubilees*[2] and another as applied to Mark's understanding of discipleship and mission.[3] An earlier version of the section that concerns this parable in chapter 3 (Sower and Soil) appears in the inaugural issue of *Canadian Theological Review*.[4] Readers will note degrees of overlap (sometimes extensive) between all three antecedents and parts of the ensuing study, which takes the discussion further by considering lines of continuity between Jesus' testimony to the life-giving power of God and similar testimony on the part of the preacher.

In yet a further sense, Christian preaching is "parabolic" insofar as it traces the experiential and theological contours delineated by Jesus' "descent" from divine glory into incarnation, crucifixion, and death, with this movement ultimately reversed by resurrection and final exaltation (so Phil 2:6–9). It will thus be "cruciform," not only in the sense that Paul understands his own and all Christian experience to follow the same pattern of abasement and redemption, but also with regard to the fact that every human effort to expound the things of God must recognize its own inadequacy—even fail and fall silent—before it can be authenticated by the One of whom it speaks.

A similar logic explains the arrangement of the chapters that follow. Part One ("God's Field") largely concerns the fact that God is the sole source of life—hardly a controversial claim, but one anchored in this case in the teaching of Jesus (his agricultural parables in particular) and a view of the natural world that he shares with the Judaism of his day. The argument of this section is that Jesus tells parables about seeds and wheat, vineyards and fields, in order to alert and turn his hearers toward the life-giving power of God. Here, theology has implications for method: just as seeds come to life only as God grants them the ability to do so, so words—whether Jesus'

2. Knowles, "Abram and the Birds in *Jubilees* 11," 145–51.

3. Knowles, "Mark, Matthew, and Mission," 64–92 (esp. 73–76). By way of a more general antecedent to this study, I am also deeply indebted to students at McMaster Divinity College who have shaped my understanding of the parables in classroom discussion and debate in the course of the past decade.

4. Knowles, "Sowing Seeds," 52–64.

own or those of the preacher—depend for their power on the same divine agency of which they speak. Acknowledging God as Creator implies God's continued role in sustaining creation as much with regard to discipleship and ministry as in the realm of nature.

Part Two ("God's Body, God's Building"), again in large measure exegetical, explores Paul's theology of the cross and its implications for Christian ministry (preaching included). This section will argue that Christian preachers are not go-betweens or gatekeepers for the kingdom of heaven and the new life that it brings; on the contrary, even in the process of preaching we join Jesus at the cross, yielding our own presumptions of spiritual authority to the sole prerogative of God. In other words, if Jesus provides not only the focus and content of our preaching but also its model, our homiletic testimony to the life that God bestows will need to proceed by way of crucifixion. Far from imagining ourselves to be essential instruments of God's purpose or the builders of God's kingdom, we who preach must abandon all pretensions of spiritual importance, dying to ourselves in order to demonstrate, as Paul says, "that the transcendent power belongs to God and not to us" (2 Cor 4:7 RSV).

Then, third, the final section ("God's Word") will propose a possible way forward. It will seek to balance God's prerogative regarding the gift of life against the fact that proclamation of the gospel remains a human responsibility. In conversation with other preachers and theorists who have made similar proposals, these final chapters will offer a more detailed analysis of preaching as a variety of "testimony" that bears witness to transformative divine power. In particular, the concluding section will argue for ways in which faithful preaching both responds to and awaits divine action in order to make its words effective. In this way, the book as a whole not only develops a theology of Christian preaching, but also—perhaps more importantly—explores the spirituality that such a theology implies.

Notwithstanding its extensive discussion of theory and theology, this book is written more for practitioners than for theorists alone, and in particular for those who find preaching to be an especially frustrating task. Pastoral theologian Andrew Purves discerns a deep theological purpose in the seeming impossibility of Christian ministry, preaching included:

> I suspect there are two major crucifixions or seasons of dying in ministry. The first happens early on, as studies now show. After seven years of higher education, great expectations of service in the Lord's vineyard often turn to sad and angry disappointment. About one third of those in early ministry leave, never to return. This a major death, full of deep disenchantment and at

times embittered recrimination. It is a personal, familial, fiscal and ecclesiastical disaster.

The second crucifixion is more subtle and less dramatic. It moves in on us more slowly and insidiously than the rapid, stunning disillusionment of the first crucifixion. It is more profound and in its way more deadly. . . . [S]omewhere along the way—ten, fifteen, twenty years out, who knows when or what circumstances precipitate the process—a terrible awareness begins to dawn . . . *I can't do this.*[5]

This second encounter with Gethsemane and Golgotha goes to the heart of our pastoral and ecclesiastical identity, for it consists of the realization that we no longer have it in us to minister effectively (if indeed we ever did). This crisis is not simply a loss of confidence in our own abilities, but a loss of theological vision as well, a realization that we do not really understand how ministry "works." The study that follows will be of some help to younger preachers in the throes of that first "season of dying," but it especially has in view the later, longer, and deeper "second death" that Purves describes. It is addressed to those who have come to realize—at whatever stage of their ministerial career—that truly transformative preaching is a humanly impossible task.

As with every book, any number of shortcuts are possible: readers interested only in parables can focus on the opening section; theologically inclined readers may find the second section more to their liking; those whose primary interest is in practical outcomes can turn without delay to the final section. Nonetheless, the overriding concern that governs each component of this study is the following: in what way or ways do the teaching, ministry, death, and resurrection of Jesus bear witness to God as the source of all life? More to the point, what patterns or principles does Jesus thereby establish for Christian preaching that concerns God's gift of new life? If, as Jesus claims, he came that we might "have life, and have it abundantly" (John 10:10), what role does preaching play in bringing this purpose to fruition?

---

5. Purves, *The Crucifixion of Ministry*, 22–23 (emphasis original).

Part One

GOD'S FIELD

Chapter 1

Parables, and Parables of Growth
Who Has Ploughed These Fields Before Us?

"You know neither the Scriptures nor the power of God" (Mark 12:24).[1]

In an essay published during his tenure at the University of Chicago—to all appearances the text of a sermon from the Divinity College chapel—Paul Ricoeur confronts the challenge of preaching the parables of Jesus:

> To preach today on the Parables of Jesus looks like a lost cause. Have we not already heard these stories at Sunday School? Are they not childish stories, unworthy of our claims to scientific knowledge, in particular in a University Chapel? Are not the situations which they evoke typical of a rural existence which our urban civilization has made nearly ununderstandable? And the symbols, which in the old days awakened the imagination of simple-minded people, have not these symbols become dead metaphors, as dead as the leg of a chair? . . .
>
> To preach today on the Parables of Jesus—or rather to preach the Parables—is indeed a wager: the wager that in spite of all contrary arguments, it is still possible to listen to the Parables

---

1. Unless otherwise indicated, scriptural quotations are from the New Revised Standard Version (NRSV).

of Jesus in such a way that we are once more astonished, struck, renewed, and put in motion.[2]

The way forward, according to Ricoeur, begins with a recognition that parables cannot be reduced to principles, propositions, or concepts. Because they concern "something Wholly-Other," One who is beyond our immediate experience or control, parables appeal instead to our imagination. In speaking of this ultimate reality, Jesus intends to surprise, even to overwhelm us:

> Look at the so-called parables of Growth: Matthew 13:31–33. This unexpected growth of the mustard seed, this growth beyond all proportion, draws our attention in the same direction as finding. The natural growth of the seed and the unnatural size of the growth speak of something which happens to us, invades us, overwhelms us, beyond our control and our grasp, beyond our willing and our planning.[3]

At three levels—in terms of narrative action, analogical language, and intended reference—parables point beyond themselves, toward a reality that far exceeds the scope of individual words, intellectual categories, or human experience in general. As to narrative action, parables speak of ordinary events that lead to extraordinary outcomes; with regard to language, parables tell us what God's kingdom is *like* rather than what it *is*. Just as metaphor cannot be reduced to proposition, so parables cannot simply be mined for moral truisms, still less so systematized into conceptual abstractions. Nor, when it comes to their intended meaning, can "the kingdom of God" to which these parables refer become a merely human construct, subject to human control. In part by confronting us with the limitations of human language and surprising us with unexpected outcomes, the parables of Jesus tantalize their hearers with the possibilities of God's reign:

> To listen to the Parables of Jesus, it seems to me, is to let one's imagination be opened to the new possibilities disclosed by the extravagance of these short dramas. If we look at the Parables as at a word addressed first to our imagination rather than to our will, we shall not be tempted to reduce them to mere didactic devices, to moralizing allegories. We will let their poetic power display itself within us.[4]

---

2. Ricoeur, "Listening to the Parables," 239.
3. Ibid., 240–41.
4. Ibid., 245.

> By virtue of their elusiveness, the parables seek to engage us with the transcendent reality of God.

Over the years there have been many approaches to parable interpretation. A good example is the parable of the Good Samaritan, which has been read at different times as an allegory of Adam's journey from this world to the heavenly Jerusalem (Origen), or of the unfolding of salvation history from Israel to Christ and the counsels of Paul (Augustine of Hippo), or else as representing the conflict between law and grace in response to human sin (Martin Luther), the exile and restoration of Israel (N. T. Wright), psychological tension between id, ego, and superego (Mary Ann Tolbert), or dysfunctional family values (Richard Rohrbaugh). Or from another perspective entirely, the parable has been viewed as a "language event" that confronts its hearers with the values of the kingdom (Eberhard Jüngel, Robert W. Funk).[5] But the acid test for all such interpretations—however congenial they appear to the sensibilities of our day—is whether they would have made sense to Jesus' contemporaries. Set within their proper social and historical contexts, parables communicate by means of their arresting juxtaposition of familiar and unfamiliar: they speak of a world that Jesus' hearers immediately recognized, populated as it was by fishermen, farmers, and tax collectors; masters and servants; poor workers and ruthless landowners; rural peasants and urban elites. As Ricoeur observes,

> The first thing that may strike us is that the Parables are radically profane stories. There are no gods, no demons, no angels, no miracles, no time before time, as in the creation stories, not even founding events as in the Exodus account. Nothing like that, but precisely people like us . . .[6]

Of course, this is not quite true: neither Jesus' parables nor his original audiences consist of "people like us"; much that would have been obvious to a first-century Palestinian Jew is utterly foreign in our day. We fail to see the point of the parables at least in part because we are far removed from their most basic social and economic dynamics: the majority of readers in the global North have been urbanized for generations, with little practical experience of sheep and goats, cycles of planting and harvest, rigid social stratification, or the economic constraints of subsistence farming. Still deeper concerns include the pervasive atheism of post-Enlightenment culture, together with the characteristic modern conviction that religion is a

---

5. For a summary of these and other approaches, see Snodgrass, *Stories with Intent*, 126–28, supplemented by Kissinger, *The Parables of Jesus*, 47, 196, 204–7.

6. Ricoeur, "Listening to the Parables," 239.

matter of private and personal—rather than public or political—concern. The most pious North American farmer would not seriously entertain the idea that crop germination, seasonal weather patterns, or the business of the slaughterhouse should be directly theological concerns, as they would certainly have been for Jesus' first hearers. The divide between us is not only cultural and historical, but conceptual and theological as well.

Yet even for Jesus' original audience, recognition of the scenarios he describes might have been short-lived or incomplete, for the characters in his parables behave in ways that are frequently unexpected, enigmatic, or counterintuitive. A wildly rebellious and dissolute son is welcomed home to a lavish celebration after he has squandered a substantial portion of the family inheritance; a middle manager, fired for incompetence, ingratiates himself with those who owe his employer money, only to be praised for having done so; a penniless and powerless widow wins her case by making life intolerable for a notoriously corrupt and hardhearted magistrate. This is definitely not how things worked in the real world. Jesus tells stories that stretch the boundaries of expectation: his parables "push the envelope" in order to challenge assumptions of what is "normal" or not. Not because he intends to confuse or disorient; quite the opposite. For all the time and effort that scholars have expended in trying to identify the rhetorical features that make these odd little tales so arresting, the ultimate explanation for their impact lies neither with the language and grammar of the parables themselves, nor within the social, economic, or political dynamics of first-century Mediterranean culture. Rather, as Jesus disarmingly announces in the majority of cases, his parables concern the nature of "the kingdom of God." Thus parables (and the explanations that sometimes accompany them) are explicitly non-self-referential: they intend to point beyond themselves to a reality that is even more alarming and disruptive, which is the presence, power, and sovereignty of God.

Learning to read Jesus' parables on their own terms will require greater awareness of their original social, political, and historical context. Before we can preach from them, we will need to learn as much as possible about what Jesus and his hearers would likely have taken for granted. Certain principles of interpretation will apply to Jesus' teaching as a whole and all parables in general, others to the agricultural parables in particular. The first, and broader area of concern will occupy the remainder of the present chapter; the second, narrower consideration will be the subject of the chapter that follows. Clearing away some of the lesser mysteries occasioned by historical distance will bring into focus the much greater theological mystery of which Jesus speaks.

LEARNING TO READ

In a famous encounter attested in slightly different fashion by all three Synoptic Gospels (Matt 22:23–33; Mark 12:18–27; Luke 20:27–28), a certain group of rivals confronts Jesus on the question of the resurrection. Members of this group—Sadducees—appear to believe that the soul ceases to exist at the moment of physical death; as a result, they reject not only the resurrection but also the idea of final judgment.[7] As a strategy for investigating Jesus' position on such matters, they describe a scenario in which each of seven brothers weds the same woman, only to die without issue and be replaced by the next brother. Finally the woman herself dies. At the resurrection, they demand, whose wife will she be? In our own day, a similar chain of events might lead us to question whether all seven had died of natural causes, but the Sadducees' chief purpose is to demonstrate the absurdity of resurrection. Their challenge is presented in the form of a popular folktale, also attested in the book of Tobit, of a woman who outlives seven husbands (Tob 3:7–15). In response, Jesus does not simply disagree with his opponents or politely observe that their views seem ill-advised. Rather, his pointed rebuttal addresses the very foundations of their thinking, and of his own: "Is not this why you are wrong," he retorts, "that you know neither the Scriptures nor the power of God?" (Mark 12:24; cf. Matt 22:29). It is a clever answer, for (even though the canon is not yet fully fixed) it implicitly takes issue with the nonscriptural source of their story, while at the same time suggesting that even when they do read Scripture they fail to understand its true import.[8] More to the point, Jesus' rebuke has significant implications for the way in which we read his teaching generally, for it suggests that these two principles—one literary ("the Scriptures") and the other theological ("the power of God")—provide an immediate key to understanding the message

---

7. So Porton, "Sadducees," 892.

8. Jesus' supporting arguments make the same two points in reverse order. The first (Mark 12:25) addresses the manifestation of God's power in raising the dead. As to the second, interpreters typically contend that the argument in Mark 12:26 turns on a nicety of grammar: since God speaks of the patriarchs in the present tense ("I am the God of Abraham, and the God of Isaac, and the God of Jacob," Exod 3:6), the latter must be alive in God's presence. But Dreyfus ("L'argument scripturaire," 216–19, 221–23), citing exact parallels from *Jub.* 45:3, *Pr. Man.* 1, *T. Mos.* 3:9, and the Shemoneh 'Esreh, argues that such formulaic invocations of the patriarchal names highlight divine initiative, as distinct from any human response. Read in this light, Jesus' quotation of Exodus 3:6 emphasizes divine faithfulness as an explanation for resurrection: "He is God not of the dead, but of the living" (Mark 12:27). A rich expansion of Dreyfus' argument, again emphasizing "the Scriptures [and] the power of God," is offered by Janzen, "Resurrection and Hermeneutics."

that he brings.⁹ Nowhere does this apply more clearly than to the task of interpreting parables: familiarity with Scripture and recognition of God's life-giving power will quickly turn us in the direction Jesus intends.

Reading with an Eye to Scripture

For this reason, while archaeological and ethnographic material may help to clarify the human dimensions of Jesus' parables, two further sources of information—precisely those that he identifies in his controversy with the Sadducees—will prove invaluable for identifying their theological implications. The first source is Hebrew Scripture. Many of the stories Jesus tells refer either directly or indirectly to themes and images already found in the biblical text. Success or failure in understanding his teaching may therefore reflect a success or failure of scriptural knowledge and imagination on the part of his hearers, whether ancient or modern. In some cases the link is obvious; in others, the parable serves as a test of recognition. Not until recently, for example, have interpreters realized that behind the story of the fired manager who reduces the debt payments owed his master (Luke 16:1–9) lies the biblical prohibition against charging interest or otherwise making a profit off the misfortunes of others (Lev 25:35–38).[10] Likewise the parable of the Barren Fig Tree hinges on a curious complaint: its owner has been seeking fruit for precisely three years. The gardener advises him to wait a fourth year, only after which will he be justified in cutting it down, should it still not produce fruit (Luke 13:6–9). For these details to make proper sense, hearers must recall a passage from the book of Leviticus that contains similarly precise chronological details:

> When you come into the land and plant all kinds of trees for food, then you shall regard their fruit as forbidden; three years it shall be forbidden to you, it must not be eaten. In the fourth year all their fruit shall be set apart for rejoicing in the Lord. But in the fifth year you may eat of their fruit, that their yield may be increased for you: I am the Lord your God. (Lev 19:23–25)

---

9. In *The Gospel in a Pluralist Society*, 131–33, missiologist Lesslie Newbigin observes a similar principle in the example of Jesus' followers, for when Jesus sends out his disciples, he gives them authority to heal, to cast out demons, and to preach (Matt 10:1, 7–8). In their ministries as in his own, words of explanation (corresponding to the testimony of Scripture) and works of healing (which manifest the "power of God") are so integrally linked that each requires the other: only together do they reveal the meaning and purpose of God's gracious kingdom.

10. This insight is indebted to Derrett, "The Parable of the Unjust Steward," 48–77.

Whatever other details remain to be clarified in comparison to social customs of the day, the main force of the story of the returning prodigal derives from the astonishing conduct of his father, whose course of action ought rather to have been guided by the terms spelled out with painful clarity in Deuteronomy 21:18–21:

> If someone has a stubborn and rebellious son who will not obey his father and mother, who does not heed them when they discipline him, then his father and his mother shall take hold of him and bring him out to the elders of his town at the gate of that place. They shall say to the elders of his town, "This son of ours is stubborn and rebellious. He will not obey us. He is a glutton and a drunkard." Then all the men of the town shall stone him to death. So you shall purge the evil from your midst; and all Israel will hear, and be afraid.

That the father declines to treat his wayward son in the manner that Scripture explicitly commands is breathtaking. In a strange case of family resemblance, disobedience on the part of the child is matched by disobedience on the part of the parent, although this dynamic only emerges against the backdrop of biblical legislation. More obviously, the parable of the Good Samaritan (Luke 10:25–37) concerns the proper interpretation of Deuteronomy 6:5, "You shall love the Lord your God with all your heart, and with all your soul, and with all your might," and Leviticus 19:18, "You shall love your neighbor as yourself." Specifically, it addresses the question of how to apply these injunctions: who, exactly, is intended by the word "neighbor"? At the same time, the parable recalls an episode from the final book in the Hebrew canon, describing the aftermath of a battle between the armies of Israel and Judah. The defeated Judeans, said to number some 200,000, are first brought to the city of Samaria, where they are clothed and fed, then transported home—those who are weak by means of donkeys—to their families in Jericho (2 Chr 28:8–15). The comparison between Samarians and Samaritans is not accidental, and contributes significantly to the meaning Jesus intends.[11]

To be sure, not all of Jesus' listeners could be expected to recognize every allusion; on the contrary, the scribal class in particular seem to have prided themselves on the fact that their comprehensive knowledge of Scripture (and its proper interpretation) served to distinguish them from the unlettered majority from which Jesus' audiences were often drawn. But perhaps that is a point Jesus himself wishes to make: since the law and the Prophets represent the spiritual legacy of all God's chosen people, scripturally-based

---

11. See further Knowles, "What Was the Victim Wearing?," 147–50.

parables direct the attention of his listeners toward the true source of enlightenment and learning.

Even when not commenting directly on matters of legislative interpretation, still other parables draw certain details from the rich fund of narrative represented by both biblical and parabiblical resources. A notable example is the parable of the ungenerous debtor, or "Unforgiving Servant" (Matt 18:21–35). Many interpreters preoccupy themselves with calculating how many years of menial labour are represented by the "ten thousand talents" that the desperate courtier owes his king. But in the process, most overlook a somewhat obvious allusion to the book of Esther. In that story a malevolent, genocidal official named Haman—an enemy of the Jews comparable to Hitler in more recent history—promises to pay King Xerxes exactly ten thousand silver talents for the right to destroy God's people (Esth 3:8–11). Only in light of this parallel can we appreciate the breathtaking magnanimity of the king's forgiveness, the plausibility of the same official refusing to forgive his fellow courtier a comparatively insignificant debt, or the rhetorical force of Jesus' warning not to follow suit. Likewise, in the case of Jesus' contrast between a widow who seeks justice and a judge who metes out nothing of the sort (Luke 18:1–8), familiarity with Scripture is all-important. That Jesus depicts God as a judge is uncontroversial, since this is a common scriptural image (Deut 10:17–18, Jer 51:36, etc.), although comparison with a notoriously *corrupt* judge takes some getting used to. Even so, the key to his intended meaning lies with the interpretation of verse 7:

> "And will not God grant justice to his chosen ones who cry to him day and night? Will he *delay long* in helping them?"

Since the language of the original text (and the verb μακροθυμεῖ in particular) can have more than one meaning, should we take this to imply that God may initially be slow to help the afflicted? Or that God forbears to judge oppressors? One way or another, a passage with remarkably similar language in the book of Sirach, or Ecclesiasticus, goes a long way toward clarifying matters:

> Do not offer [God] a bribe, for he will not accept it; and do not rely on a dishonest sacrifice; for the Lord is the judge, and with him there is no partiality. . . . He will not ignore the supplication of the fatherless, nor the widow when she pours out her story. . . . And the Lord will not delay [βραδύνῃ] neither will he *be patient* [μακροθυμήσῃ] with them, till he crushes the loins of the unmerciful . . . and breaks the scepters of the unrighteous.
>
> (Sirach 35:12, 14, 19, RSV)

In fact, it seems reasonable to infer that this passage is what provided the inspiration for Jesus' parable in the first place.

Although it is possible to read the parables as self-contained, self-referential nuggets of folk wisdom, this line of interpretation is explicitly contradicted by the parable of poor Lazarus, who dies of starvation while the dogs lick his sores at the very gates of a rich man's estate (Luke 16:19–31). As the story goes, both Lazarus and the rich man die, but their ultimate destinations are in each case the opposite of what they experienced in mortal life. When the wealthy man in torment sees Lazarus being comforted by Father Abraham, he begs Abraham to send Lazarus with no more than a single drop of water to cool his burning tongue. Abraham explains why this is now impossible. Undaunted, the tormented man pleads that Lazarus be sent instead to warn his five brothers, all still living, of the dreadful judgment that awaits them. The repercussions of Abraham's response extend well beyond the meaning of this parable alone:

> Abraham replied, "They have Moses and the prophets; they should listen to them." He said, "No, father Abraham; but if someone goes to them from the dead, they will repent." He said to him, "If they do not listen to Moses and the prophets, neither will they be convinced even if someone rises from the dead."
>
> (Luke 16:29–31)

Jesus' argument—his fictional Abraham repeats it twice for emphasis—is that the biblical standard for righteous conduct, the yardstick by which the man will be judged, is revealed already in Scripture, of which "Moses and the prophets" constitute the greatest part. Moreover, he insists, should the five brothers—Abraham's descendants—be unwilling to accept the testimony of Scripture, neither are they likely to be persuaded by a manifestation of divine power such as the raising of one who has died.

Just so, understanding Jesus' message and the provocative stories that he tells begins with willingness on the part of his hearers to accept the testimony of "Moses and the prophets." Equally critical is their recognition of God's mighty intervention in human affairs, to which "Moses and the prophets" consistently bear witness. The narrative premise that Abraham is alive in heaven itself bears eloquent testimony to the life-giving power of God, whom Jesus acknowledges as "God not of the dead, but of the living; for to him all . . . are alive" (Luke 20:38).

To the extent that particular parables comment on or otherwise evoke specific biblical texts, parable interpretation focuses initially on what biblical scholars call "intertextuality." Within the context of a society that consciously defines itself in relation to scriptural tradition, newer texts entail complex interweavings of allusions to and invocations of earlier texts.[12] Accordingly, a given parable may not allude to any one text in the biblical canon: interpretation cannot be reduced to identifying a series of one-to-one equivalences between passages in Hebrew Scripture on the one hand and the Synoptic Gospels on the other. Rather, we must recall that the Judaism of Jesus' day possessed a rich and multifaceted legacy of biblical interpretation that had already developed over many generations of interpretation and application. James Kugel observes that, in many cases,

> resemblances between one exegetical source and another can hardly be explained by direct influence.... On the contrary, such resemblances can only indicate a common store of biblical exegesis inherited by diverse, and in some cases clearly antagonistic, Jewish groups and circles that flourished in Palestine and elsewhere in the centuries just before and after the start of the common era.[13]

Abraham in the parable of the Rich Man and Lazarus is one such example, since—in stark contrast to the wealthy misanthrope—he is celebrated in both Scripture and popular tradition for his exemplary hospitality (Gen 18:1–15; 'Abot R. Nat. 7).[14] Again, when Jesus tells the story of a wealthy farmer who amasses a personal fortune at the neglect of his soul (Luke 12:15–21), he is likely drawing on a tradition that depicted Cain in similar terms, all the more so as he is here responding to a request for assistance in dividing a family inheritance between two brothers (Luke 12:13).[15]

That Jesus' parables appeal to the world of Scripture, both broadly and narrowly understood, has important implications for matters of literary form, in particular the much-vexed question of the relationship between the parables themselves and the frequently allegorical interpretations that sometimes accompany them. Building on the work of David Stern, Michael Fishbane, and Daniel Boyarin, Marie Sabin identifies Jesus' method of teaching as a species of midrash, which creatively appropriates and reactualizes the meaning of Scripture for a new situation. Typical of midrashic interpretation is the *mashal*, or parable, to which in turn is appended a *nimshal*, or explanation:

---

12. For a succinct introduction to this concept, see Luz, "Intertexts," 119–24.
13. Kugel, *In Potiphar's House*, 265–66.
14. See Scott, *Hear Then the Parable*, 153–54.
15. On these traditions, see Byron, "Living in the Shadow," 263–67.

the *mashal* interprets the biblical text; the *nimshal* interprets the *mashal*. The *mashal* is constructed out of the linking of texts; it is a paradigmatic narrative, filling in the gaps between one text and another. As a narrative it conveys its meaning indirectly, by way of analogy. The *nimshal*, on the other hand, is an orienting structure, designed to amplify the context of the *mashal*. It is not itself indirect or metaphorical, but straightforwardly provides the *mashal*'s frame of reference.[16]

Notwithstanding the interpretative function of the *nimshal*, however, "It is important to recognize that the ultimate frame of reference, in one way or another, is always Scripture"; likewise, "because a *mashal* is constructed as an intertext, it cannot be understood without its textual referent."[17] Sabin argues that Jesus' parables in Mark 4, most notably the parable of the Sower and its ensuing explanation (Mark 4:3–9, 14–20), function in precisely this manner.[18] The many examples cited above suggest the same to be true of most if not all of his parables: to understand the stories Jesus tells, we will need to recognize the echoes and reflections of Scripture that they intend.

Reading with an Eye to the Kingdom

As the story of Abraham and Lazarus implies, Jesus' teaching invokes theological themes that pervade the canon as a whole, whether with respect to the character and purpose of God, the identity of Israel, or "the kingdom of heaven." That a central focus of his ministry was to proclaim and enact the inbreaking "kingdom of God" is one of the few details on which scholars of the Gospels are universally agreed. Still, since neither kingdoms nor God are especially familiar subjects in our day, the idea requires at least brief explanation. To be Jewish in the world Jesus knew was to take for granted that God was at work in the national destiny of his chosen people. Divine sovereignty was axiomatic to historical Israel's self-understanding, so much so that it is embedded in the whole of the biblical text, rather than any one passage or narrative. Nor was God's reign limited to the geography of Palestine: the biblical writers insist that their sovereign is "King" (Ps 47:2, 7), "Most High" (Ps 83:18), and "Lord of the whole earth" (Josh 3:11, 13; Ps 97:5; Mic 4:13; Zech 4:14, 6:5, etc.).

So when many of his parables begin by declaring, "The kingdom of heaven is like . . ." or "the kingdom of God can be compared to . . ." it is clear

16. Sabin, "Reading Mark 4 as Midrash," 12.
17. Ibid., 13, 23.
18. Ibid., 13–21.

that Jesus intends to weigh in on a vital contemporary debate about the exact nature of God's rule in relation to the social, religious, and political circumstances of his day. Not only had God once sent his people into exile in Babylon as a punishment for their sins, but most of Jesus' contemporaries held to the view that (despite their having returned home in a geographical sense) Israel's spiritual exile was ongoing.[19] How else, after all, could one explain the present rule of pagan Rome over Jerusalem and Judea? It could only be that this, too, was a manifestation of God's reign, however paradoxical and—hopefully—provisional. Contemporary strategies and responses ranged from taking up arms against the military occupation (the Zealot approach) to emphasizing instead the formation of a holy people (the Pharisees), withdrawal in expectation of divine intervention (apocalypticism, exemplified by the Qumran sectarians), or, at the far end of the scale, outright collaboration with Rome (Herod and his court). Such is the intensity of this debate, and the depth of passion it inspires, that at one point Jesus himself can no longer appear in public, for he learns that an unidentified group is "about to come and take him by force to make him king" (John 6:15). Anything he says on the matter must be carefully worded. According to Jesus, therefore, the kingdom of God is like a farmer seeding his field, a grain of mustard about to sprout, a handful of yeast mixed into flour, a king settling accounts with his officials, a monarch celebrating the wedding of his son. At first blush, this seems a strange way of commenting on a controversial topic. But it is a strategic approach, not only in the sense that Jesus thereby avoids fanning the flames of popular revolt, but also in the sense that his explanation of God's "kingdom" is an intentional nonexplanation. His explanations are something of a conundrum, for like the kingdom of God itself and Jesus' ministry in general, the parables are neither self-contained nor directly self-explanatory. In order to make sense either of God's rule or of parables that purport to describe that rule, we have to resort to God. This is exactly what their teller intends. Much as they are hermeneutically evasive, Jesus' parables are theologically confrontational, for they present us with the reality of God, and judge us by the measure of our response.

To summarize: Jesus tells parables that (like his ministry of healing and deliverance) concern the nature of God's reign. Since that is the case, the key to understanding them lies not in the parables themselves, but in the world of Scripture, both broadly and narrowly understood. Returning to the conflict story with which the chapter began, we might imagine Jesus responding to a listener who failed to grasp the purpose of his parables, or to understand the vision of God's kingdom that they convey, "Is not this why

---

19. See further Wright, *The New Testament*, 268–72, and the literature cited there.

you are wrong, that you know neither the Scriptures nor the power of God?" As noted already, this insight has significant implications for our own interpretation and proclamation of the parables. If Jesus intends to refer his hearers (as well as, by implication, subsequent readers of the written text) to the Scriptures of Israel, and more broadly to their revelation of the character and "power of God," then psychology, social studies, rhetorical analysis, political theory, or other such approaches will not provide the tools we need to plumb the theological depths of these odd little tales. Jesus intends to confront us by means of the parables with the paradoxical, strangely counterintuitive character of God, and of God's reign. The parables are, in this sense, "exocentric" or "allocentric"—they are not self-contained units of meaning, but refer to a reality quite outside and beyond themselves.

There are probably two main reasons for this strategy. In the context of their first telling, the parables preserve the freedom and responsibility of each hearer to respond appropriately. More specifically, the parables challenge hearers in regard to their own understanding of God's ways. This is a matter not simply of responding to Jesus and his teaching, but of evaluating his message in direct relation to the God of whom he speaks. Jesus' exposition of this principle, cited here in its Matthean form, comes in answer to a question posed by certain disciples:

> Then the disciples came and asked him, "Why do you speak to them in parables?" He answered, "To you it has been given to know the secrets of the kingdom of heaven, but to them it has not been given. For to those who have, more will be given, and they will have an abundance; but from those who have nothing, even what they have will be taken away. The reason I speak to them in parables is that 'Seeing they do not perceive, and hearing they do not listen, nor do they understand.' With them indeed is fulfilled the prophecy of Isaiah that says:
> 'You will indeed listen, but never understand, and you will indeed look, but never perceive. For this people's heart has grown dull, and their ears are hard of hearing, and they have shut their eyes; so that they might not look with their eyes, and listen with their ears, and understand with their heart and turn—and I would heal them.'"
>
> (Matt 13:10–15)

The point of citing Isaiah 6:9–10 is not that Jesus is somehow intentionally barring the way to proper understanding, even if comprehension or lack thereof initially serves as a dividing line between "insiders" and "outsiders." "The reason why some people see and hear perfectly well but without seeing or understanding is in order that they may not have to turn and it be forgiven them."[20] Conversely, accurately perceiving the "secrets" or "mysteries of the kingdom of heaven" is a matter of willingly responding to the Word of God and the revelation it entails.[21] It is in this specific sense that Jesus insists, "To those who have, more will be given, and they will have an abundance; but from those who have nothing, even what they have will be taken away" (Matt 13:12; so 25:29). How can one be deprived of what one does not already possess? Likely in the sense of Jesus' later rebuke—in this case unique to Matthew's gospel—to the "chief priests and Pharisees" who consider themselves the gatekeepers of God's dominion:

> "Woe to you, scribes and Pharisees, hypocrites! For you lock people out of the kingdom of heaven. For you do not go in yourselves, and when others are going in, you stop them."
>
> (Matt 23:13)

In Luke's version of this saying, Jesus accuses the religious leaders of having "taken away the key of knowledge" (Luke 11:52).

By contrast, when Peter confesses him to be "the Messiah, the Son of the living God," Jesus responds by declaring, "I will give you the keys of the kingdom of heaven" (Matt 16:17–19). To be sure, Peter's knowledge of such things is far from complete (perhaps, indeed, as tiny as a mustard seed or a pearl), as is that of all his fellow disciples. Even so, in addition to what they already have—an initial sense of Jesus' identity, a deepening awareness of God's power at work in him—more will be given. That is why Jesus can assure his followers, regarding their own spiritual perception, "Blessed are your eyes, for they see, and your ears, for they hear" (Matt 13:16). An equivalent contrast, once more recalling Isaiah's metaphors of seeing and hearing, appears in John's gospel:

> Jesus said, "I came into this world for judgment so that those who do not see may see, and those who do see may become blind." Some of the Pharisees near him heard this and said to him, "Surely we are not blind, are we?" Jesus said to them, "If you were blind, you would not have sin. But now that you say, 'We see,' your sin remains."
>
> (John 9:39–41)

---

20. Bowker, "Mystery and Parable," 312; similarly Snodgrass, "A Hermeneutic of Hearing," esp. 75–76.

21. This interpretation is first offered by early patristic exegetes such as Irenaeus, John Chrysostom, Cyril of Alexandria, and Victor of Antioch, as noted by Arida, "Hearing, Receiving and Entering."

A similar appeal to the presuppositions of his hearers is once more in play when Jesus goes toe-to-toe with other teachers on the question of authority:

> As he was walking in the temple, the chief priests, the scribes, and the elders came to him and said, "By what authority are you doing these things? Who gave you this authority to do them?" Jesus said to them, "I will ask you one question; answer me, and I will tell you by what authority I do these things. Did the baptism of John come from heaven, or was it of human origin?"
>
> (Mark 11:27–30)

This exchange sums up the whole of Jesus' approach: the real issue is the question behind the question—not, ultimately, the identity or authority of Jesus or of John, but rather whether his examiners are truly open to the God they claim to represent.

Whichever metaphor he employs on a given occasion—keys, secrets, kingdoms, judgment, blindness and sight—Jesus' central concern is for knowledge of God: specifically, knowledge of God's power and God's ways. Some, he avers, are indeed open to God—open to being ruled by God—while others are not (however much they may claim to be). Parables are, in effect, strategies by which Jesus' hearers reveal (and perhaps also, on occasion, come to know) their own spiritual orientation toward God, whether by their recognition of scriptural allusions or as a direct response to the power and reign of God, to which Scripture as a whole testifies.

READING PARABLES AND THE "OPEN SECRET" OF GOD'S REIGN

All this having been said, something more (and less) complex is underway in the canonical accounts of Jesus' ministry. Throughout the Gospels, Jesus warns those who witness his power not to tell anyone about it, although his instructions are frequently ignored (e.g., Mark 1:44, 5:43, 7:36, and parallels). More specifically, he is said to have admonished Peter, James, and John, who were with him on the Mount of Transfiguration, "to tell no one about what they had seen, *until after the Son of Man had risen from the dead*" (Mark 9:9). The qualification is all-important. Comparing the documents that concern Jesus with those describing two other roughly contemporary messianic claimants (the Teacher of Righteousness at Qumran and the second-century rebel leader Simon ben Koseba), Richard Longenecker observes in all three a marked reticence when it comes to proclaiming their own identity, and a particular reluctance to acknowledge the messianic acclaim accorded them by others. Longenecker cites David Flusser on this point: "From the strictly theological point of view no man can be defined as a messiah before he has accomplished the task of the anointed."[22] Hence Jesus' insistence that the disciples say nothing until after he has been divinely vindicated by being raised from death. Apart from a brief quote from Isaiah to announce his public ministry (Luke 4:17–19), Jesus therefore waits until after the resurrection to explain what the Scriptures of Israel say concerning his identity and mission (Luke 24:27).

This chronological consideration goes a long way toward explaining the confusing, even contradictory messages of the parables. On the one hand, Jesus himself appears to draw strict lines between "insiders" and "outsiders"; between those already "in the know" and those whose access to such knowledge is strictly limited. Yet the Gospels make no such distinction: on the contrary, they treat each and every reader as though they were already disciples, withholding nothing.[23] When we read of Jesus telling his inner circle, "To you it has been given to know the secrets [or 'mysteries'] of the kingdom of heaven, but to them it has not been given," the fact that we are able to read these secrets for ourselves means that the distinction between privileged "insiders" and unenlightened "outsiders" is no longer in force.[24] After all, we need only read a few verses further on to discover Jesus' answer to the very questions the disciples have put to him. They especially want to know the meaning of the parable of the Sower (Mark 4:10), and Mark helpfully provides it. Matthew makes the paradox explicit with his quotation of Psalm 78:2:

> Jesus told the crowds all these things in parables; without a parable he told them nothing. This was to fulfill what had been spoken through the prophet:
> "I will open my mouth to speak in parables;
> I will proclaim what has been hidden from the foundation of the world."
>
> (Matt 13:34–35)

22. Longenecker, "The Messianic Secret," 207–15 (here, 213).

23. For a fuller discussion of this phenomenon in Matthew's gospel, see Knowles, "Reading Matthew," 71–73.

24. This observation at least partly resolves the offense felt by many readers at Mark's ἵνα and μήποτε: "for those outside, everything comes in parables; *in order that* 'they may indeed look, but not perceive . . . *so that* they may not turn again and be forgiven'" (Mark 4:11–12). Even so, as Snodgrass ("A Hermeneutic of Hearing," 68–72) documents, drastic admonition and warning are characteristic of the language employed by Israel's prophets, Isaiah and Jesus not least among them.

At least from the perspective of the reader, what was once hidden is evidently hidden no longer, for Jesus has now proclaimed it! To make the point more obvious, his (ostensibly private) exposition of the weeds in the field follows immediately (Matt 13:36–43). More subtly, parables addressed to "insiders" and "outsiders" respectively in Matthew 13:24–50 form a concentric series of matching pairs, implying that the teaching offered to each audience is essentially identical.[25] Likewise in the Gospel of John, we read page after revealing page of Jesus' intimate conversations both with his disciples and—more remarkable yet—with God.

To gain a sense of how radical this strategy might have appeared in its own day, we need only compare the manner in which contemporary Greek and Roman "mystery religions" took care to guard the secrets of their rituals, incantations, and ceremonies.[26] Or, in a Jewish context, we may observe how in the apocryphal *Fourth Ezra*, written around 100 CE, God tells Ezra the scribe to write down and hide seventy books whose contents—apparently concerning the identity of the Messiah—will be made known only to "the wise" (4 Ezra 12:31–38, 14:44–47). Granted, Paul too can write of heavenly visions containing "things that are not to be told, that no mortal is permitted to repeat" (2 Cor 12:4). So too he describes the Christian message of salvation as a "mystery [$\mu\nu\sigma\tau\acute{\eta}\rho\iota\text{o}\nu$]" (Rom 16:25; 1 Cor 2:7–8; Eph 1:9–10, 3:4–6; Col 1:26–27, etc.), using the same term by which Jesus describes the "*secret* of the kingdom of heaven." But for the apostle such language refers to a mystery that is no longer a mystery, to the open secret of God's purposes that were formerly hidden but have now been revealed for all to see. Just so, the Gospel writers tell all, withholding nothing from their readers. The message of the gospel, we might say, has become an "open book."

Why the contradiction? Part of the answer has to do, again, with the fact that all four evangelists write in retrospect—after the meaning of Jesus' life, death, and resurrection has already been widely expounded in the preaching of the early church. At the same time, in a different sense, the open publication of teachings originally withheld from the majority represents an intentional strategy on the part of the Gospel writers. The teachings of Jesus, and the parables of the kingdom in particular, pose a challenge for hearers and readers of the Gospels not unlike Jesus' own challenge to the crowds who heard him telling these stories in person. If Jesus' purpose was to confront his hearers on the question of their openness to God's reign, this is no less the case for those who contend both with his teachings and with the testimony of his life, ministry, death, and resurrection as a theological

---

25. See further Knowles, "Reading Matthew," 65–66, 71–72.
26. See Meyer, "Mystery Religions," 941–42.

whole. If the Gospels treat us as though we were already disciples, giving us unrestricted access to "the secrets of the kingdom of heaven," then our response to that same teaching will likewise reveal the true extent—or limitations—of our practical openness to God. Again, when Jesus tells parables about "the kingdom of God," the evangelists go one step further and provide all the elucidations to which only true disciples once had access. What we make of this will reveal our spiritual character as accurately as if we had met and heard Jesus in person—whether, that is, we ourselves have any sense of "the Scriptures," and "the power of God" to which they bear witness.

One immediate problem, of course, is that comparatively few in our own day know much about either subject. Even as lifelong churchgoers, we are not nearly as familiar with the Hebrew canon as some of Jesus' first hearers would have been. Echoes and allusions that are woven throughout every book in the New Testament fall frequently on deaf ears, not least because we read our sacred canon in translation, at one or more removes from the Hebrew, Aramaic, and Greek of the biblical tradition in Jesus' day. Cross-references and marginalia to the English text provide some assistance, but even then we do not always know what to do with them. Yet all is not lost. On the contrary, the issue for our reading of Jesus' parables remains the same as it has always been. Whether we are biblically literate or not, theologically alert or otherwise, our challenge is the same: the parables of Jesus confront us with the question of God, and of our willingness to enter God's "kingdom." And according to the one who first told them, that is as it should be.

As the initial focus of our study is on parables that concern agriculture and growth, we turn now to a discussion of two considerations that "fill in the blanks" concerning their theological background, explaining premises or principles that Jesus and his hearers would have likely taken for granted. The first (as an expression of the "power of God") has to do with what we would today call a "theology of providence." In a prescientific age, how did Jewish farmers and vinedressers understand the natural processes by which seed sprouted, rain fell, fruit trees blossomed, and vines bore fruit? This, after all, is critical background information for parables that describe these very processes in order to illustrate God's reign. Second, and more specifically, what was the significance of "seed," both literally and metaphorically, in Scripture and the Jewish world of Jesus' day? More to the point, what did such language imply about God, God's character, and God's relationship to the world? Answering these questions will set the stage, one chapter further on, for a fresh reading of the agricultural parables themselves.

Chapter 2

"I Will Watch over Them to Build and to Plant"

Nature and Nation in the World of Jesus' Day

> "For the vineyard of the Lord of Hosts is the house of Israel,
> and the people of Judah are his pleasant planting" (Isaiah 5:7).

"YOU VISIT THE EARTH AND WATER IT": GOD AT WORK IN THE WORLD

Theophrastus (ca. 371–287 BCE), who took over direction of the Athenian academy, or Lyceum, from Aristotle in 322, is today known as the greatest biologist of the ancient world. In the course of his wide-ranging inquiries into the workings of the natural realm, he especially pondered questions of propagation and regeneration: how plants and animals were able to bring forth new life. Some plants, he observed, reproduce using seeds or bulbs, roots or suckers, or else by means of detached tendrils or cuttings, whereas in other cases the generation of a new sprout appeared spontaneous. Philosophers had been unable to agree on the cause of the latter:

> Anaxagoras says that the air has seeds of all and that these are carried down with the rain water and generate plants; Diogenes

> says plants are produced when the rain water decomposes and acquires a certain mixture with the earth, and Clidemus that plants are formed of the same components as animals.[1]

Particularly when it came to spontaneous generation, Theophrastus could offer no fuller insight than any of his predecessors: "this kind," he concludes, "is rather outside the grasp of our senses."[2] Judaism, by contrast, offered a much simpler explanation: seeds, trees, and all the processes by which nature brought forth new life provided direct and concrete evidence of God's covenant love in action. Within the world of Second Temple Judaism, a constellation of loosely related agricultural images and metaphors that express such an outlook provides a comprehensive background for interpreting Jesus' agricultural parables.[3]

Jewish notions of divine providence in the natural world derive, of course, from the book of Genesis, and more particularly from day three of creation:

> Then God said, "Let the earth put forth vegetation: plants yielding seed, and fruit trees of every kind on earth that bear fruit with the seed in it." And it was so. The earth brought forth vegetation: plants yielding seed of every kind, and trees of every kind bearing fruit with the seed in it. And God saw that it was good.
>
> (Gen 1:11–12)

But this is not the disinterested cosmic "clockmaker" of deism, a God who simply sets things in motion and thereafter leaves them to run their natural course. Far from it: the people of Israel thought of wind and rain, seasonal changes, and the fruits of harvest as being under direct divine control. So much so, in fact, that celebrating God's ordering and provision in nature formed a staple of their corporate worship:

> You visit the earth and water it, you greatly enrich it;
> the river of God is full of water;
> you provide the people with grain, for so you have prepared it.
> You water its furrows abundantly, settling its ridges,
> softening it with showers, and blessing its growth.
> You crown the year with your bounty;

---

1. Theophrastus, *De Historia Plantarum* 3.1.4, cited in Theophrastus, *De Causis Plantarum*, 1:34 note c.

2. Ἀλλ' αὕτη μέν ἀπηρτημένη πώς ἐστι τῆς αἰσθήσεως (author's translation); Greek text in Theophrastus, *Enquiry into Plants*, 1:163; cf. *De Causis Plantarum*, 1.1–2, 5.1–2.

3. For a survey of this imagery (with particular attention to the Second Temple period), see Elliott, *The Survivors of Israel*, 329–44, and the literature cited there.

> your wagon tracks overflow with richness.
> The pastures of the wilderness overflow,
> the hills gird themselves with joy,
> the meadows clothe themselves with flocks,
> the valleys deck themselves with grain,
> they shout and sing together for joy.
>
> (Ps 65:9–13)[4]

This meant that life itself was a gift that God could either bestow or withhold. Everything, according to the psalmist, lay in God's hands alone:

> O Lord, how manifold are your works!
> In wisdom you have made them all; the earth is full of your creatures . . .
> These all look to you to give them their food in due season;
> when you give to them, they gather it up;
> when you open your hand, they are filled with good things.
> When you hide your face, they are dismayed;
> when you take away their breath, they die and return to their dust.
>
> (Ps 104:24, 27–29; cf. Amos 4:7–9)

For Israel, therefore, the fruits of field and orchard and vineyard were by no means automatic: while the bounty of nature was an expression of God's faithfulness towards creation, it could nonetheless be impaired or impeded by a lack of reciprocal obedience on the part of his people. God tells the first humans, "See, I have given you every plant yielding seed that is upon the face of all the earth, and every tree with seed in its fruit; you shall have them for food" (Gen 1:29). It seems only fitting, therefore, that their sole responsibility on earth is "to till . . . and keep" the garden that God has planted in Eden (Gen 2:8, 15). Yet when Adam and Eve disobey—by misappropriating the fruit of a tree!—the penalty imposed on them is that the earth will no longer yield its fruit so freely, and their own efforts to bring forth new life will forever be marked by pain:

> To the woman he said,
> "I will greatly increase your pangs in childbearing;
> in pain you shall bring forth children . . ."
> To the man he said . . .
> "Cursed is the ground because of you;
> in toil you shall eat of it all the days of your life;

---

4. Compare also Job 38:12–38.

> thorns and thistles it shall bring forth for you;
> and you shall eat the plants of the field.
> By the sweat of your face you shall eat bread until you return to the ground ..."
>
> (Gen 3:17–19)

God's sentencing of Cain for the murder of his brother repeats the same motif: "When you till the ground, it will no longer yield to you its strength" (Gen 4:12). But in the aftermath of the glood, God decides that there will be a limit to such punishments:

> And when the Lord smelled the pleasing odor, the Lord said in his heart, "I will never again curse the ground because of humankind, for the inclination of the human heart is evil from youth; nor will I ever again destroy every living creature as I have done. As long as the earth endures, seed [זרע/σπέρμα] and harvest, cold and heat, summer and winter, day and night, shall not cease."
>
> (Gen 8:21–22 NRSV alt.)

Still, the basic principle holds: obedience and disobedience on the part of the covenant people each carry their own reward. Keeping faith with God brings forth all the blessings of the earth:

> Blessed shall be the fruit of your womb, the fruit of your ground, and the fruit of your livestock, both the increase of your cattle and the issue of your flock. Blessed shall be your basket and your kneading bowl.... The Lord will command the blessing upon you in your barns, and in all that you undertake; he will bless you in the land that the Lord your God is giving you.... The Lord will make you abound in prosperity, in the fruit of your womb, in the fruit of your livestock, and in the fruit of your ground in the land that the Lord swore to your ancestors to give you. The Lord will open for you his rich storehouse, the heavens, to give the rain of your land in its season and to bless all your undertakings.
>
> (Deut 28:4–5, 8–9, 11–12; cf. Prov 3:9–10)

For biblical Israel, the converse remains equally true: failure to keep the covenant results just as surely in the withdrawal of divine blessing:

> You shall carry much seed into the field but shall gather little in, for the locust shall consume it. You shall plant vineyards and dress them, but you shall neither drink the wine nor gather the

grapes, for the worm shall eat them. You shall have olive trees throughout all your territory, but you shall not anoint yourself with the oil, for your olives shall drop off. You shall have sons and daughters, but they shall not remain yours, for they shall go into captivity.

(Deut 28:38–41)

Thus when God pronounces judgment on the iniquities of King Ahab, it is the land and its produce that suffer first: "As the Lord the God of Israel lives, before whom I stand," declares Elijah, "There shall be neither dew nor rain these years, except by my word" (1 Kgs 17:1).[5] Likewise for the prophet Haggai, who writes to a community newly returned from exile, recent crop failures are not due to inclement weather, poor soil conditions, or inadequate cultivation. It is not that farming skills have been forgotten in the generations of servitude. Rather, the nation is hungry because it remains under judgment (Hag 1:5–6, 9–11). Conversely, rejuvenation of the land and the return of abundant harvests are unmistakable signs of forgiveness and the restoration of God's blessing:

> I struck you and all the products of your toil with blight and mildew and hail; yet you did not return to me, says the Lord. Consider from this day on, from the twenty-fourth day of the ninth month. Since the day that the foundation of the Lord's temple was laid, consider: Is there any seed left in the barn? Do the vine, the fig tree, the pomegranate, and the olive tree still yield nothing? From this day on I will bless you.
>
> (Hag 2:17–19)

The prophet Zechariah offers similar testimony concerning the day of God's future victory on behalf of his chosen nation:

> On that day the Lord their God will save them, for they are the flock of his people;
> for like the jewels of a crown they shall shine on his land.
> For what goodness and beauty are his!
> Grain shall make the young men flourish, and new wine the young women.
>
> (Zech 9:16–17)

---

5. So Adar, *The Biblical Narrative*, 81–83 [with mispagination].

In place of this more prosaic rendering, however, the NJPS translation brings to the fore a sense in which the people themselves are the evidence of God's life-giving work in their midst:

> The Lord their God shall prosper them on that day. . . .
> How lovely, how beautiful they shall be,
> *Producing young men like new grain,*
> *Young women like new wine!*

Likewise in the prayers and praise of Israel, the fertility of fields and families provides a very concrete indication of divine favor:

> May our sons in their youth be like plants full grown,
> our daughters like corner pillars, cut for the building of a palace.
> May our barns be filled, with produce of every kind;
> may our sheep increase by thousands, by tens of thousands in our fields. . . .
> Happy are the people to whom such blessings fall;
> Happy are the people whose God is the Lord.
>
> (Ps 144:12–13, 15)

God, then, is the source of all life: not only are the "forces of nature"—sun, wind, and rain—under God's direct command, so too are what we would today think of as purely "natural" processes: fertilization, growth, and fruitfulness of plants, animals, and people alike.[6] Directly challenging the fertility religions that have drawn Israel away, God declares in Hosea 14:8, "I am like a cypress ever green, all your fruitfulness comes from me" (JB).

With a sense that life itself reflects the grace of God, and conscious of being daily sustained by God, the people of Israel apply this understanding of divine providence within the "natural order" as a metaphor for national identity. Often taken to be one of the earliest poems in the Hebrew canon, the "Song of the Sea" in Exodus 15 celebrates God's miraculous deliverance of his chosen people from the armies of Egypt. Using an analogy from nature, the hymn looks forward to a settled future rooted metaphorically on Mount Zion:

> You brought them in *and planted them* on the mountain of your own possession,
> the place, O Lord, that you made your abode,
> the sanctuary, O Lord, that your hands have established.
>
> (Exod 15:17)

---

6. Matthews ("Treading the Winepress," 24 and 28–29) points out that such dynamics are common within the literature of the Ancient Near East. Cf. *1 En.* 80:2–3.

Biblical and post-biblical texts alike frequently speak of God's people in these terms: the nation is often described as a vine or vineyard that the Lord has planted:

> You brought a vine out of Egypt; you drove out the nations and planted it.
> You cleared the ground for it; it took deep root and filled the land....
> Turn again, O God of hosts; look down from heaven, and see;
> have regard for this vine, the stock that your right hand planted.
>
> (Ps 80:8–9, 14–15)[7]

In terms of material culture, "the vine is a frequent figure on coins and ceramics from the Maccabean period on."[8] Many scriptural passages employ such imagery either in the context of national judgment and exile—the parable of the Lord's vineyard in Isaiah 5 is a prominent example—or to describe the promise of restoration. Jeremiah 31, for instance, expands on its promise of a new covenant by appealing to agricultural imagery:

> The days are surely coming, says the Lord,
> when I will sow the house of Israel and the house of Judah
> with the seed of humans and the seed of animals.
> And just as I have watched over them to pluck up and break down,
> to overthrow, destroy, and bring evil,
> so I will watch over them to build and to plant, says the Lord.
>
> (Jer 31:27–28)

Indeed, just as Jeremiah 2:3 identifies Israel as "the first fruits of his harvest," so too the righteous of Israel are likened to fruitful trees, even to the point of straining the metaphor:

> The righteous flourish like the palm tree, and grow like a cedar in Lebanon.
> They are planted in the house of the Lord; they flourish in the courts of our God.
> In old age they still produce fruit; they are always green and full of sap ...
>
> (Ps 92:12–14)[9]

---

7. Compare Num 24:5–6; 2 Sam 7:10; 1 Chr 17:9; Ps 44:2; Isa 5:1–10, 60:21; Jer 2:21, 11:17, 17:8, 45:4, 24:6, 32:41, 42:10; Ezek 15:1–8, 17:5–10, 22–24; Hos 9:13, 10:1, 14:6–7; Amos 9:15, etc.

8. Beasley-Murray, *John*, 272; further discussion of this image in Second Temple Judaism in Brown, *The Gospel According to John XIII–XXI*, 669–72, 674–75.

9. Other prominent examples include Ps 1:3, Isa 53:2, 61:3, and Jer 17:8.

Further examples from intertestamental literature illustrate the continued currency of such imagery in the centuries leading up to the time of Jesus and the New Testament. The following passage, from the Thanksgiving Hymns of the Qumran community, likely originated in the second century BCE or earlier. Here a messianic symbol (the "Shoot," from Isaiah 11:1) is combined with imagery symbolizing the Edenic character, abundant growth, and cosmic significance of the community of the righteous as a whole:

> And Thou hast sent out a sprouting as a flower that shall bloom forever,
> that the Shoot may grow into the branches of the eternal planting.
> And its shade shall spread over all [the earth
> and] its [top] reach up to the heavens and its roots go down to the Abyss.
> And all the rivers of Eden [shall water] its [bou]ghs
> and it shall become a mighty forest,
> [and the glory of] its forest shall spread over the world without end,
> as far as Sheol [for ever].[10]

From another collection of hymns, the so-called *Psalms of Solomon*, which respond to the crisis occasioned by Rome's capture of Jerusalem in the first century BCE, comes a similar description of God's holy people:

> The Lord's paradise, the trees of life, are his devout ones.
> Their planting is firmly rooted forever;
> they shall not be uprooted as long as the heavens shall last,
> for Israel is the portion and inheritance of God.
>
> (*Pss. Sol.* 14:3–5)[11]

Finally, *Fourth Ezra*, which we first encountered in the previous chapter, offers a description of faithful Israel that (in its full form) combines images of forests, trees, flowers, rivers, birds, and flocks in immediate succession. Still, the agricultural imagery remains prominent:

> And I said, "O sovereign Lord, from every forest of the earth
> and from all its trees you have chosen one vine, and from all
> the lands of the world you have chosen for yourself one region,
> and from all the flowers of the world you have chosen for yourself one lily . . . and from all the multitude of peoples you have

---

10. 1QH 14.15–17, quoted from Elliott, *The Survivors of Israel*, 337 (but using standardized column and line references). On the use at Qumran of agricultural imagery for the community of the faithful, see further Brooke, "4Q500 1 and the Use of Scripture," 268–75.

11. This and other intertestamental examples are noted by Schweitzer, *The Good News*, 327.

gotten for yourself one people; and to this people, whom you have loved, you have given the Law which is approved by all . . ."

(4 Ezra 5:23–27)[12]

In each case, God's chosen people are a plant, a tree, a vine whose abundance signifies the divine source of their life. So central is this kind of imagery to the self-understanding of Israel in this period that, according to the Jewish historian Flavius Josephus (ca. 37–100 CE), vines of pure gold, with "grape clusters as tall as a man," hung above the gate of the sanctuary in the Jerusalem temple (*War* 5.210; cf. *Ant.* 15.395).[13]

To summarize the discussion thus far, God alone makes the earth bring forth abundance, or else withholds abundance as a sign of displeasure; God "plants" a chosen people in the land of promise; the faithful in particular are "the planting of the Lord." Such imagery is integral to Jewish self-understanding in Jesus' day: life and blessing come from the hand of God alone.

> If now ye will have your prayers heard before Almighty God for the increase of your corn and cattle, and for the defence thereof from unseasonable mists and blasts, from hail and other such tempests, love equity and righteousness, ensue mercy and charity, which God most requireth at our hands. . . . He will repress the devouring caterpillar, which should devour your fruits. He will give you peace and quiet to gather in your provision, that ye may "sit every man under his own vine" quietly, without fear of the foreign enemies to invade you. He will give you, not only food to feed on, but stomachs and good appetites to take comfort of your fruits, whereby in all things ye may have sufficiency. Finally, he will bless you with all manner [of] abundance in this transitory life, and endue you with all manner [of] benediction in the next world, in the kingdom of heaven, through the merits of our Lord and Savior. To whom with the Father, and the Holy Ghost, be all honour everlastingly. Amen.
>
> Concluding "Exhortation" from "A Homily for the Days of Rogation Week"
> *Second Book of Homilies* (London: 1562)[14]

---

12. Cited from the translation by Metzger, *OTP* 1:533; fuller discussion in Elliott, *The Survivors of Israel*, 341–43.

13. This detail is confirmed by the Roman historian Tacitus (56–117 CE), *Hist.* 5.5, as well as by *m. Mid.* 3:8.

14. Quoted from Howse, *Best Sermons Ever*, 42.

"HOLY SEED": GOD'S PEOPLE SOWN IN GOOD EARTH

One further development, rooted in a specific set of vocabulary, completes our survey of this wide-ranging set of metaphors in the Hebrew Bible and intertestamental literature, as God's promise of fecundity for the *land* is applied in turn to the fertility of the *nation*. In Hebrew and Aramaic alike, the word (זרע) can designate either the "seed" that a farmer sows in the ground or the "seed" both of humans and of animals.[15] In the latter case most modern English versions translate this word as "offspring" in order to avoid confusion. Appearing first to Abram, YHWH promises him, "To your seed I will give this land" (Gen 12:7).[16] Such is the influence of this language that it ultimately becomes conventional: in literature of the Second Temple period, as Samuel Sandmel observes, "The seed of Abraham is synonymous with the word Jew."[17] The same promise holds for the next generation, as God tells Isaac: "I will make your seed as numerous as the stars of heaven, and will give to your seed all these lands; and all the nations of the earth shall gain blessing for themselves through your seed" (Gen 26:4). Later still God promises Jacob at Bethel, "The land that I gave to Abraham and Isaac I will give to you, and I will give the land to your seed after you" (Gen 35:12).[18] God's people are sometimes referred to as the "seed" of all three patriarchs combined.[19] This equivalence is so commonplace that the *targumim*—Aramaic paraphrases of the biblical text with roots in the Second Temple era—regularly translate references to "seed" as "sons."[20]

In at least two instances, recognizing this equivalence provides a key to proper interpretation of the biblical narrative. Only a single chapter of Genesis is devoted to Isaac, the "middle" patriarch between Abraham and Jacob, narrated in such a way as to highlight God's ultimate assurance of fertility and prosperity in the family line.[21] The chapter opens with famine,

---

15. The verb "to sow" consists of the same Hebrew letters.

16. Cf. Gen 13:15–16, 15:3–5, 13, 18, 17:9; Exod 33:1; Josh 24:3; 2 Chr 20:7; Ps 105:6; Isa 41:8; Sir 44:21; *T. Levi* 8:15; 3 Macc 6:3; 4 Macc 6:22, 18:1; *Pss. Sol.* 9:9, 18:3; so Luke 1:55; Acts 3:25; Rom 4:13–18, 9:7–8, 11:1; 2 Cor 11:22; Gal 3:16–29; Heb 2:16; *m. Ned.* 3:11, etc.

17. Sandmel, *Philo's Place in Judaism*, 37; cf. 33, 93–94.

18. Cf. Gen 28:3–4; Num 23:10; Ps 22:24; Isa 45:19, 65:9; Jer 33:26; Ezek 20:5; 4 *Ezra* 8:16, 9:30.

19. So Exod 32:13, 33:1; Deut 1:8, 34:4; Tob 4:12; *m. B. Qam.* 8:6; *m. B. Meṣ'ia* 7:1, etc.

20. Wilcox, "The Promise of the 'Seed,'" 3–6.

21. More fully than can be summarized here, Nicol ("The Narrative Structure") proposes that resolution of impediments to the promise of divine blessing provides a

following which an account of Isaac and Rebekah in the territory of Abimelech is framed by matching promises of bountiful "seed" (Gen 26:3–4, 24). Prospects of fulfillment seem dim, both because of conflicts over water rights and because Isaac tries to pass off his wife as his sister. Nonetheless, "Isaac sowed seed in that land, and in the same year reaped a hundredfold. The Lord blessed him, and the man became rich" (Gen 26:12–13). We will return to this passage in the following chapter, as it has an important bearing on Jesus' parable of the Sower, but for the moment it will suffice to observe that such a bountiful blessing on *agricultural* seed provides immediate evidence of what God ultimately intends for Isaac's human progeny: one form of "seed" functions as a metaphor for the other.

According to one reading of this text, the crop in question is barley, foreshadowing another drama of threatened lineage that is played out in the context of a barley harvest. Sometime in late spring, the widowed Ruth gleans leftovers from the barley harvest in fields belonging to Boaz, a distant relative by marriage. She approaches him for protection as he sleeps on (note!) a threshing floor; then in the morning Boaz pours six measures of barley into her shawl, lest she return to her mother-in-law empty-handed. Just so, she soon becomes his wife, and those who bear witness pray that God will also grant them "seed" (Ruth 4:12, the only occurrence of this word in the book). The narrative concludes with the birth of a son whose own grandson, David, will one day become king (4:17). In this second narrative also, one "seed" serves as a transparent metaphor for the other.[22]

As with the imagery of plants and planting, "seed" language can be applied to the righteous in particular, who are identified more specifically as "*holy* seed." Such terminology first emerges, it would appear, at the time of the return from exile in Babylon, as the community reasserts its distinctive identity. In the days immediately following their arrival in Jerusalem, Ezra is moved to repentance by the people's infidelity to God's covenant, which finds expression in their willingness to intermarry with non-Israelites:

> The officials approached me and said, "The people of Israel, the priests, and the Levites have not separated themselves from the peoples of the lands with their abominations, from the Canaanites, the Hittites, the Perizzites, the Jebusites, the Ammonites, the Moabites, the Egyptians, and the Amorites. For they have taken some of their daughters as wives for themselves and for their sons. Thus the *holy seed* has mixed itself with the peoples

unifying theme to the chapter as a whole.

22. Cf. Hubbard, *The Book of Ruth*, 261–62. (I owe this reference to my colleague Mark Boda.)

> of the lands, and in this faithlessness the officials and leaders have led the way."
>
> (Ezra 9:1-2)

Likely taking its cue from this passage and the theological debate that it reflects, "holy seed" (alternatively, "righteous" or "eternal seed") serves in the Second Temple period as code language for the faithful of Israel, particularly in texts that discourage or prohibit marriage with non-Israelites.[23] For example, the book of *Jubilees* (essentially a visionary retelling of Genesis and the opening chapters of Exodus, from the second century BCE) specifies that Isaac is born "on the feast of the first fruits of the harvest" (*Jub.* 16:13), thereby identifying him as the initial fulfillment of God's promise to establish Abraham's "seed." As Abraham tells his chosen heir, "God Most High . . . brought me out from Ur of the Chaldees so that he might give me this land to inherit it forever and to raise up a holy seed . . ." (*Jub.* 22:27). That Isaac and his offspring in turn are to be the sole inheritors of God's blessing is what distinguishes them from the elder patriarch's other sons, and from all the other nations of the earth:

> And all of the seed of [Abraham's] sons would become nations. And they would be counted with the nations. But from the sons of Isaac one would become a *holy seed* and he would not be counted among the nations because he would become the portion of the Most High and all his seed would fall (by lot) into that which God will rule so that he might become a people (belonging) to the Lord. . . . [F]rom [Abraham] there would be a righteous planting for eternal generations and a *holy seed* so that he might be like the one who made everything.
>
> (*Jub.* 16:17-18, 26)

In similar fashion the sectarians of Qumran identified themselves with the "holy seed" of Isaiah 6:13 (so 1QIsa[a] 6:13), much as Targum Jonathan finds a reference in Isaiah 6:13 to the remnant of the faithful who will at last end Israel's long years of exile:

> So the exiles of Israel shall be gathered together,
> and they shall return to their land;

---

23. In addition to the passages treated below, cf. Tob 4:12; *Jub.* 22:11-12, 25:3, 30:7-10; 4QMMT 84; 11Q ApPsa iv.6; Aramaic *Testament of Levi* a 17-18; 1 *En.* 65:12, 84:6; fuller discussion in Kugel, "The Holiness of Israel," 23-24, 27-29; Hayes, "Intermarriage and Impurity," 9-30, expanded in Kugel, *Gentile Impurities and Jewish Identities*, 68-91, Himmelfarb, "Levi, Phinehas, and the Problem of Intermarriage," 4-12, and Elliott, *The Survivors of Israel*, 314-28.

for the holy seed is their plant.[24]

Therefore on the day of judgment, according to the apocalyptic work known as *First* (or *Ethiopic*) *Enoch*, when the Son of Man is revealed in glory, "The congregation of the holy ones shall be sown, and all the elect ones will stand before him" (1 *En.* 62:8 mg.).[25] Gentile "seed," by contrast, is destined for eradication, as Isaac himself warns his son:

> Be careful, my son, Jacob, that you do not take a wife from any of the seed of the daughters of Canaan, because all of his seed is destined for uprooting from the earth; because through the sin of Ham, Canaan sinned, and all of his seed will be blotted out from the earth.
>
> (*Jub.* 22:20–21)

Even the "seed" of Esau "will be rooted out from under heaven" (*Jub.* 26:34). Likewise the preaching of John the Baptist seems to invoke the notion of a pure or "holy seed": "His winnowing fork is in his hand, and he will clear his threshing floor and will gather his wheat into the granary; but the chaff he will burn with unquenchable fire" (Matt 3:12 // Luke 3:17).

According to Marcus Borg, "A 'quest for holiness' or a 'quest for purity' was the dominant cultural dynamic in the Jewish homeland in the first century. It created a social world order as a purity system, one with sharp social boundaries."[26] This meant, as Kent Brower observes, that "To a greater or lesser degree, all of Second Temple Judaism is concerned with purity. God is holy and therefore dangerous and only dwells safely with his people under conditions of holiness."[27] That this critical dynamic is articulated by means of agricultural imagery will prove significant for our reading of Jesus' agricultural parables, since it again suggests that for Jesus to speak of "seeds" and their growth as an expression of God's kingdom evokes the question of the identity of the true Israel.

As a further, not entirely separate development of the same concept, both Jews and Jewish Christians of the Second Temple period thought of the Messiah in particular as the "seed of Abraham" or "seed of David" par excellence.[28] Paul, for instance, interprets God's promises to Abraham and his

---

24. Evans, *To See and Not Perceive*, 72–73.

25. Isaac, "1 (Ethiopic Apocalypse of) Enoch," 43. The language of this verse likely reflects Hosea 2:25.

26. Borg, *Conflict, Holiness and Politics*, 8, quoted by Brower, "The Holy One and His Disciples," 70.

27. Brower, "The Holy One and His Disciples," 70.

28. Wilcox, "The Promise of the 'Seed,'" passim; as an alternative extension of

"seed" (in the singular) as references to the Christ (Gal 3:16), and calls Jesus the "seed of David according to the flesh" (Rom 1:3). Moreover, declares the apostle, insofar as those who belong to the Messiah are beneficiaries of God's promise, they inherit the title previously reserved for ethnic Israel alone: "If you are of Christ, then you are the *seed of Abraham*, heirs according to promise" (Gal 3:29, author's translation). Notwithstanding his frequent use of agricultural imagery, it does not appear that Jesus intended seed imagery as any kind of indirect self-reference. Nonetheless, his followers' identification of him as God's messianic "seed" could only have encouraged them to interpret his parables in something other than literal terms.

"SEED FOR SOWING AND BREAD FOR EATING": EVIDENCES OF DIVINE LOVE

Since Jesus ministered in a society for which the cycle of seasons and rains and harvest provided the basic rhythms of community life, we would expect his language to reflect agricultural motifs. But even for New Testament writers, whose ministries were likely oriented toward an urban context, such images and ways of thinking represented an essential feature of their vocabulary. From the preaching of Paul and Barnabas at Lystra comes this explanation of the natural order:

> "We are mortals just like you, and we bring you good news, that you should turn from [idolatry] to the living God, who made the heaven and the earth and the sea and all that is in them. In past generations he allowed all the nations to follow their own ways; yet he has not left himself without a witness in doing good—giving you rains from heaven and fruitful seasons, and filling you with food and your hearts with joy."
>
> (Acts 14:15–17)

In his own letters, when Paul wants to encourage generous giving in support of the collection for the Jerusalem church, he turns once more to agricultural imagery:

> God is able to provide you with every blessing in abundance, so that by always having enough of everything, you may share abundantly in every good work.... He who supplies seed to the

---

agricultural symbolism first applied to the nation as a whole, the Messiah is a "vine" (*2 Bar.* 39:7).

sower and bread for food will supply and multiply your seed for sowing and increase the harvest of your righteousness.

(2 Cor 9:8–10)

Paul's language brings us at last to the ultimate focus of our present investigation, and to the claim that appeared on the opening page of this chapter, namely that for Jesus and his contemporaries, God's provision of "seed to the sower and bread for food" represents a direct expression of divine love. Most readers will be familiar with Jesus' instructions in the Sermon on the Mount regarding love of enemies:

> "You have heard that it was said, 'You shall love your neighbor and hate your enemy.' But I say to you, love your enemies and pray for those who persecute you, so that you may be children of your Father in heaven; for he makes his sun rise on the evil and on the good, and sends rain on the righteous and on the unrighteous."
>
> (Matt 5:43–45)

Jesus holds that there should be a "family resemblance" between his followers and the one whom they (following his lead) call "Father." More specifically, they are to demonstrate abundant, generous love even to those who reject them, because this is how God also acts. Here the illustration that Jesus chooses is all-important: "he makes his sun rise on the evil and on the good, and sends rain on the righteous and on the unrighteous." Nature itself, for Jesus, is a demonstration of divine love. Even more familiar, perhaps, is his expansion of the same principle as it applies to the anxieties of daily living:

> "Therefore I tell you, do not worry about your life, what you will eat or what you will drink, or about your body, what you will wear. Is not life more than food, and the body more than clothing? Look at the birds of the air; they neither sow nor reap nor gather into barns, and yet your heavenly Father feeds them. Are you not of more value than they? And can any of you by worrying add a single hour to your span of life? And why do you worry about clothing? Consider the lilies of the field, how they grow; they neither toil nor spin, yet I tell you, even Solomon in all his glory was not clothed like one of these. But if God so clothes the grass of the field, which is alive today and tomorrow is thrown into the oven, will he not much more clothe you—you of little faith?"

(Matt 6:25–30; cf. Luke 12:22–38)

The illustrations that anchor his argument are again drawn from nature, and from a theology of divine providence. More specifically, his statements employ a fortiori reasoning: if God so cares for flowers and birds, the flora and fauna of the natural world, think *how much more so* God can be expected to provide for the human creatures who place their trust in him. Indeed, the comparison extends still further. Seasonal cycles of sowing and reaping and gathering into granaries, as we have seen, imply a practical dependence on the life-giving generosity of God that undergirds the whole of creation. Yet birds, says Jesus, rely on none of these: "they neither sow nor reap nor gather into barns, and yet your heavenly Father feeds them." In fact, they are like Adam and Eve prior to their expulsion from Eden, for whom God provided by means of a biosphere that yielded its bounty without constraint. Just so, says Jesus, will their heavenly Father provide for all who receive his words. Such promises are not merely material or mechanistic, but speak to the very nature of God, and the specifically filial character of such reliance.

The same premise is captured (if rather simplistically) by a nineteenth-century children's hymn still in use to this day:

> God sees the little sparrow fall,
> It meets His tender view;
> If God so loves the little birds,
> I know He loves me, too.
> *He loves me, too, He loves me, too,*
> *I know He loves me, too;*
> *Because He loves the little things,*
> *I know He loves me, too.*
> He paints the lily of the field,
> Perfumes each lily bell;
> If He so loves the little flow'rs,
> I know He loves me well.[29]

The issue at stake is not heavenly provision of the necessities of life for their own sake, but rather (as in the Lord's Prayer: "Give us this day our daily bread"), the fact that the acceptance of such provision implies direct reliance on the loving-kindness of God. Such is his confidence in God's favor and generosity that Jesus promises his listeners abundant divine provision of a sort that has not been theirs since the ground of Eden was cursed, and Adam and Eve expelled from the garden.

---

29. By Maria Straub (1838–1898), originally published in Straub, *Crown of Glory*, 43.

Granted, the conviction that the workings of the natural order reveal God's character and purpose is not original to Jesus. Already in the second century BCE, *First Enoch* cites the evidence of stars and sun and seasons, of rain and trees and fruit, as one source for universal knowledge of God's ways, and therefore as a basis for God's judgment of the wicked (*1 En.* 2–5; this view is shared, incidentally, by the Apostle Paul in Rom 1:19-20). As another, nearly contemporary parallel to Jesus' saying about rain that falls on righteous and unrighteous alike, David Flusser notes a tradition attributed to Johanan ben Zakkai, perhaps the most influential Jewish teacher of the first century CE. According to ben Zakkai, the last verse of Psalm 65 ("the meadows clothe themselves with flocks, the valleys deck themselves with grain, they shout and sing together for joy" [Ps 65:13]) and the first verse of Psalm 66 ("Make a joyful noise to God, all the earth") both refer to rainfall. Since Jew and Gentile benefit equally from the fruit of the earth, both rejoice (although, by implication, only one of the two groups acknowledges the true source of God's bounty).[30] Sounding very much like Jesus, the fourth-century Palestinian rabbi Joshua ben Nehemiah declares, "God causes the sun to shine both upon Israel and upon the nations, for the Lord is good to all."[31] The growing divide between church and synagogue makes it unlikely that ben Nehemiah is quoting from Jesus of Nazareth. In fact, both express a view of sun, rain, and seasons that was typical of contemporary Judaism. As Craig Keener observes, summarizing a range of rabbinic evidence, "Jewish sages saw God's gift of rain as one of his ultimate acts of power and beneficence."[32]

Still, it is possible to be even more specific about the workings of divine love in the realm of nature. The earliest compilation of rabbinic teaching is the Mishnah, from around 200 CE; the earliest representative of rabbinic tradition within that document is said to come from "Simeon the Just," one of two high priests by the same name who held office about a century apart, in 300 BCE and 200 BCE respectively.[33] Although it is no longer possible to know which of these is meant, it is clear that the Mishnah understands Simeon's authority to be preeminent. His teaching, at least two centuries prior to the time of Jesus, is summarized in a single saying:

---

30. Flusser, "Johanan ben Zakkai and Matthew," 490-92; different forms of the story appear in *Deut. Rab.* 7:7 and *Gen. Rab.* 13:6.

31. *Pesiqta Rabbati* 195b, quoted in Montefiore and Loewe, eds., *A Rabbinic Anthology*, 43.

32. Keener, *A Commentary on the Gospel of Matthew*, 204 n.126; cf. Davies and Allison, *The Gospel According to Saint Matthew*, 1:555-56.

33. See Strack and Stemberger, *Introduction to the Talmud and Midrash*, 63.

> The world rests on three things:
> Torah, *Avodah*, and deeds of loving-kindness.
>
> (Mishnah *Pirqe 'Abot* ["Sayings of the Fathers"] 1:2)

That is, the three basic components that together represent the faith and faithfulness of Israel are the law given to Moses at Mount Sinai (*Torah*), the worship of God in the Temple at Jerusalem (*Avodah*), and deeds of "loving-kindness" (or "steadfast love," *hesed*).[34] From one point of view, all three describe the ways in which God's people express their obedience and allegiance to God. Yet all three are in the first instance divine gifts rather than simply human responses, none more so than "deeds of loving-kindness." Just as *Torah* and *Avodah* were first given to Israel on Mount Sinai, so God's own deeds of loving-kindness are what inspire imitation on the part of the faithful. According to Jesus, then, divine love and generosity are revealed in the bounty of sun and rain, in God's provision of food for birds and adornment for flowering plants; according to Johanan ben Zakkai, in rain and grain, and sheep on hillsides; according to a later commentary on Simeon's proverb, in all the works of creation. The work in question, a collection from the third to fourth centuries CE known as *The Sayings of the Fathers according to Rabbi Nathan*, bases this opinion on a creative rendering of Psalm 89:2: "From the very first the world was created only with mercy, as it is said.... *The world is built with mercy* [*hesed*]; *in the very heavens Thou dost establish Thy faithfulness.*"[35] To be sure, these texts do not all belong to the same time period, but precisely for that reason they indicate that such ideas remain prevalent before, during, and well after the time of Jesus.

BACK TO "NATURE"

Where, then, does all of this leave us? For urban dwellers of the twenty-first century, parables about seeds and fields, trees and farming appear to be little more than artifacts of a distant time and place—social, cultural, or historical curiosities far removed from the workings of our own everyday lives. For us, seeds come previously packaged or potted: we encounter them as popcorn kernels ready for the microwave, crunchy bits in bread, or preboiled rice ready for the dinner table in just two minutes. We may acknowledge (as a

---

34. Finkel, "Prayer in Jewish Life," 44–49.

35. *'Abot de Rabbi Nathan* §4, in Goldin, *The Fathers According to Rabbi Nathan*, 34 (emphasis original); cf. Davies, *The Setting of the Sermon on the Mount*, 305–6; on the dating of *'Abot*, see Strack and Stemberger, *Introduction to the Talmud and Midrash*, 227.

local slogan has it) that "Farmers feed cities," but few of us feel much sense of connection to the world of sowing and planting, reaping and harvest. Still less do we think of God as actively at work in the processes of an apparently "natural" world. When it comes to science and nature, we are functionally deist, whatever theological convictions we may profess. Profound conceptual disjunctions between ourselves and the creation of which we are a part, as between creation and its Creator generally, render us oblivious to some of the fundamental presuppositions that underlie Jesus' agricultural parables. For his first hearers, God is the immediate source of all life, and nature as a whole is (at least notionally) a moral realm, directly reflecting the goodness, justice, and generosity of its Creator. The nation of Israel is God's "planting" and its people are "seed," in fact "holy seed" whose ethnic purity and ethical virtue are meant to reflect the righteousness of the One who sustains them. This interconnected series of foundational concepts provides a unique and refreshing point of departure for interpreting—perhaps even preaching from—the parables that now command our attention.

Chapter 3

"Consider the Lilies"
Reading Jesus' Agricultural Parables

"To you has been given the secret of the kingdom of God" (Mark 4:11).

The argument of this chapter is that Jesus' "parables of growth" constitute an invitation for hearers both ancient and modern (preachers foremost among them) to encounter and acknowledge the life-giving power of God. At the same time, the parables in question offer an account of the hearers' own identity as the people of God, those whose life is given and shaped by a vitality not of their own making. The parables accomplish this not by means of subversive rhetoric, psychological insight, narrative winsomeness, or even by virtue of Jesus' personal authority, but ultimately because they appeal to what would have been—at least for their original audience—a common and widespread understanding of the way God works in the everyday world. Doubtless this is true in some measure for all of Jesus' parables, some of which will require at least passing comment in the course of our discussion, but here we are primarily concerned with the Sower (Matt 13:3–9, 18–23 // Mark 4:2–9, 13–20 // Luke 8:5–8, 11–15), the Seed Growing Secretly (Mark 4:26–29), the Mustard Seed (Matt 13:31–32 // Mark 4:30–32 // Luke

13:18–19), the Wheat and Weeds (Matt 13:24–30, 36–43), the Barren Fig Tree (Luke 13:6–9), and, from John's gospel, the True Vine (John 15:1–8). Reflections on the parable of the wealthy but spiritually obtuse farmer (Luke 12:16–21) will provide a transition to the next section of our study.

MANY THINGS IN PARABLES AND MANY WAYS OF READING THEM

Interpreters have tended, in large measure, to regard Jesus' parables as metaphors of human obligation and response—in a manner, that is, precisely opposite the reading proposed here. The parable of the Sower provides an obvious case in point. Among the early church fathers, Augustine of Hippo (354–430 CE) is representative:

> Work diligently the soil while you may. Break up your fallow with the plough. Cast away the stones from your field, and dig out the thorns. Be unwilling to have a "hard heart," such as makes the Word of God of no effect. Be unwilling to have a "thin layer of soil," in which the root of divine love can find no depth in which to enter. Be unwilling to "choke the good seed" by the cares and the lusts of this life, when it is being scattered for your good. When God is the sower and we are the ground, we are called to work to be good ground.[1]

Notwithstanding their emphasis on unmerited grace, churches of the Reformation continue in much the same vein. In homilies on Luke's version of the parable from the first two centuries of German Lutheranism, for example, a high estimation of the preached word and introspective preoccupation with the signs of personal regeneration combine to produce an emphasis on the moral responsibility of the hearer—even, in some cases, to the point of devaluing the power of the gospel itself.[2] Just so, Helmut Thielicke's wartime sermon on "the Seed and the Soils" comes to its climax with a pointed moral challenge:

> No battle, no cross, no crown. He who does not toil and sweat and does not daily fall in line for service to God is exposing his inner man to decay.

---

1. Augustine, "Sermons on New Testament Lessons" 73.3, cited from Oden and Hall, *Mark*, 57; further, Wailes, *Medieval Allegories*, 98–100.
2. Westendorf, "The Parable of the Sower (Luke 8:4–15)."

> God's grace is no cheap grace; you must pay for it with all you are and all that you have. You can loaf your way into hell, but the kingdom of heaven can only be seized by force.[3]

The primary appeal of this line of interpretation is that it preaches well: it gives the preacher something to insist on and the hearers something to do in response. Everyone leaves church feeling that something has been, or could be, accomplished. So compelling and apparently self-evident is this approach that it will only be overturned by careful and consistent attention to the conceptual backgrounds outlined so far in our study.

It seems fair to ask why, if the approach advocated here is as self-evident as claimed, it has not gained favor before now. At least in the modern era, the answer may be due in some measure to an influential article by Norwegian scholar Nils Alstrup Dahl, which explicitly rules out the sort of interpretation proposed in this study. Although Dahl also prioritizes divine action over human endeavor in the parables of growth, he understands organic imagery and "the idea of growth" to represent nothing more than the certainty of God's triumph in history. Commenting on the parable of the Budding Fig Tree (Mark 13:28–29), he observes:

> There is a fixed plan and order for the eschatological chain of events, which can be illustrated by the process of growth. But what happens is not due to an historic development following an immanent necessity, but to the creative activity of God, who, according to his own plan, leads history towards its goal. . . . The pictures taken from organic growth illustrate the divine order and eschatological necessity of what is happening.[4]

For Dahl the point of such parables is not divine agency per se so much as the inexorable unfolding of historical progress to which that agency gives rise:

> To the growth which God in accordance with his own established order gives in the sphere of organic life corresponds the series of events by which God in accordance with his plan of salvation leads history towards the end of the world and the beginning [of] the new aeon. This should, however, not be taken to mean that we must seek the point of the parables in this idea of growth. Rather, it is presupposed as a matter of course.[5]

---

3. Thielicke, *The Waiting Father*, 60.

4. Dahl, "The Parables of Growth," 145. On the paradigmatic character of Dahl's article, see Scott, "Parables of Growth Revisited," 3–6.

5. Dahl, "The Parables of Growth," 146.

In contrast to an emphasis on life-giving divine power, Dahl assumes the main purpose of these parables to be historical and eschatological, which (ironically) threatens to distance them from the historical setting in which they were first articulated. Certainly they engage eschatological themes and interests, but the final triumph of God's kingdom is not to be confused with the broader character of the kingdom in all its various dimensions. Stated differently, growth in nature, the growth of the kingdom, and even its ultimate eschatological manifestation all depend fundamentally upon the power of God: no single expression of divine agency can take precedence over another, for all point equally to the same theological source.

For John Dominic Crossan, on the other hand, references to eschatological consummation are later additions. Once shorn of historical overtones, the four "seed" parables instead become "ontologico-poetic metaphors," by which Crossan means that they represent "the primary and immediate expression of [Jesus'] own experience of God."[6] On such a view, religious experience is the cause, not the consequence, of his ministry: "Jesus' actions and controversies, and eventually Jesus' death, are the result and not the referent of the parables, they are the effect and not the cause of these images." By means of such parables, Jesus also summons his hearers to action: the parabolic revelation of God's gracious providence calls for "resolution" and "response":

> The sower and the mustard-seed articulate the gift of the kingdom's advent and the joyful surprise of its experience: despite all the problems of sowing there is the abundant harvest, and despite the smallness of the seed there is the shady peacefulness of the grown plant. The seed growing secretly and the tares are images of resolute and prudent action, of the farmer who knows how and when to move. They are parables of the response demanded by the kingdom's advent. Together the four parables contain in contrasted images the revelation of the kingdom's presence and the resolution that presence demands.[7]

Yet the logic of Crossan's analysis appears (at the very least) incomplete, posing a difficult challenge for the reader. If Jesus' religious experience, expressed in parables, is indeed what motivates his teaching, surely his hearers will require similar inspiration if they are to respond in kind. For this we will need to look beyond the parables themselves: insofar as Jesus' experience of God underlies his ministry, we will want to examine the theological origins

---

6. Crossan, "The Seed Parables of Jesus," 261 n.62, 265.
7. Ibid., 266.

of the experience itself. Parables that invoke a life-giving divine vitality seem uniquely suited to such an inquiry.

Although it seems counterintuitive for readers such as ourselves (accustomed as we are to an emphasis on human responsibility), understanding the agricultural parables as open allusions to divine power suggests that their primary purpose is to depict the nature and ways of God. The distinction is subtle, yet essential, and its implications profound. Rather than emphasizing human endeavor, Jesus appeals in the first instance to *divine* action, thereby raising the question of divine identity. By alluding to divine identity, he also raises the question of *human* identity, and the identity of his hearers in particular. In other words, the most critical consideration for his audience is one not of moral responsibility ("What should we do?") but of theological identity, in both its divine and human dimensions: "How does God act?"; therefore, "Who is God?", and therefore in turn, "What does it mean to be the true people of God?"

The reason for this theological orientation is not difficult to discern. These parables were originally addressed to various first-century Palestinian Jews: not, that is, to Stoics, Cynics, Zoroastrians, initiates of some Hellenistic "mystery" religion, or any other contemporary audience outside the narrow confines of what Jesus himself calls "the *lost* sheep of the house of Israel" (Matt 10:6, 15:24). That is to say, the parables are directed in the first instance to those who already consider themselves to be members of the covenant of Moses and inheritors of the patriarchal promises. Who is or is not a true member of that covenant and what covenant fidelity should consist of are crucial points of contention, not only for Jesus but for just about everyone in the Judaism of his day. Obviously, each set of proponents considers their own position to be of greatest faithfulness, and those of their various opponents erroneous—otherwise debate would be unnecessary. All without exception would claim, "We are the people of his pasture and the sheep of his hand" (Ps 95:7). Whether or not they are indeed "lost sheep," as Jesus contends, is therefore the issue at stake.

In this light, Jesus' rhetorical strategy (which must be distinguished from the *theological* function of his parables) becomes all-important. Jesus frequently argues his point not by insisting that his own position is correct, but by appealing instead to the perspectives of his hearers. The clearest examples of this approach are the stories and sayings that begin with him asking, "Which of *you* . . . [τίς ἐξ ὑμῶν]?"

> "Which of you by being anxious can add one cubit to his span of life?"
>
> (Matt 6:27 // Luke 12:25)

"Which of you who has a friend will go to him at midnight and say to him, 'Friend, lend me three loaves . . .'?"

(Luke 11:5)

"What man among you, if his son asks him for bread, would give him a stone?"

(Matt 7:9; cf. Luke 11:11)

"What man among you, if he has only one sheep and it falls into a pit on the Sabbath, will not lay hold of it and lift it out?"

(Matt 12:11; cf. Luke 14:5)

"For which of you, desiring to build a tower, does not first sit down and count the cost, whether he has enough to complete it?"

(Luke 14:28)

"What man among you, having a hundred sheep and losing one of them, does not leave the ninety-nine in the wilderness and go after the one that is lost until he finds it?"

(Luke 15:4)

"Who among you would say to your slave who has just come in from plowing or tending sheep in the field, 'Come here at once and take your place at the table'? Would you not rather say to him, 'Prepare supper for me, put on your apron and serve me while I eat and drink; later you may eat and drink'?"

(Luke 17:7–8)

According to Matthew he sometimes asks, emphasizing the personal pronoun, "What do *you* think?" (e.g. Matt 17:25; 18:12; 21:28; 22:42). Jesus' logic is that the hearers' own convictions should make the answer to each question obvious.[8]

So also (even in the absence of such direct appeal) when it comes to parables about "the kingdom of God." Even if Jesus considers some of them to be straying or "lost sheep," most members of his audience would surely have numbered themselves among the chosen people—possibly not the most perfect or pure members of God's chosen people, but in any event not what Paul dismissively refers to as "Gentile sinners" (so Gal 2:15; cf. Matt 18:17). As a matter of rhetorical strategy, then, Jesus takes such an

---

8. A similar logic applies to Jesus' use of folk sayings (Matt 16:23, John 4:35), or in circumstances that imply self-incrimination (Matt 26:25; Matt 26:64 // Luke 22:70; Matt 27:11 // Mark 15:2 // Luke 23:3).

assumption as his starting point. If the hearers to whom he addresses kingdom parables believe themselves to be members of the covenant, inheritors of the patriarchal promises, and subjects of God's gracious reign, Jesus will (at least for the purpose of teaching) treat them as such. To borrow a phrase from modern legal practice, he will appeal to what they "know or reasonably ought to know" about the ways of God. This is not to deny that he is equally capable, on occasion, of taking the opposite approach ("Get behind me, Satan" [Mark 8:33]; "faithless and perverse generation" [Matt 17:17 // Luke 9:4]; "Woe to you . . . hypocrites!" [Matt 23:13], etc.). But at least in these parables he will speak of a theologically vibrant world in which the mighty word of God is the source of all life; where the power of God makes the sun shine, the rain fall, the grain ripen, and the trees bear fruit; where the hearers themselves depend on God's own goodness and generosity for life. He will assume everything, in short, that provided the focus of the previous chapter. Likewise he will assume—until forced to some other conclusion—basic familiarity with "the Scriptures [and] the power of God" on the part of his hearers, and tell parables that constantly invoke these two sources of interpretation. Given this approach, the audience's comprehension or lack thereof becomes a matter of spiritual diagnosis, self-assessment, perhaps even judgment. The purpose of this strategy is that by virtue of their response to such teaching, his hearers will reveal whether or to what degree they indeed recognize the ways of the One whom Jesus calls "Father." Hence, incidentally, his astonishment when his closest followers ask him to interpret the parable of the Sower: "Do you not understand this parable? Then how will you understand all the parables?" (Mark 14:13; cf. 9:19). Because he has chosen them, because they are closest to him, they of all people should have been able to grasp his meaning without difficulty.

With regard to contemporary ministries of preaching and teaching, preachers likewise do well to assume that their hearers are children of God and inheritors of the kingdom. Not, perhaps, the most perfect of saints. Nor, necessarily, because the preacher altogether endorses this sunny assessment. On the contrary, the preacher may (not unlike Jesus) entertain grave doubts as to the sanctity of certain congregants. But no matter. Insofar as the hearers have shown up to church, identify themselves as "Christians," and are willing (however grudgingly) to endure the Sunday morning sermon, the preacher should address them as faithful followers of Christ. As with Jesus, however, this *rhetorical* approach entails a deeper *theological* stratagem. By addressing them *as* disciples, proclamation of Jesus' life and teaching will reveal whether or in what sense they actually *are* disciples. This, as we saw in our first chapter, is how the Gospels also function, treating all readers as "insiders" so as to proclaim the "open secret" of the gospel and thereby declare the full import of God's reign. In this manner the Gospels, the parables within them, and the preaching to which they give rise call for repentance and faith on the part of every hearer. Far from assuming that we have nothing more to learn, it is a call for us to turn again and again from every less sufficient offer of life, identity, or sustenance, and toward their true source in God.

Having thus broached the topic of parabolic language in relation to the larger context of Jesus' ministry, and its possible implications for preaching today, we turn now to consider the parables themselves. Here our contention will be that the content and purpose of Jesus' agricultural parables offers a model for preachers to imitate, even though that model will challenge many of our assumptions and expectations about the nature of Christian proclamation.

SOWER AND SOIL (MATT 13:3-9, 18-23 // MARK 4:2-9, 13-20 // LUKE 8:5-8, 11-15)

"The Sower Goes out to Sow . . ."

The parable of the Sower and the Soil commands disproportionate attention not only because it is typically understood to describe the ministry of proclamation but also because of its paradigmatic role. As many interpreters note, Jesus' response to his uncomprehending followers identifies it as a "parable of parables," a model for the way in which all such stories function: "He said to them, 'Do you not understand this parable? Then how will you understand *all the parables*?'" (Mark 4:13).

Most view this parable as a straightforward, if largely pessimistic description of Christian ministry, applying its exposition to all preachers of the gospel:

> The sower sows the word. These are the ones on the path where the word is sown: when they hear, Satan immediately comes and takes away the word that is sown in them. And these are the ones sown on rocky ground: when they hear the word, they immediately receive it with joy. But they have no root, and endure only for a while; then, when trouble or persecution arises on account of the word, immediately they fall away. And others are

> those sown among the thorns: these are the ones who hear the word, but the cares of the world, and the lure of wealth, and the desire for other things come in and choke the word, and it yields nothing. And these are the ones sown on the good soil: they hear the word and accept it and bear fruit, thirty and sixty and a hundredfold.
>
> (Mark 4:14–20)

The comments of Halford Luccock in the mid-twentieth century are representative:

> It is a true picture of every teacher's experience, whether the teaching is done in pulpit, classroom, or in the contacts of daily life.... There are different kinds of soil; much seed will not come to fruit.[9]

Equally characteristic are the title and thesis of an article from the *Journal for Preachers*: "Sowing Seeds in Difficult Soil: Preaching to Those Who Won't Listen."[10] On such a view, the parable emphasizes human responsibility: "Jesus' purpose seems to have been primarily that of warning against the habits which make void the hearing of the word."[11] No doubt this forms part of his intended meaning, but whether it is primary is another matter altogether. Donald Juel, for instance, comments on the nonhortatory character of the parable, quoting a student whose perceptive observations were shaped by the experience of having grown up on a farm:

> How strange, she noted, that we use the image of soil to exhort people to change. Soil is a passive image. A farmer who began every day exhorting his fields to produce would seem a fool. The soil awaits activity it cannot generate. How, she asked, do we turn this parable into exhortation?
>
> The question is quite appropriate. Jesus' parable includes no imperatives—except for the command to "listen" (4:9). The parable simply describes how things are. And how is it with the Kingdom? The Kingdom is like a tiny seed that, once planted, will become an enormous shrub (vv. 30–32). It is like a farmer who plants, then can only wait for the growth to occur until the harvest arrives (vv. 26–29).[12]

---

9. Luccock, "St. Mark: Exposition," 696.
10. Carter, "Sowing Seeds in Difficult Soil."
11. Luccock, "St. Mark: Exposition," 698.
12. Juel, "Encountering the Sower," 278.

Emphasizing the responsibility of hearers to bring forth good fruit entails two critical assumptions. The first is that Jesus' own ministry and that of his later followers operate under the same or similar conditions. Preachers, in other words, are equally sowers, not merely recipients of what Jesus' brother calls the "implanted word" (Jas 1:21). Although the question of continuity between Jesus' ministry and that of various later representatives is necessarily complex and nuanced, the theological temerity of invoking messianic authority for the preaching of the church should not be underestimated. Second, an emphasis on human responsibility implies that success in bearing spiritual fruit lies within the power of the hearers, and that the goal of Jesus' teaching is therefore, in some sense, moral fortitude or reform in the face of worldly distractions and outright persecution. To be sure, moral responsibility and moral endeavor are not exact equivalents. Nonetheless, a simple test applies: to what extent do the original twelve themselves succeed in manifesting the good fruit of which the parable speaks?

The answer is unexpected. Mark consistently employs the language of the parable to describe responses to Jesus' teaching, particularly so when it comes to his closest followers.[13] Like the sower in the parable, Jesus proclaims "the word" (2:2) to all who will listen:

> With many such parables he spoke the *word* to them, as they were able to hear it; he did not speak to them except in parables, but he explained everything in private to his disciples.
>
> (Mark 4:33–34)

Again, private exposition for the benefit of his inner circle includes the "word" of his impending death (8:32). This elicits a rebuke from Peter, whom Jesus identifies with "Satan" (8:33), no doubt because Peter is trying to suppress or deny the truth of what he has said (cf. Mark 4:14). Later a wealthy man will be dismayed at the "word" (10:22) that Jesus speaks concerning treasure in heaven and the dangers of worldly goods, yet the disciples themselves are no less astonished (10:23–26). Once more Jesus must explain his meaning to those who should have no difficulty understanding:

> "Truly I tell you, there is no one who has left house or brothers or sisters or mother or father or children or fields, for my sake and for the sake of the good news, who will not receive

---

13. Drury, *The Parables in the Gospels*, 51–52; Tolbert, *Sowing the Gospel*, 121–230 (also Tolbert, "How the Gospel of Mark Builds Character," 351–55); Heil, "Reader-Response," 275–80; and Keegan, "The Parable of the Sower," 507–16, all propose more general, thematic similarities (rather than specific verbal links) between the parable or its interpretation and Mark's depiction of discipleship.

a *hundredfold* now in this age—houses, brothers and sisters, mothers and children, and fields, with *persecutions*—and in the age to come eternal life."

(Mark 10:29–30)

In keeping with the prospect of imminent persecution, Jesus admonishes his follows not to be "ashamed of me and my *words*" (Mark 8:38), yet the evangelist reports that "All of them deserted him and fled" (14:50). At each of these junctures, the vocabulary of Mark's narrative reflects the language of the parable, but in a manner that specifically reflects the disciples' limitations and failures.[14]

More broadly, Jesus appoints the twelve "to preach and to have authority to cast out demons" (Mark 3:14–15), yet they achieve only limited results. Although Mark 6:13 relates that the disciples "cast out many demons, and anointed with oil many who were sick and cured them," their subsequent inability to heal the boy with a "spirit of dumbness" is considerably more prominent (Mark 9:14–29). By betraying his Lord, Judas in particular succumbs to the "lure of wealth" (Mark 14:11). In largely failing (at least within the Gospel narratives) to manifest the fruitfulness of which the parable speaks, all twelve fall far short of expectation. Indeed, the Gospels offer little evidence of moral achievement on their part. No more are the blessings they anticipate of their own making. The Markan wording—disciples who suffer the loss of all things will "*receive* a hundredfold"—suggests divine provision in the face of persecution rather than personal accomplishment or the reward of faithful endurance. In short, Mark's correlation between the language of Jesus' explanation and subsequent failures on the part of his closest followers makes it unlikely that he intended the parable as a template for Christian ministry in any positive sense. Far from serving to distinguish between the faithless many and the faithful few—as it is usually read—the parable in its Markan context suggests itself as a lamentable portrait of fruitless discipleship rather than an exhortation to moral or spiritual endeavor.

"Some Thirty, Some Sixty, Some a Hundredfold..."

At the same time, a fuller sense of the meaning conveyed by agricultural metaphors within the Judaism of his day (and their scriptural background

---

14. Compare σατανᾶς in Mark 4:14 and 8:33; θλίψεως ἢ διωγμοῦ (4:17) and ἓν ἑκατόν (4:20) with λάβῃ ἑκατονταπλασίονα . . . μετὰ διωγμῶν in 10:30 (cf. θλῖψις at 13:19, 24); μέριμναι τοῦ αἰῶνος καὶ ἡ ἀπάτη τοῦ πλούτου (4:19) with πλούσιον in 10:25 (cf. 12:41–44).

in particular) suggests that this parable has more to say about divine action in the face of human failure than about moral endeavor in its own right, proper ways of responding to Jesus' teaching, or the conditions of Christian ministry. The central premise in this section of our study is that understanding "the Scriptures [and] the power of God" provides an essential key to the meaning Jesus intends, whether for his first audience or for readers of any subsequent age. Accordingly, what echoes of Scripture or intimations of divine power are to be discerned in the parable of the Sower and its interpretation? For Marie Sabin, all three parables of Mark 4 evoke the word by which God sows life in the opening chapter of Genesis.[15] Birger Gerhardsson argues that the three types of soil reflect the three spheres of responses envisaged by Deuteronomy 6:5: "You shall love the Lord your God [1] with all your heart, [2] with all your soul, and [3] with all your might."[16] Taking his cue from the citation of Isaiah 6:9-10 in Mark 4:12, John Bowker understands the parable as a midrash on the "holy seed" of Isaiah 6:13, although the similarities he proposes are thematic rather than textual.[17] Alternatively, Craig Evans sees here the thematic concerns of Isaiah 55:10-11, to which we will return in due course.[18] Particular details may also reflect biblical motifs: Rudolf Pesch suggests that an allusion to LXX Jonah 4:6-8 heightens the narrative force of the parable's withering sun (Mark 4:6).[19] According to Dale and Patricia Miller, Mark "might have expected informed Jewish readers of his time to understand thorns in light of Jer. 4.3, Mic. 7.4, 2 Sam. 23.6, and Prov. 24.30-31, in which thorns are a symbol for sin."[20] Already in *Jubilees*, paraphrasing the book of Genesis two centuries prior to Jesus, Mastema (another name for Satan) sends birds to consume the seed scattered by an adolescent Abraham in his father's field (*Jub.* 11.10-24).[21] The episode serves as a parable in its own right, depicting cosmic opposition to the people of God, the "seed" of Abraham to whom God has given this land.[22] But none of these proposals can account for the thrust of the parable as a whole, or for its perplexing conclusion.

15. Sabin, "Reading Mark 4," 21-22, 25-26.
16. Gerhardsson, "The Parable of the Sower," esp. 175-79, 192.
17. Bowker, "Mystery and Parable," 311-12, 315, followed by (inter alia) Snodgrass, "A Hermeneutic of Hearing," 72.
18. Evans, "On the Isaianic Background."
19. Pesch, *Das Markusevangelium*, 233. Pesch identifies further scriptural antecedents for the imagery of roots, thorns, and fruit-bearing.
20. Miller and Miller, *The Gospel of Mark*, 143.
21. See further Knowles, "Abram and the Birds."
22. Cf. Elliott, *The Survivors of Israel*, 399; Crawford, "Abraham/Ravens Tradition

Taking the parable and its interpretation together, each of the first three elements has a corresponding explanation. The seed consumed by the birds is likened to Satan snatching the word from the hearer; the seed sown in rocky soil and withered by the sun illustrates "trouble or persecution"; the thorns that choke the seed cast into their midst represent "the cares of the world, and the lure of wealth, and the desire for other things"—an escalating series of first one, then two, then three sources of opposition. By contrast, "these are the ones sown on the good soil: they hear the word and accept it and bear fruit, thirty and sixty and a hundredfold." Here the contrast is not only between failure and fruitfulness, but also between the explanations for each previous outcome and the fact that neither Jesus nor the evangelist offers any equivalent accounting for the fecundity of the "good earth" and the circumstances, personal qualities, or forms of response that it might represent. Those who prove fruitful are merely said to "hear" and "receive" or "accept" the word. The prospect of fruitfulness proved difficult even for its earliest interpreters: Matthew finds it necessary to add that "this is the one who hears the word *and understands*" (Matt 13:23), while Luke 8:15 makes sense of the outcome by attributing it to "hearing with an honest and good heart," as well as to "perseverance" in bearing fruit.

Joel Marcus argues in an article by this name that "Blanks and Gaps in the Markan Parable of the Sower" are intentional: the absence of critical information constitutes a "gap," an ambiguity intentionally designed to provoke reflection on the part of hearers and readers of the text.[23] This particular "gap" is certainly provocative, yet clues to the missing explanation lie within the size of the unexpected yield. According to Robert McIver, realistic estimates suggest that "a four-fold or five-fold yield is probably typical of much of the Mediterranean world in antiquity, especially in Palestine." Accordingly, "even the grain that gave a yield of thirty-fold was not only exceptional, it was miraculous in first-century Palestine."[24] In his study of contemporary social and economic conditions, Douglas Oakman observes that contrary to the vigilance, diligence, and back-breaking labor required of every peasant farmer, divine providence alone would be sufficient to

in *Jubilees* 11," 93–95, 97.

23. Marcus, "Blanks and Gaps," 247–62.

24. McIver, "One Hundred-Fold Yield," 607–8; cf. Marcus, *Mark 1–8*, 292–93. These estimates are confirmed by Hamel, *Poverty and Charity*, 125–37. Conversely, the Roman scholar Marcus Terentius Varro (116–27 BCE) cites reports of hundred-fold returns (including Syrian Gadara), notwithstanding normal wheat yields of ten- or fifteen-fold (*Rerum Rust.* 1.44.1–2); similarly Theophrastus, *Hist. Plant.* 8.7.4, and Pliny the Elder (29–73 CE), *Nat.* 18.21.4–5, cited by Payne, "The Authenticity of the Parable of the Sower," 185–86.

produce such an abundant crop.²⁵ Detailed knowledge of the biblical text only confirms this interpretation. In Genesis 26, Isaac undergoes a series of experiences reminiscent of his father's life: like Abraham before him, he too suffers through famine, receives a divine visitation (complete with the promise of blessing for his "seed"), and passes off his wife as a sister in order to avoid conflict with the subjects of Abimelech (Gen 26:1–11). Thereupon, according to Genesis 26:12, "Isaac sowed seed in that land, and in the same year reaped a hundredfold, for the Lord blessed him."²⁶

This is the only passage in Hebrew Scripture to describe a hundredfold multiplication of seed. The Hebrew text (שְׂעָרִים מֵאָה) can be pointed either with šîn: שְׂעָרִים ("one hundred *measures*") or with śîn: שְׂעֹרִים ("*barley* a hundredfold"). The Septuagint reflects the latter option, while indicating (more clearly than do most English translations) the sense of the Hebrew that the cause of this extraordinary yield is God's blessing: "Isaac sowed in that land and in that year found barley bearing a hundredfold; for the Lord blessed him."²⁷ Philo of Alexandria (ca. 20 BCE–50 CE) likewise understood this verse (in typically allegorical fashion) to emphasize divine blessing over human attainment (*Mut.* 268–69; *QG* 4.189), while Josephus's explanation of Abimelech's animosity in Genesis 26 hints at a similar interpretation: "For seeing that God was with Isaac and showered such favors upon him, he cast him off" (*Ant.* 1.260).²⁸ That a hundred-fold yield is a particular mark of divine favor is confirmed, incidentally, by the account in the *Sibylline Oracles* (from the mid-second century BCE) that briefly describes the Exodus and the giving of the law (*Sib. Or.* 3:248–60), then, with an abrupt change of subject, concludes, "For [Israel] alone the fertile soil yields fruit from one- to a hundredfold, and the measures of God are produced" (3:263–64).²⁹

25. Oakman, *Jesus and the Economic Questions*, 100–102, 107–9.

26. The parallel is noted by, inter alia, Dahl, "The Parables of Growth," 153; Jeremias, "Palästinakundliches zum Gleichnis vom Säemann," 53; and Hultgren, *The Parables of Jesus*, 188; cf. Payne, "The Authenticity of the Parable of the Sower," 182.

27. Ἔσπειρεν δὲ Ισαακ ἐν τῇ γῇ ἐκείνῃ καὶ εὗρεν ἐν τῷ ἐνιαυτῷ ἐκείνῳ ἑκατοστεύουσαν κριθήν· εὐλόγησεν δὲ αὐτὸν κύριος (author's translation).

28. Cf. Nodet, trans., *Les Antiquités Juives*, I.B 57 n.2; *Tg. Neof.* Gen 26:12.

29. ἐξ ἑνὸς εἰς ἑκατόν, τελέθοντό τε μέτρα θεοῖο. The translation is that of Collins, *OTP* 1:368; on the dating of *Sib. Or.* 3, see *OTP* 1:355. Although rabbinic references to Genesis 26:12 postdate Mark's gospel by at least a century—and considerably more—they are, nonetheless, illuminating. Albeit with an emphasis on meritorious reward rather than spontaneous divine generosity, a tradition attributed in *t. Berakhot* 6:8 to Rabbi Meir (T3; ca. 130–160 CE) cites Genesis 26:12 as evidence for the extent to which God's blessing multiplies seed grain in the land of Israel, even a hundred times one hundred: "Isaac expounded and said, 'Since a blessing is earned only through one's actions ...' he arose and sowed, as Scripture states ... [Gen 26:12]" (quoted from

Whether one is simply a rural Palestinian—one of the *'am ha-aretz*, the unlettered "people of the land"—or one well-versed in Scripture and familiar with its traditions of interpretation, one might reasonably be expected to recognize that the seed in this parable and the "word" in the life of the hearer multiply thirty, sixty, and a hundredfold not through the efforts of the farmer or because of any intrinsic merit or ability on the part of the recipients, but simply because the Lord blesses them, just as God blessed Isaac in the book of Genesis.[30] All the more so in light of Mark's use of this parable to highlight failure on the part of the disciples, the parable draws attention to God's role in bringing the seed to fruitfulness, precisely because human efforts alone are incapable of doing so. In Pauline terms, the parable is about the frequent failure of the "word" as a means of human communication, in contrast to the triumph of grace.[31]

Stated in the strongest possible terms, then, words themselves have no inherent power to produce the life that God intends, any more than hearers have it in themselves to triumph over spiritual adversity, bring forth spiritual fruit, or raise themselves up from death. No more can preachers expect their own words—however artfully delivered—to be capable of transforming their hearers. In context, there could be no more striking illustration of this principle than the unexpected fact that Jesus' own words fail initially to bear fruit in the lives of his closest disciples, who succumb to the very obstacles against which the parable clearly forewarns them. Although our first instinct as preachers is the desire for authority—a share in Jesus' power—this parable reminds us that to preach as he did will require us to share his

---

Neusner and Sarason, eds., *The Tosefta*, 37); cf. *t. Soṭ.* 10:6; *b. Ketub.* 112a; *Num. Rab.* 12:11. Again, an anonymous opinion recorded in *Genesis Rabbah* 73:8 interprets the same verse to mean that "Wherever the righteous go, a blessing accompanies them," while *Gen. Rab.* 86:6 attributes to a contemporary of Rabbi Meir, Simeon ben Yoḥai, the interpretation, "Wherever the righteous go, the *Shekinah* accompanies them" (quoted from Freedman and Simon, eds., *Midrash Rabbah: Genesis*, 2.673, 804).

30. Even if the parable enumerates numbers of grains per head of wheat rather than bulk returns relative to the quantity of seed sown (so White, "The Parable of the Sower," 301–2, followed by, e.g., Scott, *Hear Then the Parable*, 355–57), divine intervention is not thereby obviated.

31. Just so, emphasizing the contrast between human frailty and divine power, the earliest post-biblical interpretation of this parable (from the late first or early second century) views it as an allegory of bodily death and resurrection, doubtless under the influence of John 12:24: "The sower goes forth and casts into the earth each of the seeds. They fall into the dry and bare ground, and decay. Then out of their decay the majesty of God's providence raises them up, and from being one seed, many grow up and bring forth fruit" (1 Clem. 24:5, quoted from Oden and Hall, *Mark*, 50).

weakness also. As Jesus himself insists, "A disciple is not above the teacher, nor a slave above the master" (Matt 10:24).

Seeds, Words, and the People of God

One important detail remains to be clarified: what, exactly, does the Sower sow? Curiously, the parable does not actually mention "seed"; it simply says "*Some* fell by the roadside . . . *others* fell on shallow soil," and so on.[32] Nonetheless, the interpretation begins clearly enough: "The sower sows *the word*" (Mark 4:14). Yet the line immediately following introduces a different explanation: "These are the ones on the path, where the word is sown: when they hear, Satan immediately comes and takes away the word that is sown in them" (Mark 4:15). How can "seed" represent both "the word" and (as elsewhere in biblical tradition) people in whom the word is "sown"? On the assumption that Jesus' methodology will reflect the conventions of his day, Bowker offers the helpful—and delightfully understated—observation that "It is by no means uncommon for there to be an inexact match in the component parts of rabbinic explanation."[33] Still, the Apostle Paul offers a more specific clue. In contrasting Adam and Christ, with their respective legacies of death and resurrection, Paul also speaks repeatedly—and unexpectedly—of seeds and sowing:

> What you sow does not come to life unless it dies. And as for what you sow, you do not sow the body that is to be, but a bare seed, perhaps of wheat or of some other grain. But God gives it a body as he has chosen, and to each kind of seed its own body. . . .
> So it is with the resurrection of the dead. What is sown is perishable, what is raised is imperishable. It is sown in dishonor, it is raised in glory. It is sown in weakness, it is raised in power. It is sown a physical body, it is raised a spiritual body.
> (1 Cor 15:36–38, 42–44)

Paul can speak in this way because Adam himself is the "seed" first sown by God's life-giving word, formed from earth and eventually returned to earth, who in his lifetime sows seed of his own, notwithstanding the thorns that frustrate his labors and the offspring who turn aside from God's ways, sometimes in pursuit of prosperity and other worldly concerns. Adam is

---

32. Juel ("Encountering the Sower," 274) also notes the discrepancy between references to seed by means of neuter pronouns in the parable, but masculine pronouns in the interpretation.

33. Bowker, "Mystery and Parable," 310.

both sower and sown, the "seed" who proceeds from God's life-giving word who must "go forth and multiply" across the face of the earth. Just so, the sower in the parable "sows the word," says Mark 4:14, and Luke 8:11 makes the meaning unmistakable: "The seed is the word of God." Yet in the verses immediately following the seed is no longer simply the thing preached, but also those who hear and forget, rejoice only to fall away, listen at first but become distracted, or ultimately bear fruit. Despite initial appearances, the emphasis is less on soil conditions than on the nature of the seed. Words become seeds and seeds become people because behind the parable—as Paul would have known—lies the story of Adam, into whom God first spoke the word of life.

Moreover, a fluid conceptual link between sown seed, God's word, and God's people emerges elsewhere in texts that were current in the Second Temple period. According to Bowker, this overlap is already present in Isaiah 6, which Jesus quotes by way of explanation, where "the function and purpose of the prophetic word [is] in making unequivocally clear the nature of those who hear it."[34] More obvious is Isaiah 55, as noted by Evans:[35]

> For as the rain and the snow come down from heaven,
> and do not return there until they have watered the earth,
> making it bring forth and sprout,
> giving seed to the sower and bread to the eater,
> so shall my word be that goes out from my mouth;
> it shall not return to me empty,
> but it shall accomplish that which I purpose,
> and succeed in the thing for which I sent it.
>
> (Isa 55:10–11)

Strictly speaking, Isaiah identifies God's word with the *rain* that brings forth seed, rather than with the seed itself (as in Heb 6:4–8). Yet it might well be that the parable of the seed that flourishes despite all manner of impediments—and the triumph of God's word that it conveys—represents Jesus' own meditation (or midrash) on this passage from Isaiah 55.

Linking word and seed more directly is 1 Peter 1:23–25:

> You have been born anew, not of perishable but of imperishable seed, through the living and enduring word of God. For "All flesh is like grass and all its glory like the flower of grass. The

---

34. Ibid., 312.
35. Evans, "On the Isaianic Background," 466–67.

grass withers, and the flower falls, but the word of the Lord endures forever." That word is the good news that was announced to you.

Likewise, Marcus observes how "the seed that God sows" becomes in 4 *Ezra* 8:41 "the human beings he has planted in the world," just as the book elsewhere depicts both knowledge of God (8:6) and God's law (9:31–37) as seed that is sown in the human heart in order to bring forth fruit.[36] Marcus goes so far as to suggest that the identification of God's word as seed is sufficiently familiar that it would have been recognized even prior to the explanation.[37]

In sum, shifts in meaning both between the parable and its interpretation and within the interpretation itself give evidence of creativity and conceptual fluidity rather than "clumsy or careless speaking,"[38] shoddy editing, or differences in authorship. The sower who sows brings forth life by means of words, just as God first spoke life into Adam, then his "seed" in turn. Once again, recognizing the origins of this dynamic metaphor in the legacy of Israel's Scriptures (and the life-giving generosity of God of which the Scriptures speak) proves essential to proper interpretation. Accordingly, the identification of seed with both proclamation and people will apply not only to the sower, but to other seed parables as well, especially those that follow immediately in both Mark and Matthew.

Words and God's Word in the Life of the Church

What possible guidance might this parable offer for contemporary ministries of preaching, teaching, and (to whatever extent they can be characterized as such) "sowing the word"? An initial answer has to do with a gap in the parable's explanation that can only be filled by knowledge of the biblical text, and the appeal to divine blessing that it implies. If our own words are to bear fruit, by implication, it will only be by virtue of grace. This is frustrating, to be sure, because even though preaching is hard work, there is no necessary correlation between the amount of effort we expend and the results that ensue. Nonetheless there is a certain elegance—even a degree of irony—in this observation. Those who preach and teach God's "word" require their hearers to recognize the blessing to which the sacred text bears witness. Yet if preachers themselves fail to recognize that same blessing—if preachers fail to rely on the one true source of life and spiritual

---

36. Marcus, *The Mystery of the Kingdom*, 48.
37. Ibid., 50.
38. Cranfield, "St. Mark 4:1–34," 408.

transformation—it will leave them laboring anxiously over their structure and diction and delivery, pursuing the latest preaching fads and fearful of a failed harvest, like the farmer who fails to see that all the worry in the world cannot cause the grain to germinate, much less produce a life-giving harvest. Offering a rare exception to the response-oriented tendencies of most academic (as well as popular) exegesis, Charles Cranfield acknowledges that "four kinds of hearers are indicated," but adds an injunction to prayer:

> None of us can be good soil of himself, none of us can by his own power and wisdom and goodness hear God's Word aright. Only God can make us good soil (cf. Mark 10:27 . . .). So the summons of this passage is to prayer, that God may forgive us our superficiality, instability, [and] distractedness, and make our hearts to be good soil, that we may hear and receive His Word and faithfully live by it.[39]

Perhaps a measure of failure is inevitable: Mark, at any rate, seems curiously pessimistic about the sanctity or moral fortitude of Jesus' first followers. This commends a measure of caution when subsequent disciples seek to evaluate their own potential (or that of others) for spiritual or ministerial success. The Apostle Paul would not disagree (1 Cor 10:12). According to Luke, some of the same failed disciples later experience such unexpected success that they at once disavow responsibility for it. Peter's response to the apparent acclaim of bystanders after the healing of a lame man in the temple is, "Men of Israel, why do you wonder at this, or why do you stare at us, as though by our own power or piety we had made him walk?" (Acts 3:12). The wisest of preachers, likewise, know better than to take credit when blessing attends their preaching. Even so, the promise of an impossible harvest cannot be ignored:

> This last picture is full of assurance for the Church, for it reveals that with the coming of Jesus the seeds of God's Kingdom have not only been planted, but will in the end bear a marvellous harvest, well beyond our wildest dreams. . . . It is a parable for all God's people. It says that in spite of many disappointments and setbacks in doing his work through the Church in the world, there will be a reward, a harvest.[40]

The experience of the Chinese church in the last century provides a salutary illustration: notwithstanding the apparent failure of all previous missionary endeavors, the official atheism of Mao's regime, and ultimately, the terrors

---

39. Ibid., 414.
40. Dale, "The Sower," 308.

of the Cultural Revolution, its adherents number "anywhere between 50 and 90 million today."[41]

One way or another, this parable offers little support for a high view of human agency in the preaching of God's "word." Post-resurrection examples to the contrary—Peter and Paul in the book of Acts, or the Apostle Paul's characterization of his own preaching as the "word of God" (1 Thess 2:13)—do not justify a selective exclusion of Mark's vision of human frailty, however challenging it may prove. Stated differently, preachers seeking to invoke the authority of Jesus for their own proclamation have to reckon equally with the weakness and failure that he no less exemplifies. At least in Protestant contexts that value sermonic proclamation above all, preachers are easily convinced of the importance of their own ministry. The authority of Scripture is applied to preaching, which in turn invests the preacher with unique authority over the life of the congregation. This position comes to maximal expression in the words of Heinrich Bullinger and the Second Helvetic Confession of 1566, "*Praedicatio verbi Dei est verbum Dei*"—"The preaching of the Word of God *is* the Word of God."[42] Indeed, Bullinger's claim can appeal to the authority of Jesus himself, who in Luke 10:16 tells the seventy disciples as he sends them out to preach, "He who hears you hears me." Yet it is far from clear that echoing or imitating Jesus results in any exaltation of the preacher: the parable of the Sower seems suited rather to a theology of the cross.

Recognizing what might have been more evident to a first-century audience tends to confirm N. T. Wright's contention that the parable of the Sower amounts to a retelling of the story—the history—of God's people.[43] Accordingly, the imagery in this parable of seed that largely fails to bear fruit implies further questions that remain current for the church of today: "Who are the true people of God?"; "Who are the true *seed* of God's promise and planting?"; and, above all, "How is it that this seed, this planting, this people can come to bear spiritual fruit of their own, even in face of weakness and failure?" Our answer to such questions must invoke the conclusions of the preceding discussion: the true people of God are those whose identity is not principally shaped by cultural allegiance or denominational pedigree or confessional conformity or (above all) moral achievement, but by the fact that their lives depend—actively and practically and immediately—on God's gift of life in all its powerful splendor. From Adam and Eve onward, this is the most basic principle of human existence, applying as much to preachers and their ministries as to congregations and the life of the church as a whole.

41. Jenkins, *The Lost History of Christianity*, 255.
42. *Confessio Helvetica Posterior* I, 4, quoted in Greidanus, *The Modern Preacher*, 9.
43. Wright, *Jesus and the Victory of God*, 230–39.

The theological challenge of the parable and its attendant explanation cannot, therefore, be minimized, for—as noted earlier—it challenges us with the grace of God. Donald Juel summarizes the matter well:

> Our text makes a remarkable claim. It suggests that stories like the parable of the Sower that speak only of promises and not of requirements may be heard differently. Some will hear the stories as promises and will take heart; others will hear them as demands and take offense. The Bible proposes that Jesus' words are capable of hardening people against the possibility of faith. And the actual experience of the parable in classes and congregations bears out the claim. When interpretation fails to bring the text under control, listeners are left at the mercy of God without any way of controlling how the encounter will turn out. . . . The God we encounter in the parable is one we cannot manage—and cannot endure.[44]

Thus the ultimate challenge of this parable—indeed of all Jesus' parables, the "word" that he proclaims, and sermons that follow suit—concerns "the character of God," and the questions that every reader, every hearer must answer: can this God be trusted? Can we live by the mercy, grace, and life-giving power of this God?[45] More pertinently, can we learn to preach in such a way as to rely more on divine mercy than the supposed power of our own voices?

SEED THAT GROWS OF ITS OWN ACCORD (MARK 4:26–29)

Mark's ensuing parable, concerning seed that grows of its own accord, pushes the premise of the previous illustration nearly to the point of absurdity. Grain farming in the ancient world was such an exhausting, labor-intensive occupation that for Israel its frustrations served as a perfect illustration of creational disharmony and the consequences of human sin (Gen 3:17–19). Just so, the parable of the Sower depends for narrative tension on its appeal to the familiar adversities faced by every farmer in Jesus' circle of hearers: hungry birds, scorching heat, thin soil, ever-present weeds. Who but a powerful, generous God could finally overcome such daunting obstacles to fruition? Mark's second parable makes the same point, but this time by obviating the labors of the farmer almost entirely. By this account the farmer

---

44. Juel, "Encountering the Sower," 281–82.
45. Ibid., 283.

need only sow, sleep, and harvest: there is no mention of tilling, weeding, watching anxiously, or praying for timely rain. But this is neither laziness nor willful inattention. As was the case in Matthew 6:26 with "the birds of the air [who] neither sow nor reap nor gather into barns, and yet [their] heavenly Father feeds them," so here the sower appears to be exempt from God's sentence on Adam: "Cursed is the ground because of you; in toil you shall eat of it. . . . By the sweat of your face you shall eat bread" (Gen 3:17, 19). Sleeping and waking day after day, he seems the very picture of contentment, an apt expression of obedience to Jesus' own command:

> "Therefore do not worry, saying, 'What will we eat?' or 'What will we drink?' or 'What will we wear?'. . . But strive first for the kingdom of God and his righteousness, and all these things will be given to you as well."
>
> (Matt 6:31-33)

Although sleep can hardly be considered striving, the farmer appears to recognize that once the seed has been sown, his work is over for the time being, since "the earth produces of itself [αὐτομάτη]" (Mark 4:28). This is the opposite of the way things normally appear, with the peasant fretting furiously and seeds lying inert in the ground. Now the situation is reversed: "In contrast to the farmer's odd passiveness, the seeds are jumping."[46]

The precise nuance of Mark's vocabulary is all-important, on which Marcus is worth quoting in full:

> The Greek term *automatē*, from which we get "automatic," is frequently used in the OT and later Jewish texts to refer to that which is worked by God alone; in Lev 25:5, 11, for example, it designates crops that grow up in the sabbatical year and thus display God's sovereign care for his people. *Automatē*, moreover, often has a nuance of the miraculous; in 4 Kgdms 19:29, for example, it is part of a divine sign of deliverance from the Assyrian foe, and in several passages in Philo's *On the Creation* (40-43, 80-81, and 167), it is used for the paradisiacal conditions of Eden. . . . It is thus appropriate that Mark uses it to describe the divinely energized, miraculous growth that is creating the new Eden . . .[47]

---

46. Duke, *The Parables*, 20.

47. Marcus, *Mark 1-8*, 328, citing Stuhlmann, "Beobachtungen und Überlegungen zu Markus iv.26-29," 154-56, and Klauck, *Allegorie und Allegorese in synoptischen Gleichnistexten*, 221-22. Similarly LXX Joshua 6:5, Wisdom 17:6, and Acts 12:10, cited by Scott, *Hear Then the Parable*, 368.

In his own paraphrase of Genesis 3, Josephus has God explain to a crestfallen Adam that "spontaneous" abundance had been his original purpose for creation:

> "I had decreed for you to live a life of bliss, unmolested by all ill, with no care to fret your souls; all things that contribute to enjoyment and pleasure were, through my providence, to spring up for you *spontaneously* [αὐτομάτῃ], without toil or distress of yours; blessed with these gifts, old age would not soon have overtaken you and your life would have been long."
>
> (*Ant.* 1.46)

According to the parable, it is this lost bounty that Jesus intends to restore.

Perhaps there is a touch of irony, even comedy, in the fact that the farmer "does not know how" the germination and growth of the seed take place (Mark 4:27). Far from celebrating incomprehension, the point of the parable, with its downplaying of the farmer's contribution, is to underscore the miraculous, life-giving agency of God, which listeners and readers alike are invited to recognize.[48] All that now remains is the satisfying labor of harvest, a task the man takes up as soon as the grain is ripe (4:29). It would seem as though—at least in the present parable—this is the first real effort the fortunate farmer has had to expend.

Again, an audience's awareness of scriptural echoes would make this premise more evident. Most obvious, as with the Sower and Seed, is the parable's evocation of Genesis 3 and the labors of Adam. Nor was Jesus the first to draw a contrast between the unfortunate legacy of Adam and the blessings reserved for God's people. Together, Psalms 127 and 128 describe abundant divine provision for those who walk in faithfulness; in particular, Psalm 127:2 juxtaposes the labor (עצבון), "toil, pain" (Gen 3:17) by which Adam's descendants are condemned to gain their daily bread and the apparently carefree rest that is the legacy of the blessed:

> It is in vain that you rise up early and go late to rest,
> eating the bread of anxious toil [לחם העצבים];
> for he gives to his beloved sleep.

Whether the psalm indicates that God provides sleep itself (NRSV, above), or gives his provision while his beloved ones slumber (so JB: "since he

---

48. Citing, inter alia, Song 6:12, 2 Macc 7:22, and John 3:8, Sahlin ("Zum Verständnis von drei Stellen im Markusevangelium," 55–57) argues that the sower "not knowing how" serves to indicate miraculous divine intervention rather than genuine ignorance or misunderstanding; cf. Stuhlmann, "Beobachtungen und Überlegungen," 155.

provides for his beloved as they sleep"; NRSV mg., NJPS, etc.) makes little difference to the intended contrast between burdensome human exertion and divine bounty. It is at least possible, as Anderson proposes, that "the reference [in this verse] is to the growth of crops and flocks," but if so, such a conclusion can only be inferred from the context.[49] Alternatively, Sabin compares Ecclesiastes 11:4–6 ("Sow your seed in the morning, and don't hold back your hand in the evening, since you don't know which is going to succeed . . . or if both are equally good"), which "inculcates trust in the power and goodness of God" as the source of all life.[50]

Whether or not the progress from sprout to seed head to full grain can be taken to imply stages of development in the growth of the kingdom need not detain us here, for the main premise of the parable is that even the minimum human activities of sowing and reaping would be neither possible nor necessary without the God-given power of germination already hidden within the seeds. So it is with God's dominion. This is equally the sense of Jesus' rebuff to Pilate in the Gospel of John: "My kingdom is not of this world" (John 19:36), meaning that the realm of which he speaks is neither established nor defended by human might. That the "harvest" in question conveys eschatological overtones is almost certain, given both the general tenor of Jesus' language elsewhere (e.g., Matt 9:38 // Luke 10:2) and the allusion in Mark 4:29 to Joel 4:13, announcing the "day of the Lord."[51] But at least in its present context, the parable's primary focus is neither the manner in which the kingdom is manifest nor even the certainty of final harvest, but rather—given the theological overtones of the imagery in question—the fact of divine power invisibly at work in the world. For Mark the previous interpretation ("the sower sows *the word*," Mark 4:14) likely applies here as well. Just so, in the view of Emil Brunner, "The theme of the parable is the mysterious power of God's Word."[52] Likewise the conventional equivalence of seed and people is probably once more in play, in which case the seed that grows of its own accord speaks not of some abstract divine reign, or of any general assurance that God will work things out in the end, but more specifically of the living community that God births and nurtures by means well beyond the power of human agency alone. Perhaps we should take this to mean that if God's people are seed, then God's work in them is neither ostentatious nor even necessarily overt, but rather hidden, obscure,

---

49. Anderson, *The Book of Psalms*, 2:868.
50. Sabin, "Reading Mark 4 as Midrash," 16.
51. Dupont, "La parabole de la semence," 379–80; cf. Rev 14:15.
52. Brunner, "Two Parables About the Kingdom of God," in *Sowing and Reaping*, 27.

even mysterious. In this sense they reflect the characteristics of the kingdom itself, as expressed in Luke 17:20: "Once, having been asked by the Pharisees when the kingdom of God would come, Jesus replied, 'The coming of the kingdom of God is not something that can be observed . . .'" (TNIV). As their pastors and preachers would freely admit, Jesus' comment provides an accurate description of many a local congregation!

Viewed against the social and theological backdrop of its day, the implications of this parable are inescapable. Sentiments of the sort expressed by 2 Peter appear to have been widespread, with active preparation on the part of God's people deemed essential for ushering in the day of final divine victory:

> Since all these things are to be dissolved in this way, what sort of persons ought you to be in leading lives of holiness and godliness, waiting for *and hastening* the coming of the day of God, because of which the heavens will be set ablaze and dissolved, and the elements will melt with fire?
>
> (2 Pet 3:11–12)

Whether such preparation should take the form of Torah observance, moral reformation, withdrawal from society, or military insurrection represented a key point of contention, but the pivotal role of God's people was generally agreed. According to the parable, by contrast, the faithful are no more responsible for the flourishing of God's kingdom than a farmer's diligent care could make a sterile seed bear fruit. The maturation of grain and the manifestation of the kingdom are the sole prerogative of God.[53] The German harvest hymn "Wir pflügen und wir streuen," well-known from its nineteenth-century English translation, makes this very point:

> We plough the fields, and scatter the good seed on the land,
> But it is fed and watered by God's almighty hand;
> He sends the snow in winter, the warmth to swell the grain,
> The breezes and the sunshine, and soft refreshing rain.
> *All good gifts around us*
> *Are sent from heaven above,*
> *Then thank the Lord, O thank the Lord*
> *For all His love.*[54]

---

53. That the growth of the seed implies ongoing (albeit covert) divine agency, in contrast to the patient inactivity of the sower, speaks against Dupont's contention that the conduct of the protagonist represents that of God: Dupont, "La parabole de la semence," 382–85; see also his "Encore la parabole de la Semence," 107–8.

54. Matthias Claudius (1740–1815), "Wir pflügen und wir streuen" (1782); the English translation is by Jane Montgomery Campbell; see further Glover, ed., *The*

Employing the same metaphor, Paul comes to similar conclusions with respect to the work of ministry, initially conceding a greater role for human agency only to declare it all but inconsequential: "I planted, Apollos watered, but *God gave the growth*. So neither the one who plants nor the one who waters is anything, but *only God who gives the growth*" (1 Cor 3:6–7).

Preachers, as we have observed, are often highly enamored of their own role in proclaiming God's reign—even those who do not subscribe to the liberal conviction that our task is one of actually "building" the kingdom. The parable of the seed growing of its own accord once more counsels both caution and humility in this regard, for it indicates that all the preaching in the world will not by itself create new life in its hearers. That role is reserved for the "living and active" Word of God alone (Heb 4:12); to the extent that the parable illustrates their task, preachers can do no more than proclaim the message of the gospel, leaving the results up to God. Jesus takes the same approach in telling parables like this one. As Helmut Thielicke observes in his own sermon on the parable of the Hidden Seed:

> So, because Jesus knows which way the switches are set, because he knows what the outcome of growth and harvest will be, the words he speaks are not prepared, tactical propaganda speeches. The propaganda of men, even when it masquerades as a kind of evangelism and becomes an enterprise of the church, is always based on the accursed notion that success and failure, fruit and harvest are dependent upon our human activity, upon our imagination, energy, and intelligence. Therefore . . . pastors must beware of becoming religious administrators devoid of power and dried up as far as spiritual substance is concerned.[55]

Pastors can take neither responsibility nor credit for the power of the preached word and the gift of life that it entails: "We may think of ourselves as religious professionals, but we're just people throwing seed."[56] According to this parable, we do well simply to "sleep and rise," day after day, patient and confident in the assurance that God alone accomplishes what we ourselves cannot. The patent absurdity of such a proposal, at once contradicted by the interminable burdens and anxieties of pastoral ministry (or even the difficulty of composing a good sermon), corresponds exactly to the incredulity with which we may imagine its first audience would have greeted this story. Therein consists its power to confront us with the unexpected reality of God. As Paul Simpson Duke insists,

Hymnal 1982 Companion, 559–61.

55. Thielicke, *The Waiting Father*, 89.
56. Duke, *The Parables*, 25.

To know such a word would send us into the pulpit freer, less anxious about ourselves, less inclined to take constant measurements, less needy of affirmation, more at ease in the potent and finally hilarious mystery of God. This is not only how to preach this parable; it is how this parable teaches us to preach.[57]

THE MUSTARD SEED (MATT 13:31-32 // MARK 4:30-32 // LUKE 13:18-19)

Following immediately in Mark, the parable of the Mustard Seed picks up where the previous one left off. In rabbinic discourse the mustard seed is a proverbial symbol of minimal measure: according to the parable, it "is the smallest of all the seeds on the earth" (Mark 4:31; cf. Matt 17:20 // Luke 17:6).[58] In point of fact, mustard is no more the smallest seed on earth than the shrub it produces is the largest, as numerous commentators observe. But this is the realm of rhetoric, not plant classification: the point of comparison is the obvious contrast between small and large, emphasized all the more by the fact that the parable concerns only "a [single] grain of mustard." But having understood the metaphor, modern observers may still overlook its underlying premise: for Jesus and his hearers the difference between a tiny seed and an enormous bush was not a matter of cell division, photosynthesis, adequate hydration, or nutrient transfer, but rather the life-giving power of God. As with the seed that multiplies with neither encouragement nor assistance from the well-rested peasant, so here the full-grown mustard shrub is of obviously miraculous dimensions relative to its humble beginning: such transformation can only bespeak the handiwork of God.[59] Again, modern commentators debate various details having to do with consequences or outcomes, and the meaning Jesus intended for each. Since the tiny seed grows disproportionately enormous, so must be the ultimate power and significance of God's kingdom, or the community of believers, either in Jesus'

---

57. Ibid., 26.

58. So *m. Ṭehar.* 8:8, *m. Nid.* 5:2, *m. Naz.* 1:5, cited by, e.g., McArthur, "The Parable of the Mustard Seed," 201; cf. Hunzinger, s.v. σίναπι, *TDNT* 7:288; Schellenberg, "Kingdom as Contaminant?," 536–37.

59. According to Gerhardsson, "The mystery lies not in the contrast between the beginning and the end, but in the fact that a powerful process, with immense consequences, is set in motion when a little seed is placed, hidden, buried, in the ground.... The mustard seed is the smallest of all seeds, *but when it is sown in the field* it shows its miraculous power and reaches its fulfilment" ("The Seven Parables," 21–22; emphasis original). But this creates a false contradiction: the difference between "the beginning and the end" is the consequence, precisely, of miraculous divine power.

ministry or at the time of final judgment; the cause-and-effect continuity between seeds and shrubs represents "the *organic unity* between Jesus' present ministry in Israel and the coming kingdom of God"; even as birds find shelter beneath its branches, so disciples—possibly Gentile nations, or humanity in general—find shelter in the kingdom that the parable proclaims.[60] Nor is this tendency a recent trend: Pheme Perkins cites a sermon by John Chrysostom (ca. 347–407 CE) in which the growth of the mustard seed represents the universal spread of the Christian message: "Even so it shall be with respect to the gospel . . . for his disciples were weakest and least of all; but nevertheless because of the great power that was in them, it has been unfolded in every part of the world" (*Homilies on Matthew* 46.2).[61]

To be sure, Jesus would have wanted to encourage his disciples with the promise and prospect of a disproportionate outcome for their inauspicious beginnings, and the early church would have had every motivation to find a similar meaning in his words. Craig Keener notes,

> Far from baptizing the wicked in fire and overthrowing nations at his first coming, Jesus had come as a meek servant, wandering around Galilee with a group of obscure disciples, healing some sick people. The Romans took no notice of him until angry Jewish aristocrats brought him to their attention, and even this did not happen until Jesus attacked the temple system. In a world with governments in turmoil and full of wandering teachers and magicians, Jesus' initial arrival as a meek and politically inconspicuous servant rendered his mission as opaque as his parables, except to disciples bearing the insight of faith.[62]

Moreover, this theme undoubtedly links the parables of the Leaven (Matt 13:33 // Luke 13:20–21), the Treasure in the Field (Matt 13:44), and the Pearl (Matt 13:45–46), each of which concerns something relatively small or hidden being of incommensurate consequence or effect. While by no means excluding such lines of interpretation, however, the emphasis proposed here is less one of consequence than of *cause*, without which the envisaged outcomes would not be possible in the first place.

As has been the case with each previous interpretation, the burden of proof for our proposed reading must be borne in part by whatever biblical allusions undergird the parable. These are not difficult to find, even if

---

60. These and other approaches are summarized by Snodgrass, *Stories with Intent*, 221–27; the quotation is from 225 (emphasis original), an unacknowledged citation of Dahl, "The Parables of Growth," 148.

61. Perkins, "Mark 4:30–34," 311.

62. Keener, *Matthew*, 387.

they are more thematic than textually precise: as Klyne Snodgrass points out, identifying allusions is the single most difficult question posed by the parable.[63] From Ezekiel comes the allegory of a "shoot" or "sprig"—itself a familiar messianic metaphor—that grows into a mighty tree:

> Thus says the Lord God: I myself will take a sprig from the lofty top of a cedar . . .
> On the mountain height of Israel I will plant it, in order that it may produce boughs and bear fruit, and become a noble cedar. Under it every kind of bird will live; in the shade of its branches will nest winged creatures of every kind.
>
> (Ezek 17:22–23; cf. 17:3–6)

Later the prophet describes proud Assyria in closely similar terms:

> Consider Assyria, a cedar of Lebanon . . . [which] towered high above all the trees of the field; its boughs grew large and its branches long. . . . All the birds of the air made their nests in its boughs; under its branches all the animals of the field gave birth to their young; and in its shade all great nations lived.
>
> (Ezek 31:3, 5–6)

Daniel in turn borrows the same imagery for the nation of Babylon:

> There was a tree at the center of the earth, and its height was great. . . . The animals of the field found shade under it, the birds of the air nested in its branches, and from it all living beings were fed.
>
> (Dan 4:10, 12; cf. 21)

The enormous size of each tree represents the power and influence of the nation in question, whether past, present, or future: "the image of a large tree with birds resting in it or under it was a traditional symbol for a great kingdom."[64] At the same time, the major premise of all three passages and their agricultural imagery is that every nation on earth is raised up or cast down by the power of God alone, as much as with the living cedars of Mount Lebanon.[65] In each case, the point is unmistakable: "Thus says the

---

63. Snodgrass, *Stories with Intent*, 224.

64. Davies and Allison, *Matthew* 2:420. The tradition behind Matthew and Luke has enhanced the allusion by amending Mark's "greatest of all shrubs [λαχάνων]" (Mark 4:32) so that it "becomes a tree [δένδρον]" (Matt 13:32; cf. Luke 13:19); so Funk, "The Looking Glass Tree," 5.

65. Similarly Carter, "Matthew's Gospel," 198–200.

Lord God: I myself will take a sprig . . . I will plant it . . ." (Ezek 17:22); "I made it beautiful with its mass of branches . . . I have cast it out" (Ezek 31:9, 11); "This sentence is rendered . . . in order that all who live may know that the Most High is sovereign over the kingdom of mortals" (Dan 4:17). Since it too describes the "kingdom" (Mark 4:30)—and therefore the people—of God, Jesus' parable of the burgeoning grain of mustard takes its place alongside other examples from contemporary Jewish literature that similarly envisage the messianic community as a planting made great by means of divine power.[66]

For Funk, the contrast between mighty cedars (evoked by allusions to Ezekiel) and the humble mustard plant lends the parable "the character of serious satire. . . . The Kingdom is asserted with comic relief."[67] On the contrary, the primary contrast is between the initial and ultimate states of the mustard itself, a contrast supported rather than contradicted by reference to Ezekiel. Even so, Funk captures the paradoxical quality of the kingdom that Jesus proclaims: "It will erupt out of the power of weakness and refuse to perpetuate itself by the weakness of power." And he rightly critiques the kind of ecclesiastical triumphalism that effectively abandons any need for trust or faith.[68] In much the same way, Cardinal Ratzinger—subsequently Pope Benedict XVI—takes the parables of the mustard seed and leaven as models both for the life of faith and for the conduct of Christian ministry:

> [I]f our Lord himself ends up on the Cross, one sees that God's ways do not lead immediately to measurable successes. This, I think, is really very important. The disciples asked him certain questions: What's going on, why aren't we getting anywhere? And he answered with the parables about the mustard seed, the leaven, and the like, telling them that statistics is not one of God's measurements. In spite of that, something essential and crucial happens with the mustard seeds and the leaven, even though you can't see it now. In that sense, I think we have to disregard quantitative measures of success. After all, we're not a business

---

66. Davies and Allison, *Matthew* 2.420, and Mussner, "1QHodajoth und das Gleichnis vom Senfkorn," 128–30; cf. 1QH 14.15–17 and *Pss. Sol.* 14:3–5, cited in the previous chapter.

67. Funk, "The Looking Glass Tree," 7; similarly Sabin, "Reading Mark 4 as Midrash," 21: "To the reader versed in all the great trees of Scripture, this surely comes as a jolt, even a joke"; and Perkins, "Mark 4:30–34," 313: "The substitution of a lowly plant, nowhere mentioned in the Hebrew scriptures, for the imperial cedar strikes a somewhat comic note").

68. Funk, "The Looking Glass Tree," 7–8, although his analysis emphasizes the power of language itself, and remains strangely silent on directly theological issues.

> operation that can look at the numbers to measure whether our policy has been successful and whether we're selling more and more. Rather, we're performing a service, and in the end, when we've done our job, we put it in the Lord's hands.[69]

In this regard the parables of the Sower, the Seed Growing Secretly, and the Mustard Seed are of a piece, for all three resolve into proper focus against a backdrop of weakness and failure—first that of the earliest disciples, more centrally that of Jesus' own ministry, but ultimately also that of his subsequent followers. Without in any way diminishing the distinctive character of each parable or the particular nuances conveyed by the different evangelists and their respective narrative contexts, these innocuous little stories address the concerns of the socially, theologically, and spiritually weak. Peasants under military occupation do not need to be convinced of their social insignificance or political impotence, any more than the early church would have failed to recognize the human folly of their undertaking and the legacy of defeat on which it was built. Middle-class suburbanites, tenured academics, and other socially advantaged readers of a later day, by contrast, struggle to recover points of emphasis that would have been so obvious to Jesus' first audiences as to make comment unnecessary. Whether in terms of seed that multiplies in miraculous abundance, bears fruit without the travail required of every farmer, or produces a plant so enormous that birds take shelter in its branches, these parables invoke the power of God to accomplish what human listeners obviously cannot, with equal respect to the proclamation of God's "word," the prospering of God's people, and the ultimate triumph of God's kingdom as a whole.

WHEAT AND WEEDS (MATT 13:24–30, 36–43)

Even though it shares the same basic structure and similar theological themes, the sequence of parables in Matthew 13 differs in a number of respects from Mark 4. Possibly Mark's juxtaposition of the seed that grows of its own accord (Mark 4:26–29) with a parable about mustard (4:30–32) was suggested by conventional agricultural wisdom. Among Hellenistic writers, for instance, Pliny the Elder (29–73 CE) reports that mustard (much like the seed in the first of these two parables) germinates quickly and is capable of growing "without cultivation [*nulla cultura*]" (*Nat.* 19.54.170). Expanding only slightly, the Roman farmer and landowner Columella (ca. 4–70 CE) indicates that mustard requires no cultivation other than manuring and

---

69. Ratzinger, *Salt of the Earth*, 15–16.

weeding (*Rust.* 11.3.29: "*neque est eorum cultus alius, quam ut stercorata runcentur*"). Depending on the antiquity of the traditions in question, Matthew's quite-different sequence may instead reflect characteristically Jewish concerns. In place of the seed growing unaided, his story of the Sower is followed first by a parable (unique to this Gospel) about similar-looking weeds (ζιζάνια) amidst wheat, and only then by the parable of the mustard seed. Schellenberg notes that according to the Mishnah, "Flanking a grain field with mustard is problematic because the two crops could not easily be distinguished: not only are the plants similar in appearance, but also it is prohibitively difficult to separate their seed once commingled."[70] One story concerns darnel or tares—pseudowheat sown amidst good grain—while the next addresses mustard: by means of this literary arrangement, Matthew juxtaposes not two kinds of seed but three, all of them challenging to differentiate!

Biblical legislation on such matters is unequivocal. In a single verse, Leviticus forbids in turn the commingling of animal seed, plant seed, and the produce of diverse species:

> You shall keep my statutes. You shall not let your animals breed with a different kind; you shall not sow your field with two kinds of seed; nor shall you put on a garment made of two different materials.
>
> (Lev 19:19)

Deuteronomy 22:9–11 extends and clarifies the meaning of each prohibition:

> You shall not sow your vineyard with a second kind of seed, or the whole yield will have to be forfeited, both the crop that you have sown and the yield of the vineyard itself. You shall not plow with an ox and a donkey yoked together. You shall not wear clothes made of wool and linen woven together.

Moving beyond its literal application, the injunction forbidding *sha'atnez*—the closest English equivalent is "linsey-woolsey"—took on overtones (by way of translation into Greek as κίβδηλος) of impurity and adulteration, with regard equally to character or convictions (Wis 2:16, 15:9). The prohibition against sowing a field with different kinds of seed was widely applied to questions of ethnic, and therefore religious, purity. Likewise the idea of being "mis-yoked" could be applied to religious compromise, perhaps

---

70. Schellenberg, "Kingdom as Contaminant?," 534, citing *m. Kil.* 2:8–9; cf. Scott, *Hear Then the Parable*, 381–83. For Oakman (*Economic Questions*, 124–28), the mustard, like tares, is to be considered a weed.

referring to marriage outside the faith community (2 Cor 6:14; cf. Phil 4:3).[71] Four centuries prior to Jesus, the book of Ezra records a complaint by certain unnamed officials that the returning exiles have intermarried with the very nations they were originally meant to displace: "Thus the holy seed has mixed itself with the peoples of the lands" (Ezra 9:1–2). Their choice of language directly invokes that of Leviticus 19 and Deuteronomy 22.[72] This school of interpretation remains in force throughout the Second Temple period and beyond: the angelic messenger in *2 Baruch* 42:4 refers to apostates as those "who mingled themselves with the seed of the mingled nations."[73] From Qumran, the letter of instruction known as 4QMMT applies all three biblical injunctions to the dangers of intermarriage and the need to preserve Israel's "holy seed":

> And concerning the practice of illegal marriage that exists among the people: (this practice exists) despite their being so[ns] of holy [seed], as is written, Israel is holy. And concerning his (that is, Israel's) [clean ani]mal, it is written that one must not let it mate with another species; and concerning his clothes [it is written that they should not] be of mixed stuff; and he must not sow his field and vine[yard with mixed specie]s. Because they (Israel) are holy, and the sons of Aaron are [most holy.][74]

By the time of the Mishnah, then (that is, prior to 200 CE), ethnic and ethical interpretations of "mixed kinds" evidently constitute a well-worn trope, yet the discussion in the tractate *Kil'aim* returns to more pedestrian, agricultural concerns. Still, its provisions are relevant here because the very first verse of the tractate expressly stipulates that wheat and darnel, respectively, are *not* "diverse kinds": although different, they can therefore be allowed to grow together (*m. Kil.* 1:1). Presumably this judgment was a matter of practical necessity: since wheat and darnel are difficult to distinguish, let alone separate either as seeds or seedlings, defining darnel as a "diverse

---

71. Paul's use of ἑτεροζυγοῦντες ("mis-yoked") evokes the cognate adjective ἑτερόζυγος from LXX Leviticus 19:19; see discussions in Barrett, *Second Epistle to the Corinthians*, 361, and Thrall, *Second Epistle to the Corinthians*, 2:472–74.

72. So Kugel, "The Holiness of Israel," 24.

73. Elliott, *The Survivors of Israel*, 327–28; also *1 En.* 89:75: "the sheep ... got mixed among the wild beasts" (n.54). Albeit in allegorical fashion, Philo, *Spec. Leg.* 3.46, 4.203–18, interprets Leviticus 19:19 with reference to illicit sexual unions. Cf. Sam. *Tg.* Leviticus 19:19, referring to "the garments of the 'mixed rabble' of rebellion," and the proverb attributed to R. Isaac (T4), commenting on Abraham's search for a daughter-in-law (Gen 24:2–4): "Though the wheat of your hometown be darnel [זונין], use it for seed" (*Gen Rab.* 59.8).

74. 4QMMT 78–81; Hayes, "Intermarriage and Impurity," 25–35 (here, 24).

kind" would have excluded wheat from cultivation altogether.⁷⁵ Nor can we imagine this to have been a Mishnaic innovation: the problem of "weeds in the field" is surely as old as wheat farming itself. Thus Jesus and those whose views are later codified in the Mishnah agree in their respective assessments of wheat and darnel: they are emphatically *not* "diverse kinds." But where the rabbis enforce this ruling in agricultural terms, Jesus applies its implications metaphorically, weighing in on centuries of debate that identifies the people of God as "holy seed."

To be more precise, the parable and its interpretation make several key assertions regarding the nature of such "seed," some familiar and others quite distinctive. First, they assume the customary equivalence of agricultural and human "seed": "the good seed are the sons of the kingdom; the weeds are the sons of the evil one" (Matt 13:38). Second, they affirm that "the kingdom of heaven" is to be defined primarily in ethical rather than ethnic terms ("they will collect out of his kingdom all causes of *sin* and all *evildoers*. . . . Then the *righteous* will shine like the sun in the kingdom of their Father," 13:41, 43).⁷⁶ Yet, third, the kingdom is characterized—at least in the short term—by its paradoxical inclusion of the rebellious and disobedient. With a timely pun, Duke underscores the significance of this premise for Jesus' wider ministry: "Some, especially Pharisees, would have found his seedier associates a rank contradiction of the claim that God's kingdom was dawning in his work."⁷⁷ Most unusually, fourth, the parable insists that it is not the prerogative of the citizens or "sons" to maintain the purity (whether ethical, ethnic, or otherwise) of God's domain. Commentators complain that the servants' expression of surprise is unrealistic: surely tares are to be expected in a field of wheat.⁷⁸ Bernard Brandon Scott objects that if the idea of deferred judgment was "meant to defend Jesus' calling the outcast,

---

75. On the treatment of darnel in ancient agricultural practice, see Oakman, *Economic Questions*, 116-18. The interpretation offered here answers the objection by Blomberg (*Preaching the Parables*, 120) that the farmer's command not to pull up the weeds is "very unrealistic."

76. The parable's strongly dualistic tone speaks against the otherwise-similar interpretation of Instone-Brewer (*Prayer and Agriculture*, 198) that "The Pharisees attempt to avoid all *mixtures*, but a strange mixture is allowed in the Kingdom in order to help more outsiders to enter."

77. Duke, *Parables*, 69.

78. See Catchpole, "John the Baptist, Jesus and the Parable of the Tares," 563-64, and the literature cited there. Similarly misdirected is the view of Oakman (*Economic Questions*, 121-23) that the parable critiques sloppy agricultural practice on the part of the landowner, for this is to confuse his role with that of the nocturnal "enemy."

it offers them little hope at the final coming."[79] But these are points that the parable itself intends: just as, at the outset, darnel is impossible either to distinguish or to eradicate, so the saints lack discernment as to the true character of those in their midst. In contrast to strenuous efforts on the part of many among his contemporaries to safeguard the purity of God's "holy seed," Jesus maintains that such efforts are the sole prerogative of God's avenging angels on the day of final judgment.[80] The parable of the Net makes a similar argument: "at the end of the age, the angels will ... separate the evil from the righteous" (Matt 13:49). The wisdom of this position is once more rooted (as it were) in the realities of practical experience: "in gathering the weeds you would uproot the wheat along with them" (13:29).[81]

Prior even to its implications for mission and evangelism, or for safeguarding the pious from "the world," reading the parable in this manner today unexpectedly contradicts one of the core principles of Protestantism. The Protestant Reformation was impelled in large measure by its desire to return an ostensibly corrupt and wayward church to the perfection and purity of its earliest origins. Accordingly, the Pauline admonition, "Wherefore come out from among them, and be ye separate, saith the Lord, and touch not the unclean thing" (2 Cor 6:17; KJV) has informed the identity and outlook of more than a few preachers and their congregations. There is an old joke about the preacher who encounters a parishioner in her garden. Marveling at the splendor of her careful arrangements, the preacher expostulates on the wonder and beauty of God's creation. "Oh yeah?" responds the gardener, "You shoulda seen it when God was looking after it by himself!" Such is the view of every reformer, that without considerable exertion—weeding out moral turpitude, pruning back spurious doctrinal growth, fencing out unwholesome intruders—the church loses its proper holiness, indeed its very character as the true people of God. John the Baptist, no less, appears to relish the prospect of wheat being winnowed from chaff, whose destiny is "unquenchable fire" (Matt 3:12). Jesus, by contrast, contends that (notwithstanding the legitimate demands of righteousness, or the certainty that trees are indeed known by their fruit) the holiness and character of God's children is maintained above all by the one who is the

---

79. Scott, "Parables of Growth Revisited," 5.

80. Similarly Dahl, "Parables of Growth," 152.

81. For an illustration of what Jesus may have had in mind we need look no further than the testimony of Matthew 11:12 ("From the days of John the Baptist until now the kingdom of heaven has suffered violence, and the violent take it by force"), if that verse indeed describes those who sought to establish Jewish independence by military means. Given the disastrous outcome of the first Jewish War, the evangelist and his contemporaries might well have read this parable as a denunciation of such methods.

source of their life. To press the metaphor more firmly, his point is that wheat fields do not—cannot—weed themselves: if the saints truly are God's seed and God's sowing, then they are in no position to usurp God's own prerogatives as landowner, householder, even "Lord of the harvest" (Matt 9:38 // Luke 10:2).[82] Preaching on this parable, Emil Brunner states the matter succinctly: "All coercive means are ruled out in the community of Christ. Faith and force are mutually exclusive."[83]

Once again, absurdity seems the order of the day, not least because the parable of the darnel flies in the face of the very dangers on which the earlier story of the Sower was built. Perhaps it is just as well that Matthew has omitted Mark's parable of the seed growing "automatically," for here the enemy's nocturnal sabotaging of the wheat crop (Matt 13:25) indicates only too well what can happen while farmers and careless farmhands slumber! Barbara Brown Taylor constructs an entire sermon—at once hilarious and brilliant—out of the fact that in such a situation, weeds and wild plants quickly take over.[84] Against the apparent thrust of this parable, every community of faith (including Matthew's own) knows the importance of asserting internal order and thereby maintaining its distinct identity.[85]

All the same, the outlook of the wheat and the weeds is of a piece with Jesus' ministry as a whole. Every religious tradition is acutely aware that sanctity is fragile: contagion no larger than the size of a mustard seed (*m. Nid.* 5:2) is sufficient to render the clean, unclean or what is holy, unholy. By contrast, the holiness of Jesus proves curiously robust, even contagious. Notwithstanding the consternation such actions occasion, he welcomes, touches, even blesses known sinners, for the sanctity he embodies is potent enough to overcome evil, error, and uncleanness alike (so, notably, Mark 5:25–34 and parallels).[86] In this encounter between holiness and corruption it is the sinners and the impure, not Jesus, who come away changed. Even while conceding that the devil himself will sow seed in their midst, the

---

82. In the view of Doty ("An Interpretation," 192), "The believer is free to go about his task—here being a good farmer—without intensive, extensive, frenetic justifying and judging and rooting-out of the 'enemy' or his deeds." On the contrary, the point Jesus intends is that the children of God are, precisely, *not* farmers: they are simply "seed."

83. Brunner, "The Weeds Among the Wheat," in *Sowing and Reaping*, 73.

84. Taylor, "The Gardener in Question," 782.

85. McIver ("The Parable of the Weeds among the Wheat," esp. 652–53) argues cogently for an "ecclesiological" interpretation of the parable, resolving in particular the apparent contradiction (so, e.g., Davies and Allison, *Matthew* 2.428) between this parable and Matthew 18:15–17.

86. Cf. Brower, "The Holy One and His Disciples," 72–73.

parable of the Weeds among the Wheat extends a similar assurance to the children of God. Despite the note of warning sounded earlier by the parable of the Sower (and Mark's recognition of such dangers for even the closest disciples), Matthew's parable of the Weeds among the Wheat encourages confidence that true seed will ultimately flourish because God has sown it, even to fruition and final harvest. On this reading, the parable suggests that any ministry presuming to model itself after the example of Jesus will be characterized more by confidence in God's ability to enliven and safeguard the community of faith than by damaging rearguard actions designed to shield its members from the apostate and the impure.

OF FIG TREES AND FRUIT (LUKE 13:6-9)

Yet another aspect of Jesus' teaching about God's kingdom emerges from the parable of the Barren Fig Tree (unique to Luke but with a parallel of sorts in Mark 11:12-14). Like vines and vineyards (to which we will turn momentarily), the fig tree serves as a symbol for Israel (Hos 9:10); its fruitfulness indicates divine blessing (Joel 2:22, Hag 2:19), while lack thereof betokens judgment (Isa 34:4, Joel 1:12, Amos 4:9, Hab 3:17). More specifically, the fruitless fig tree is for Jeremiah a symbol of Jerusalem's spiritual barrenness:

> When I wanted to gather them, says the Lord,
> there are no grapes on the vine, nor figs on the fig tree;
> even the leaves are withered, and what I gave them has passed
> away from them.
>
> (Jer 8:13)[87]

The Lukan parable combines two sets of imagery: "A man had a *fig tree* planted in his *vineyard*; and he came looking for fruit on it and found none" (Luke 13:6). But while biblical symbolism provides a general backdrop, the action of the parable hinges rather on a question of timing:

> So he said to the gardener, "See here! For three years I have come looking for fruit on this fig tree, and still I find none. Cut it down! Why should it be wasting the soil?" He replied, "Sir [κύριε], let it alone for one more year, until I dig around it and put manure on it. If it bears fruit next year, well and good; but if not, you can cut it down."

---

87. Cf. Micah 6:9, 7:1: "The voice of the Lord cries to the city ... Woe is me! For I have become like one who, after the summer fruit has been gathered, after the vintage has been gleaned, finds no cluster to eat; there is no first-ripe fig for which I hunger."

(Luke 13:7–9)

The possibility of an allusion to Leviticus 19:23–25, which stipulates that the produce of a newly-planted fruit tree may not be eaten for the first three years, at first seems confusing:

> When you come into the land and plant all kinds of trees for food, then you shall regard their fruit as forbidden; *three years* it shall be forbidden to you, it must not be eaten. In the *fourth year* all their fruit shall be set apart for rejoicing in the Lord. But in the *fifth year* you may eat of their fruit, that their yield may be increased for you: I am the Lord your God.

Such is the importance of this legislation that the *Mishnah* and Gemaras dedicate an entire tractate—*Orlah* (which David Instone-Brewer translates as "Forefruit")—to its interpretation.[88] Since even fourth-year produce must be consecrated to God and the man has already been expecting fruit for three years, commentators speculate that as many as six, seven, or more years may have passed since planting.[89] While such objections are not unreasonable, they nonetheless seem to overinterpret the text, which attributes just two sets of actions to the owner: planting and looking for fruit. Further expanding the leisure of Mark's well-rested peasant, the simplest reading of this narrative envisages planting followed by a three-year wait, which upon intervention from the gardener will now be extended to four.

Even apart from a possible allusion to Jeremiah 8:13, the similarity between this parable and the message of John the Baptist, on the one hand ("Every tree . . . that does not bear good fruit is cut down and thrown into the fire," Matt 3:10 // Luke 3:9), and Jesus' enacted parable of rebuking a fig tree for being fruitless at the hour of his coming, on the other (Matt 21:18–19 // Mark 11:12–14), makes it certain that the narrative implies the prospect of imminent judgment. As for individuals, so for the people of God as a whole: "the tree is known by its fruit" (Matt 12:33 // Luke 6:44). In characteristically prophetic fashion—like John before him—Jesus demands that his hearers "bear fruits that befit repentance" (Matt 3:8 RSV), but finds none. This is equally the message of the parable of the Wicked Tenants, in which a man plants a vineyard, then leases it out: "*When the season came*, he sent a slave to the tenants in order that they might give him *his share of the produce* of the vineyard" (Luke 20:10 // Mark 12:2 // Matt 21:34).[90] Like any

---

88. Instone-Brewer, *Prayer and Agriculture*, 379.

89. For the range of possibilities, see Hultgren, *Parables of Jesus*, 243–44.

90. For a similar parable attributed to a rabbi of the second century CE, this one using the metaphor of an unproductive wheat field, see *'Abot R. Nat.* 16 (cited by Scott,

grower with new plant stock, the man in Luke 13 watches over the fig tree year after year, impatient for a return on his investment that will provide food for family and market. But knowing what obedience to Torah requires, he has no expectation of an early harvest. Then, having waited the required interval, and notwithstanding his disappointment at the initial lack of produce, he allows himself to be talked into waiting yet another year: even if it will still be too early to use them for himself, with figs in the fourth season he can make an offering of firstfruits to the Lord.

The barren tree is an enigma precisely because it fails to produce: not that it bears the wrong fruit (as envisaged by Matt 7:16–20 // Luke 6:43–44), but that it bears none whatsoever. As the source of all life and fruition, might God be to blame? Two answers are possible. On the one hand, the fig tree's bare branches could be a sign of divine judgment, in keeping with any number of scriptural precedents. In this case, however, the "Lord" of the parable (hence the ambiguous κύριε) fully expects to find fruit. If God abundantly provides life to all who will receive it, he cannot be the cause of such lack. No more could a farmer who sowed only good seed be blamed for counterfeit crops springing up in his field. Therefore the tree itself must be somehow responsible: against all expectation it is prematurely, inexplicably dead (cf. Jude 12). By implication, the objects of Jesus' prophetic denunciation are not judged for their failure to manifest "good works" or "deeds of loving-kindness" as ends in themselves, or for any other lack of piety in its own right. Rather, his contention is that those who claim to be God's planting, God's true people, fail by virtue of their barrenness to give evidence of divine life in their midst. Since God is indeed the source of Israel's prosperity—in all its senses—absence of fruit implies the functional irrelevance of God. The real issue is not the works themselves, but lack of openness to the life of God. Still, the parable concludes without resolution because it is a word of dire prophetic warning rather than of outright condemnation: there is still time for the arid and barren to be restored. Once again, given the theological richness of the agricultural imagery in question, a twofold appreciation of "the Scriptures [and] the power of God" permits the full dimensions of this parable's intended meaning to emerge.

VINES AND VINEYARDS (JOHN 15:1–8)

Corresponding to the critique implied by Luke's parable of the fig tree is an equally pointed challenge from the Gospel of John, as Jesus tells his

Hear Then the Parable, 337–38). Also similar is the *Story of Ahiqar* 8:35, of uncertain date.

disciples, "I am the true vine" (John 15:1). In a previous chapter we noted Josephus's description of an enormous golden vine, replete with clusters of gold grapes, hanging over the portico of the sanctuary in the Jerusalem temple, vividly representing a key biblical symbol for fruitful Israel. In the Synoptic Gospels, the tenants in the vineyard (Matt 21:33-46 // Mark 12:1-12 // Luke 20:9-19) reflect the specific influence of a similar parable in Isaiah 5, but this stock biblical image for the community of God's people equally undergirds the parables of the Workers in the Vineyard, hired at different hours (Matt 20:1-16), the Two Sons (Matt 21:28-31), and the Fruitless Fig Tree (Luke 13:6-9). Although the two metaphors are closely related, here we are dealing with a vine (ἄμπελος) rather than a vineyard (ἀμπελών); while both represent Israel in biblical and post-biblical literature alike, the vine additionally conveys messianic overtones.[91]

Jesus' claim to be the *true* vine surely implies criticism of all other claimants, if not also an assertion of messianic identity (cf. *2 Bar.* 39:7, cited earlier). Even so, this passage focuses primarily on the organic, life-giving unity that allows vine branches to bring forth grapes and (by analogy) disciples to bear spiritual fruit:

> "I am the true vine, and my Father is the vine grower. He removes every branch in me that bears no fruit. Every branch that bears fruit he prunes to make it bear more fruit.... Just as the branch cannot bear fruit by itself unless it abides in the vine, neither can you unless you abide in me. I am the vine, you are the branches. Those who abide in me and I in them bear much fruit, because apart from me you can do nothing. Whoever does not abide in me is thrown away like a branch and withers; such branches are gathered, thrown into the fire, and burned."
>
> (John 15:1-6)

Although more explicit here than in other New Testament passages, and more clearly linked to the person of the Messiah, the underlying theological dynamics of this symbolism are present already within the agricultural imagery itself and the broad scriptural heritage that it invokes. Of foremost importance is the idea that God is the sole origin of life and fruition for the whole of creation. In particular, just as Israel is the vine of God's planting, so Jesus refers to his heavenly Father as the gardener, or viticulturist, thereby clearly identifying the source of his own life. As the true vine, drawing his vitality from God, Jesus becomes the source of life and fruition for disciples who have access to the Father through him. Indeed, the loving intimacy

---

91. Jaubert, "L'image de la Vigne (Jean 15)," 93-95.

that binds Father and Son is reflected in the intimacy between Jesus and his disciples: "As the Father has loved me," he urges them, "so I have loved you; abide in my love" (John 15:9).[92] Moreover, says Jesus, just as the vinedresser prunes the vine, so likewise will his Father tend and propagate the messianic stock, or else cast off and burn those branches that fail to bear fruit (a motif that recalls both the preaching of John the Baptist and the parable of the fig tree in the vineyard). Where this imagery differs from Luke's parable, however, is that the criterion of fruitfulness and the judgment implied by pruning are both applied *within* the community of Jesus' disciples, rather than to those defined as being outside their number. The "fruit" in question is not clearly identified, any more than it is in the previous passage, but in both cases the underlying principle is the same—that fruition is only made possible by means of organic union with the divine source of life.

As previously, "fruit" borne by the faithful is not an end in itself, but serves rather as evidence of a deeper potency at work, in this case pointing to the life of the Messiah: "My Father is glorified by this, that you bear much fruit and so prove to be [γένησθε; NRSV "become"] my disciples" (John 15:8 RSV). Of particular importance here is the concept of "abiding" or "remaining" in the vine, which implies an essential theological passivity, even receptivity, with regard to a source of vitality other than oneself:

> "*Abide* in me as I *abide* in you. Just as the branch cannot bear fruit by itself unless it *abides* in the vine, neither can you unless you *abide* in me. . . . Those who *abide* in me and I in them bear much fruit, because apart from me you can do nothing."
>
> (John 15:4–5)

This last declaration—"Apart from me you can do nothing"—articulates more clearly (albeit with reference to the Messiah) a principle that has been at least implicit in each of the parables reviewed thus far, whether concerning seed that fails to flourish until blessed by God, grows up inexplicably without assistance from the farmer, produces a plant out of all proportion to its tiny size, or prevails despite competition from noxious weeds. It likewise underlies Jesus' parabolic critique of the barren fig tree, as well as his claim, earlier in the same passage, to be the "true vine" of God's planting. Following a review of parables unique to each of Matthew (the Wheat and Weeds), Mark (the Seed growing unaided), Luke (the Fig Tree), and John (the Vine), as well as from the triple tradition (the Sower and soil, the Mustard Seed), it seems fair to conclude not only that agricultural motifs pervade the traditions of Jesus' teaching and ministry, but also that every

---

92. This theme is sensitively explored in ibid., 96–97.

layer of this tradition acknowledges a theology of direct divine providence as integral to the reign of God and the life of God's people. As if to illustrate its comprehensive scope, the Gospels expound this perspective with reference to three major crops—wheat, figs, and grapes—that represent Israel's three main forms of agricultural produce: grains, tree fruits, and plants of the field. Not even spices escape mention!

THE WEALTHY FARMER (LUKE 12:16-21)

Thus far, in no small measure as a corrective to the strongly anthropocentric and typically moralizing tendencies of parable interpretation (especially where preaching is concerned), our study has focused on questions of divine initiative and causality with respect to the life of God's people. Even so, what forms of response does Jesus envisage? According to these parables in particular, what might an appropriate faith, piety, or obedience consist of, whether for their first audiences or for those who hear and preach them anew?

One form of response implied by all the agricultural parables comes to clearer expression in Jesus' tale concerning a wealthy farmer overtaken by sudden death. Here the operative theological dynamic, identified throughout the whole of our discussion, is present from the outset in the parable's opening line: "The land of a rich man brought forth plentifully" (Luke 12:16). The remainder of the parable concerns an inappropriate human response: rather than exhibiting gratitude or acknowledging his dependence on the generosity of God, the man imagines that his security lies in the material wealth he has managed to amass for himself. As is evident both from the narrative context and from a likely allusion to traditions concerning Cain and Abel, the parable at one level addresses questions of human greed or covetousness. When a man asks Jesus to arbitrate between him and his brother on a matter of family inheritance,[93] Jesus responds first to the petitioner—"Friend, who set me to be a judge or arbitrator over you?" —then to the bystanders: "Take care! Be on your guard against all kinds of greed; for one's life does not consist in the abundance of possessions" (Luke 12:14-15). As with the parable of the Persistent Widow, the "Wisdom of Jesus ben Sirach" may have inspired this story:

---

93. The petitioner's request for assistance implies that he is a younger brother (so Marshall, *The Gospel of Luke*, 522), a situation closely parallel to the parable of the Prodigal (Luke 15:11-12), except that here the father is evidently no longer alive to intercede for him.

> Good and evil, life and death, poverty and riches, are from the Lord.
> The Lord's gift remains with the just; his favor brings lasting success.
> A person may become rich through a miser's life, and this is his allotted reward:
> When he says, "I have found rest, now I will feast on my possessions,"
> He does not know how long it will be till he leaves them to others and dies.
>
> (Sir 11:14, 17–19)[94]

But identifying a moral fault is not the same as providing its solution, something the parable never spells out in detail. In fact, resolving the anxiety that gives rise to materialism and avarice requires discernment concerning the nature of true security, the theological source of which hearers must discover for themselves behind the parable's agricultural imagery. To this end, another scriptural allusion helps to identify the "power of God" at work in the story.

In Jewish tradition, Cain and Abel are archetypal opposites, one a man of violence and greed, the other a model of martyred righteousness.[95] Abel is the epitome of virtue, an example to all who love God, the prototype of those who cry out for God to requite their unjust suffering, and ultimately, in the Second Temple-period *Testament of Abraham*, the one who judges humanity immediately after death, separating the righteous from the wicked.[96] Cain, by contrast, is the epitome of wickedness and self-love; in Targumic tradition he explicitly rejects the possibility of any judgment, reward, or retribution after death.[97] In Josephus's retelling of Genesis 4, Cain accumulates possessions by means of robbery and violence, inventing weights and measures so as to defraud others; all that interests him is the endless accumulation of wealth. Accordingly, Josephus takes his name to mean "Acquisition" (*Ant.* 1.52–53, 60–61). For Philo, "The central flaw in Cain's character . . . was his failure to recognize that all possessions belonged

---

94. Cited in part by Buttrick, *Speaking Parables*, 188; here the translation is from Skehan and Di Lella, *The Wisdom of Ben Sira*, 235–36. Cf. *1 Enoch* 97:8–10, cited by Scott, *Hear Then the Parable*, 133 n.21.

95. In Philo, for example, "The types of Cain and Abel are presented as two aspects of the human soul, representing the human capacity for good and the human capacity for evil"; so Najman, "Cain and Abel as Character Traits," 107; further, 113–18.

96. Byron, "Living in the Shadow of Cain," 263–65; see *1 En.* 22:6–7; *T. Ab.* 13:3–9.

97. See Vermès, "The Targumic Versions of Genesis 4:3–16," 96–99.

to God rather than to him."[98] Josephus offers a similar explanation for God accepting Abel's offering rather than that of Cain:

> The brothers having decided to sacrifice to God, Cain brought the fruits of the tilled earth and of the trees, Abel came with milk and the firstlings of his flocks. This was the offering which found more favour with God, who is honoured by things that grow *spontaneously* [αὐτομάτοις] and in accordance with natural laws, and not by the products forced from nature by the ingenuity of grasping man.
>
> (*Ant.* 1.54)

Responding to another dispute between brothers, Jesus tells a parable whose protagonist bears a striking resemblance to Cain. This character is not, say, a cloth merchant, a money lender, or a tax agent, for none of these occupations entails immediate dependence on the providence of God. Certainly the man is avaricious and self-satisfied, taking no thought for the state of his soul or the prospect of divine judgment. But the fact that he cultivates wheat or grain—σίτος can mean either—suggests these to be symptoms of a deeper spiritual malaise. His fundamental error is lack of theological perception, an inability to recognize the true source of his bounty. Nothing, in fact, prevents him from filling new granaries to overflowing, for the riches they contain are not of his own making. His sin is not avarice per se, but garnering agricultural produce for his own security, and thereby failing to recognize that his crops illustrate his contingency, his human dependence on the blessings of a bountiful God. Accordingly, Bernard Brandon Scott entitles this parable "How to Mismanage a Miracle."[99] Philo, incidentally, concurs that the issue at stake is acknowledgment of divine generosity as opposed to relying on human resourcefulness and exertion, although he assigns grain farming to the latter category in keeping with the curse of Genesis 3:17–19. As much as a more theologically astute farmer would know that the wealth he amasses comes directly from the hand of God, so the newly orphaned petitioner would do well to recognize that his family inheritance is no more than a gift, therefore to be received with gratitude rather than greed. Even without it, God will still provide for him. To underscore this point for his own audience—and with it the theology of natural providence on which

---

98. Byron, "Living in the Shadow of Cain," 265; cf. 265–68.

99. Scott, *Hear Then the Parable*, 127; cf. 134–35, noting the similarity to God's provision for the sabbatical year (Lev 25:2–4, 20–21) and suggesting that a bumper crop implies responsibility to share its bounty with the poor (followed by Buttrick, *Speaking Parables*, 189).

the argument is built—Luke next relates Jesus' exhortation for disciples to consider the birds, the flowers, and the grass of the field, all of which God generously nurtures and sustains (Luke 12:22–28 // Matt 6:25–30).[100] By virtue of this narrative arrangement, the Lukan Jesus at once explains to his disciples (perhaps also the petitioner) what the parable's spiritually myopic landowner ought to have recognized all along.

Notwithstanding its context in Luke, or the circumstances to which the parable was first addressed, the rich man's lack of perspective is typical of a more widespread failure of vision, the very predicament that various parables about seeds, fields, vines, and trees seek to resolve. Whether for Jesus' first audience or for us as we read—and preach—these parables, discipleship requires that we recognize the extent of our dependence on God. Even beyond its application to questions of material wealth, the dichotomy of Jesus' concluding denunciation implies as much: "So is he who lays up treasure *for himself*, and is not rich *toward God*" (12:21; cf. 12:33–34). This is a matter not of recognition alone, but also of active reliance on God's grace.

To summarize once more: Jesus tells parables that evoke a theology of divine providence, inviting hearers to rely (in communion with him) upon the life-giving power of a generous God. This dynamic is intrinsic to the loving trust that he exemplifies, expressing in practice what it means to call God "Father." At the same time, the appeal of the parables to something beyond the power of words themselves suggests a possible model for preaching. Like life itself—at least as envisaged in Jesus' description of the kingdom of God—preaching depends for its power not on the authority of the preacher, the cleverness of its rhetoric, or even its ability to articulate theological truth. Rather, truly transformative preaching requires active intervention from the same God of which it claims to speak. This is not a counsel of despair, as though there were now nothing left for preachers to do. On the contrary, desiring to preach to others requires that we first submit ourselves to the same conditions of which these parables speak. In this regard there is no real distinction between preachers and their audiences, since both must hear and receive the seed that is God's word, and both must yield equally to the life-giving prerogative of God.

In much the same vein, Snodgrass introduces his interpretation of the parables with an incisive comment that aptly summarizes the results of our own study:

> The parables do not need to be curtailed, rewritten, domesticated, psychologized, theologized with foreign christological

---

100. The link is made explicit by the catchword ἀποθήκη (Luke 12:18, 24): whereas the farmer gathers produce into granaries, the ravens do not.

and atonement contributions, decontextualized, or controlled. They need to be allowed to speak, and they need to be heard. Some parables are clear as bells, and, while we may discuss nuances and backgrounds in lengthy treatises, they do not need explanation so much as implementation. They in effect say to us, "Stop resisting and do it," or "Believe it."[101]

Clifton Black has an even more pointed word of admonition for preachers, derived from the same texts that have occupied our attention:

> Remember that your job is to plant what you cannot germinate: seeds that grow in secret, invisibly, and find root in a mere fraction—yet bloom there beyond calculation. As with silver tongued Apollos (Acts 18:24–28) and Paul, who by his own admission could not preach his way out of a paper sack (2 Cor 11:6), so too with us: one plants, another waters, but God alone gives growth (1 Cor 3:6).[102]

How preachers might yield to this call, learning to speak from the perspective expressed by Jesus' agricultural parables in particular, will be the subject of the next two chapters.

---

101. Snodgrass, *Stories with Intent*, 3.
102. Black, "Preaching from the Gospels and Acts," 6.

Part Two

GOD'S BODY, GOD'S BUILDING

Chapter 4

"Not with Plausible Words of Wisdom"
Preaching Shaped by the Cross

> The crucified Christ therefore remains the inner criterion of all preaching which appeals to him. So far as it points to him, it is tested by him; so far as it reveals him, it is authorized by him.
>
> —Jürgen Moltmann (1926–)[1]

If we take Jesus' agricultural parables as our model, transformative preaching will depend for its effectiveness on a power well beyond anything words alone can achieve. This is less a question of theological *content* than of theological *method*. Our proposal is that these parables cite the dual testimony of Scripture and the "natural" world as an invitation for hearers to recognize and rely upon the life-giving power of God in their own lives. For preachers to follow suit has implications both for spirituality—one's general disposition toward God—and for the specific practice of preaching. These subjects will provide the focus for the next two chapters, the argument of which is relatively straightforward. Specifically, if Christian preaching invites hearers to trust in the transformative agency of God, the same will necessarily hold true for the preacher, as for the act of preaching itself. Not surprisingly, Jesus himself provides the model for a life of utter reliance on God.

---

1. Moltmann, *The Crucified God*, 75.

"THE SON CAN DO NOTHING ON HIS OWN": JESUS AND THE LIFE OF GOD

At the end of the previous chapter we briefly reviewed Jesus' apparent prescription for ministerial success:

> "Abide in me as I abide in you. Just as the branch cannot bear fruit by itself unless it abides in the vine, neither can you unless you abide in me. I am the vine, you are the branches. Those who abide in me and I in them bear much fruit, because apart from me you can do nothing..."
>
> (John 15:4–5)

While this is familiar territory, it is less often recognized that John's gospel sets out the specific dynamics of the disciples' practical reliance on him by analogy to Jesus' own relationship with the Father. According to John, Jesus' relationship with the Father forms the model for our own relationship with Jesus. And since Jesus' relationship with God provides the immediate basis for his ministry, so that relationship serves in turn as a model for pastoral ministry that is based on our own relationship with Christ. So when Jesus commands his disciples, "Abide in me as I abide in you," his own relationship with the Father models what that "abiding" looks like in practice: rather than simply telling them what to do, he demonstrates it in his own life, and death.

"Like Father; Like Son": Ministry as Loving Dependence

Although this dynamic may take some getting used to for readers more comfortable with a "high" Christology, the Gospel of John emphasizes Jesus' complete inability to accomplish the works of God in and of himself. Jesus' first statement to this effect seeks to explain his controversial practice of healing on the Sabbath. The justification for such actions, he says, is that "My Father is still working, and I also am working" (John 5:17). In principle, then, Jesus' ministry takes its cue from the unceasing providence of God. We may take this to mean that even as the Sabbath is intended for human benefit in general (as in Mark 2:27), so his ministry of healing achieves the same end. Or, since Jesus refers to God "working" while his people rest (as with the seed that grows while the farmer sleeps), his intention is more likely that even on the Sabbath the sun comes up as usual, the rain falls in season, the vines blossom, the grain continues to ripen, and the trees grow ever more heavy with fruit. All these reflect the immediate and unceasing generosity of God, which not even the Sabbath interrupts.

Philo, a near contemporary, offers a similar explanation of the Sabbath and its origins in God's seventh-day "rest." Following the Greek (LXX) text of Genesis 2:2, he avers that God did not actually "rest" when creation was complete; indeed, he says, "God never leaves off making" (*Alleg. Interp.* 1 §5 [LCL]).[2] Rather that ceasing his own creative activity, God *caused to rest* the works of creation that he had previously set in motion:

> For he makes things to rest which appear to be producing others, but which in reality do not effect anything; but he himself never ceases from creating. On which account Moses says, "He caused to rest the things which he had begun."
>
> (*Alleg. Interp.* 1 §6)[3]

To illustrate what he has in mind Philo then cites the cosmic cycles of days and months and years, marked by the rotation of planets and stars, and the human life cycles of birth and death (§7-8, 16). As he explains in another passage, also concerning Sabbath and creation:

> The cause of all things is by nature active; it never ceases to work all that is best and most beautiful. God's rest is rather a working with absolute ease, without toil and without suffering.
>
> (*Cher.* §87 [LCL])

Nor is Philo alone in finding God exempt from the requirements of Sabbath respite: as Raymond Brown observes,

> There are a whole series of rabbinic statements to the effect that Divine Providence remained active on the Sabbath, for otherwise, the rabbis reasoned, all nature and life would cease to exist.... Since only God could give life (II Kings v 7; II Macc vii 22-23) and only God could deal with the fate of the dead in judgment, this meant that God was active on the Sabbath.[4]

Contemporary and subsequent debate about the implications of divine providence in relation to Sabbath rest offers an illuminating context for

---

2. Cf. Hoskyns, *The Fourth Gospel*, 266-67; Barrett, *John*, 213.

3. Although his interpretation is perhaps grammatically forced, Philo distinguishes between the simple form of the verb, παύειν, and the intensive κατέπαυσεν found in LXX Genesis 2:2-3. Here the translation is that of C. D. Yonge, *The Works of Philo Judaeus*, 1:53, which is clearer at this point than the Loeb edition.

4. Brown, *John I-XII*, 217.

understanding Jesus' claim to imitate God. He continues with an extended defense of such actions:

> "The Son can do *nothing* on his own, but only what he sees the Father doing; whatever the Father does, the Son does likewise. For the Father loves the Son, and shows him all that he himself is doing.... Indeed, just as the Father raises the dead and gives them life, so also the Son gives life to whomever he wishes."
>
> (John 5:19–21)

Here the content of Jesus' "nothing" is quite specific. Notwithstanding the fact that he is defending the particular action of having healed a lame man, he characterizes the whole of his ministry as one of bestowing life (cf. John 1:4). The importance of this assertion is suggested by a comment attributed to the third-century Rabbi Johanan bar Nappaha (*b. Ta'an.* 2a):

> Three keys are in God's hands which are given into the hand of no representative [שליח; emissary, intermediary], namely the key of the rain [Deut 28:12], the key of the womb [Gen 30:22], and the key of the resurrection of the dead [Ezek 37:13].[5]

Although this formulation is considerably later than the time of Jesus or John's gospel, it would appear from the content of the *Shemoneh 'Esreh*, or "Eighteen Benedictions" (which this section of the Talmud seeks to expound), that prior to the destruction of the Jerusalem temple, Jewish prayer already typically blessed God for the gift of life in creation, in dew and rain, and in resurrection, thereby acknowledging that the gift of life is indeed the sole prerogative of God.[6] Whether, then, in the realm of nature, in terms of human procreation, or beyond the boundaries of death, God alone holds the keys to life. And it is in serving as an instrument of this divinely given life that Jesus depends entirely upon the will and initiative of the Father. His reticence to take personal credit for the restorative power of his ministry is altogether in keeping with subsequent demurrals that acknowledge God's sole authority over such matters.

Again at the end of the same discourse Jesus repeats his contention: "I can do nothing on my own. As I hear, I judge; and my judgment is just, because I seek to do not my own will but the will of him who sent me" (John

---

5. Cited from Barrett, *John*, 216; cf. Rengstorf, s.v. ἀπόστολος, *TDNT* 1:419. For discussion of this motif in other rabbinic texts, see Aune, *Revelation 1–5*, 103-4.

6. See further Schürer, *Jewish People in the Age of Jesus Christ*, 455-63: "From its content it its evident that the Prayer did not reach its final form until after the destruction of Jerusalem in A.D. 70 ... but the underlying foundation of the Prayer is certainly much older" (459).

5:30). It is a curious defense, for it implies that Jesus is not responsible for the direction or conduct of his ministry: he is simply following the Father's lead. C. K. Barrett observes that

> Jesus is what he is only in humble obedience to and complete dependence upon the Father. He has no independent status; he even has no independent will or judgment. He does only what he sees the Father do.[7]

His ministry consists simply of beholding, understanding, copying, and participating in something initiated and altogether sustained by the saving will of the Father.

While we should not be surprised that his detractors fail to be swayed by this argument, Jesus makes similar assertions throughout John's gospel.[8] Once more forced to defend himself as opposition increases, he again insists that the authority of his teaching is dependent on the One who has commanded it. Moreover, such teaching conveys the gift of life: "the words and deeds of Jesus that the commandment directs are themselves the source of eternal life":[9]

> "I have not spoken on my own, but the Father who sent me has himself given me a commandment about what to say and what to speak. And I know that his commandment is eternal life. What I speak, therefore, I speak just as the Father has told me."
>
> (John 12:49–50)

This is likewise his response to Philip in chapter 14: while the works that he performs are authentic and persuasive in their own right, fuller discernment will acknowledge their divine origin:

> Do you not believe that I am in the Father and the Father is in me? The words that I say to you I do not speak on my own; but the Father who dwells in me does his works. Believe me that I am in the Father and the Father is in me; but if you do not, then believe me because of the works themselves.
>
> (John 14:10–11; cf. 14:24)

---

7. Barrett, *John*, 214.

8. Beasley-Murray, *John*, 75, observes that in his words (John 8:28, 12:49), his works (14:10), and his being sent into the world (7:28)—the three foundational dimensions of his earthly ministry—Jesus claims direct dependence on the Father.

9. Brown, *John I–VII*, 492.

It is worth noting that this hermeneutic is similar to the interpretative principle that underlies the parables of growth: just as the bounty of nature reflects the life-giving work of God, so Jesus' own works of provision and healing reveal the Father. In this regard, "words" and "works" serve the same purpose: in each case the onlooker or listener is invited to probe beyond the immediate evidence so as to discern its true source and origin. As this principle provides the key to understanding Jesus' own ministry, so it proves axiomatic for the ministry of his first disciples, as indeed for all those who subsequently offer their ministries in his name.

"Apart from Me You Can Do Nothing": Dependence and Discipleship

What Jesus says of the disciples—"Apart from me you can do nothing"—is antecedently true of himself in relation to God—"I can do nothing on my own." The whole of his relationship with them is to be characterized by a willing reciprocity between Master and disciple, matching that which unites Father and Son. Four statements in particular draw a series of direct comparisons between the respective relationships. The first of these concerns the source of Jesus' life, even as Jesus is the source of the disciples' life, explaining his declaration that he is "the living bread" given for the life of the world (John 6:51): "Just as the living Father sent me, and I live because of the Father, so whoever eats me will live because of me" (John 6:57). Likewise in terms of personal knowledge, Jesus promises an intimacy matching that which he enjoys with his heavenly Father: "I know my own and my own know me, just as the Father knows me and I know the Father" (John 10:14–15). No less complete is the love that binds them together: "As the Father has loved me, so have I loved you. Remain in my love" (John 15:9). Finally, Jesus compares his own commissioning of the disciples to the Father's commissioning of him: "As the Father has sent me, so I send you" (John 20:21; cf. 17:18). The most basic dimensions of these (unexpectedly) parallel relationships—spiritual life, personal love, intimate knowledge, mission and ministry—are thus each characterized by obedience to the life-giving initiative of another, out of which emerges a mutuality borne of willing submission and faithful dependence.

If the consequences of Jesus' reliance on his Father are clear—authority to declare forgiveness and proclaim God's imminent reign; power to heal, even to restore the dead to life—they are less obvious in the case of the disciples. The disciples, says Jesus, are to "bear much fruit" and thereby glorify the Father who is its ultimate source and inspiration (John 15:8). But what sort of "fruit" does he have in mind? Where neither Jesus nor John offered an immediate explanation, commentators have not hesitated to fill in the gap. The views of Matthew Henry (1662-1714), disseminated via numerous editions of his popular commentary, have influenced many:

> We must be *fruitful*. From a vine we look for *grapes* (Isa 5:2) and from a *Christian* we look for *Christianity*, this is the fruit, a Christian temper and disposition, a Christian life and conversation, Christian devotions, and Christian designs. We must honour God, and do good, and exemplify the purity and power of the Rrligion we profess, and this is *bearing fruit*. The disciples here must be fruitful as Christians, in all *fruits of righteousness*, and as apostles in *diffusing the Savour of that knowledge*.[10]

Other exegetes—ancient and modern alike—refer in similar terms to "qualities of Christian character" (Morris), "mutual love" (Augustine, Barrett, Bultmann), "good works" (Augustine, Fenton), or "effective mission" (Beasley-Murray, Lindars).[11] While this line of interpretation cannot be excluded altogether, two other Johannine references to "fruit" offer a more specific context for understanding what Jesus intends. One of these draws a parallel between the glory of Jesus' resurrection and the "eternal life" that awaits faithful disciples:

> Jesus answered them, "The hour has come for the Son of Man to be glorified. Very truly, I tell you, unless a grain of wheat falls into the earth and dies, it remains just a single grain; but if it dies, it bears much *fruit*. Those who love their life lose it, and those who hate their life in this world will keep it for eternal life."
>
> (John 12:23-25)

The other is more directly missiological, as Jesus comments on how many Samaritan villagers have come to believe that he is the Messiah:

> Jesus said to them, "My food is to do the will of him who sent me, and to accomplish his work. Do you not say, 'Four months more, then comes the harvest'? But I tell you, look around you, and see how the fields are ripe for harvesting. The reaper is already receiving wages and is gathering *fruit for eternal life*, so

---

10. Quoted from Henry, *An Exposition of the Historical Books of the New Testament*, 571 (emphasis original).

11. So Augustine, "Tractates on the Gospel of John" 82.1, 87.1, cited in Elowsky, ed., *John 11-21*, 170, 177-78; Barrett, *John*, 395; Beasley-Murray, *John*, 273; Fenton, *The Gospel According To John*, 158; Lindars, *The Gospel of John*, 489; Morris, *The Gospel According to John*, 595.

> that sower and reaper may rejoice together. For here the saying holds true, 'One sows and another reaps.' I sent you to reap that for which you did not labor. Others have labored, and you have entered into their labor."
>
> (John 4:35–38)

In each of these passages, fruit and fruition emerge out of death, loss, or some other insufficiency, even in the case of the disciples "reaping" where others have sown. Where Jesus ("the Son of Man") is glorified by death and subsequent fruitfulness (12:23), so the Father is glorified by fruitful disciples (15:8). And whether in Jesus' own experience or that of the Samaritans, "bearing fruit" appears equivalent to life itself—indeed, "eternal life"—precisely that which the disciples as "branches" derive from Jesus the true vine. On the basis of these parallels, Brown concludes that "bearing fruit [is] symbolic of possessing divine life and that secondarily it involve[s] communicating that life to others" by virtue of the love that binds the disciples to one another and their Master alike.[12]

Notwithstanding its unfortunate tendency to get sidetracked by less momentous concerns, the proper goal of Christian ministry surely involves what Jesus and John both call "eternal life." But since it is humanly impossible for us to generate spiritual life within our congregants, we are forced to rely instead on Jesus (just as he explains to his disciples in John), as well as on the power of God to which the parables consistently bear witness. If the terms that Jesus articulates are to remain in force for subsequent disciples—not just the original eleven or twelve—they will have critical implications for the conduct of Christian ministry, preaching included:

> Apart from union with Christ, ministry is cast back on us to achieve. This is a recipe for failure, for we all fall short of the glory of God. The understanding and practice of pastoral work in this case is a burden too heavy to bear and follows a path that denies the gospel. We do not heal the sick, comfort the bereaved, accompany the lonely, forgive sins, raise up hope of eternal life, or bring people to God on the strength of our piety and pastoral skill. To think that these task are ours to perform is not only hubris, but also a recipe for exhaustion and depression in ministry.[13]

Despite the fact that such dynamics are in striking contrast to the social, cultural, and psychological ideals of our day, the effectiveness of Christian

---

12. Brown, *John XIII–XXI*, 680; cf. 675–79.
13. Purves, *Reconstructing Pastoral Theology*, 45.

ministry will be predicated upon obedience, loyalty, lack of personal initiative, and what could perhaps be described as "learned theological helplessness." Ministry will rely for its success less on aptitude, proper training, or personal ability than on willing inability and loving reliance: "Just as the branch cannot bear fruit by itself unless it abides in the vine, neither can you unless you abide in me ... apart from me you can do nothing." For well-educated, skills-driven, competency-oriented religious professionals of the affluent West (preachers foremost among them), this will prove to be a difficult—even painful—lesson. Yet for all that, learning to depend on Jesus will draw us deeper into the meaning of his crucifixion: as much in the course of discipleship and ministry as in an initial experience of conversion, we will find ourselves joining him at the cross.

"I HAVE BEEN CRUCIFIED WITH CHRIST": DISCIPLESHIP, MINISTRY, AND LEARNED THEOLOGICAL HELPLESSNESS

So far the argument of our study has been that Jesus tells parables that appeal to the life-giving power of God, citing the theological testimony of Scripture and the world of nature. Just as these parables imply the need for listeners to acknowledge the source of their life in God, so Jesus makes a similar, more overt appeal for his closest disciples to find their life and sustenance in him, even as he derives his own life directly from the Father and depends for his ministry on the Father's initiative. From him, too, comes the power that enables disciples to bear "fruit." Within Jesus' human lifetime, his followers fail spectacularly in this regard. Indeed, by falling victim to the most ignominious form of execution known in the Mediterranean world, Jesus himself at first fails to manifest the divine life on which he claims to rely. Yet no less famously, Messiah and disciples alike are transformed by the reversal of this shameful defeat in Jesus' resurrection from death.

His example is salutary, in more than one sense. Taking their cue from the testimony of the evangelists (e.g., Mark 10:45 // Matt 20:28: "the Son of Man came ... to give his life a ransom for many") and the Apostle Paul, Christians of every age have understood the crucifixion and resurrection as the essential basis for salvation from sin: "Jesus our Lord ... was handed over to death for our trespasses and was raised for our justification" (Rom 4:24–25). Paul articulates this principle in distinctly personal terms both for himself ("I have been crucified with Christ; it is no longer I who live, but ... Christ who lives in me"; Gal 2:19–20) and for his hearers ("For if we have been united with him in a death like his, we will certainly be united with him in a resurrection like his" [Rom 6:5]). Likewise death and resurrection offer a pattern for moral reformation ("We have been buried with him by baptism into death, so that just as Christ was raised from the dead by the glory of the Father, so we too might walk in newness of life" [Rom 6:4]), as well as the promise of eschatological restoration ("If we have died with him, we will also live with him" [2 Tim 2:11 // Rom 6:8]). But the pattern of Jesus' death and resurrection applies to more than conversion, morality, or future glory alone. Although the origins of this interpretation are to be found in Luther's theology (if not earlier still), Michael Gorman has championed the view that what Paul articulates is not so much a conceptual framework or moral vision as—to borrow the language of Martin Heidegger—a "way of being in the world."[14] Gorman speaks of "Paul's narrative spirituality of the cross," by which he means

> conformity to the crucified Christ, showing that this conformity is a dynamic correspondence in daily life to the strange story of Christ crucified as the primary way of experiencing the love and grace of God.[15]

For Gorman, to be a follower of the crucified Messiah is to find one's whole experience, and in particular one's experience of God, given shape and meaning by the life, death, and resurrection of Jesus of Nazareth: "*the narrative of the crucified and exalted Christ is the normative life-narrative within which the community's own life-narrative takes place and by which it is shaped.*"[16] Accordingly, Christian discipleship entails ongoing conformity to the trusting obedience, self-giving service, and expectation of future glory that Jesus himself exemplified in life—the familiar Pauline triad of faith, love, and hope.[17]

---

14. Thus, as Paul Scott Wilson reminds us, "The cross and resurrection are central to the gospel, yet the gospel is larger than the events of Good Friday and Easter in that it includes the implications of these events" (*Setting Words on Fire*, 69). Wilson goes on to quote Gordon W. Lathrop (*The Pastor*, 50–51), who argues for implications that are central to our own and Gorman's work: "Preaching is a Trinitarian event: enlivened by the Spirit, the words of the preacher draw the hearer into the truth of our need, into the encounter with the Crucified-Risen One and so into faith and hope in God. . . . Faith in the triune God, after all, is faith in God coming now, into the midst of our death, and making, *giving* life" (emphasis original).

15. Gorman, *Cruciformity*, 5.

16. Ibid., 44 (emphasis original).

17. For brief summaries, see ibid., 93, and, more specifically, 153 (faith); 173, 267 (love); 347–48 (hope).

To these Gorman adds a critical fourth dimension: cruciform power. Because it is modeled on the crucifixion of God's Messiah, this is a deeply paradoxical concept:

> God's decisive act in Jesus stands all forms of power and authority on their heads.... Christ is ... the locus and revelation of divine power only as the weak, the crucified one. *Christ is, for Paul, God's power-in-weakness.*[18]

While many details of this rich and puzzling dynamic await further exploration, it will suffice for the moment to observe its relevance for Christian experience generally, and therefore to the work of Christian ministry in particular. As a matter of experiential principle, Paul declares, "Whenever I am weak, *then* I am strong" (2 Cor 12:10). Whether in terms of persecution and physical affliction, perceived lack of rhetorical skill, or failure to embody Greco-Roman ideals of power and prestige, Paul consciously identifies with the weakness and humiliation of Jesus upon the cross, confident that in the course of doing so he will also experience the power that raised Jesus from death.[19] While we are all eager to appropriate the power of Christ's resurrection in support of our present ministries, we sometimes overlook the fact that such empowerment comes only at the cost of death. At least within the relative safety of the Western church, the "death" in question may be moral or metaphorical rather than literal, but it will be demanding and difficult nonetheless. Preachers in particular must submit to the same conditions of the Christian gospel that they announce to their hearers, however challenging these may seem. As Brunner reminds us, "God's word does not stir up enthusiasm. It kills and makes alive, it calls to battle and promises victory, but at the same time it implies a costly and difficult struggle."[20]

For Paul, "the message of the cross"—indicating the core content of the Christian gospel that he preaches—represents both "folly" and "power": "folly to those who are perishing, but to us who are being saved it is the power of God" (1 Cor 1:18 RSV). He characterizes the task of preaching "the gospel of Christ" in similar terms:

> Thanks be to God, who in Christ always leads us in triumph, and through us spreads the fragrance of the knowledge of him everywhere. For we are the aroma of Christ to God among those

---

18. Ibid., 278 (emphasis original).

19. Ibid., 281–93 (here describing forms of Pauline "weakness," although the analysis offered in our present study will diverge somewhat from Gorman's understanding of cruciform "power").

20. Brunner, "The Fourfold Soil," in *Sowing and Reaping*, 15.

> who are being saved and among those who are perishing, to the one a fragrance from death to death, to the other a fragrance from life to life. Who is sufficient for these things?
>
> (2 Cor 2:14–16 RSV)

But it is not as if the folly of the cross and the proclamation of impending death apply exclusively to those who are perishing, while "those who are being saved" know only "life" and "power." On the contrary, the same "message of the cross," with its sentence of death and promise of new life, applies equally to both groups. Only from the perspective of five-point Calvinism can Paul be taken to mean that the ignominious crucifixion of Jesus presages divine condemnation for one portion of humanity, while quite another segment of the population reaps all the benefits of his resurrection. Rather, "the word of the cross" and the preaching of the gospel announce a single, twofold movement of abasement and exaltation, death followed by new life. Paul expounds these corresponding elements most clearly in his letter to the Philippians:

> He humbled himself and became obedient to the point of death—even death on a cross. *Therefore* God also highly exalted him and gave him the name that is above every name . . .
>
> (Phil 2:8–9)

Although they are distinctive in their effects, death and resurrection are nonetheless inseparable elements of a single saving initiative, the whole of which forms the subject of Paul's preaching. The difference between "those who are perishing" and "those who are being saved" is therefore largely a matter of apprehension or acceptance on the part of each constituency, as the apostle himself explains:

> We preach Christ crucified, a stumbling block to Jews and folly to Gentiles, but to those who are called, both Jews and Greeks, Christ the power of God and the wisdom of God. For God's foolishness is wiser than human wisdom, and God's weakness is stronger than human strength.
>
> (1 Cor 1:23–25 RSV)

The theological content of his message is the same in either case: "We preach Christ crucified." Where some are overwhelmed by the stench of death, for others the same wind bears also the sweet fragrance of springtime; the first group sees nothing beyond ignominy and shame, while the second recognizes in that same humiliation the paradoxical wisdom of God's folly and the triumph of divine weakness.

The comprehensive significance of Christ's work is vitally important for discipleship because the cross does not cease to be relevant once one is "saved." To be "in Christ"—Paul's most frequent description of Christian identity—means that those so inscribed are caught up into the theological whole of Jesus' crucifixion and resurrection as a single saving act. If there is any imbalance in this identification, it is that even "those who are being saved" appear at times to share more in Jesus' death and humbling than they do his exaltation. This much is implied, for example, by Paul's many physical trials, his refusal to "lord it" over his converts (κυριεύειν; 2 Cor 1:24), the strangely truncated admonition of Philippians 2 (where he exhorts his converts to imitate Jesus' humiliation but makes no immediate mention of their sharing his glory), and especially the central role of the Lord's Supper in congregational life, by means of which believers "proclaim the Lord's *death*" (1 Cor 11:26).[21] "The cup of blessing which we bless," he asks, "is it not a participation, a communion, in the *blood* of Christ?" (1 Cor 10:16). Thus, continuing to identify with Jesus' death as much as his resurrection is vital to the conduct of Christian ministry because both are essential to the ongoing experience of discipleship as a whole. As at first entry into the dominion of Christ, so in the course of its proclamation and enactment, embodying "death" will mean turning away from all misleading or insufficient promises of life as a necessary precondition for embracing its true source.

Embracing Death: The Crucifixion of Ministry

Andrew Purves commences his slim volume on pastoral practice with a provocative challenge: "Has God killed your ministry yet?"[22] However shocking, his question is also honest and refreshing, because it puts into words what many pastors instinctively know to be true: not only that effecting spiritual transformation in their congregants is well beyond their ability, but not infrequently also that the possibly modest ministerial success they experienced in earlier years has now given way to a situation in which "blessings" and "successes" (however these are defined) seem painfully rare. In fact, if they are as forthright with themselves as Purves asks them to be,

---

21. According to Engberg-Pedersen ("Proclaiming the Lord's Death," 103–32, esp. 115–20), celebration of the Lord's Supper represents an operational or enacted form of theology; as such it has a powerful effect on shaping congregational *identity* as well as congregants' self-understanding.

22. Purves, *The Crucifixion of Ministry*, 11.

it appears as though, far from affirming their ministry, Christ now seems to withhold his blessing. Struggling preachers may find such thoughts both frightening and dangerous, since entertaining them risks further alienating the very Lord whom they so deeply wish to please. Yet Purves offers a bold response: the call to die with Christ belongs as much to ministry as to conversion, and being weaned from competency-based models of ministerial proficiency represents a call to deeper communion with him, with the goal of a richer, more mature participation in his redemptive work.

We will find no more authoritative example of what Purves has in mind than the Apostle Paul himself, particularly so in the letters he wrote to his converts in ancient Corinth.[23] From the snippets of information that emerge from the apostle's defense of his pastorate, we get a picture of a preacher under fire from disaffected congregants on the one hand, and confidently dismissive rivals on the other. First Corinthians opens with repeated disavowals of "eloquent wisdom" (1 Cor 1:17; cf. 1:19–25; 2:1–5), suggesting these to be the grounds on which his ministry is being challenged.[24] The congregation's complaints seem to be less about theology per se than about styles and methods of preaching.[25] Toward the end of 2 Corinthians, Paul quotes back to them what some in the church are saying: "His letters are weighty and strong, but his bodily presence is weak, and his speech contemptible" (2 Cor 10:10). At least some of this invective originates with certain unnamed opponents and leadership rivals whom Paul describes as "false apostles" and "deceitful workers, disguising themselves as apostles of Christ" (2 Cor 11:13):

> These missionaries, whom Paul sarcastically calls "super-apostles" (2 Cor 11:5; 12:11), evidently disparaged Paul for being an ineffective speaker (10:10; 11:6), for being devoid of any demonstrable superhuman power (10:10), and for his supposed lack of external credentials like letters of recommendation (cf. 3:1; 5:12).[26]

Paul feels compelled to defend his apostolic authority. Yet countering his opponents' claims to ministerial prowess and verbal eloquence with

---

23. This theme and its implications for preaching are more fully explored in my earlier study, *We Preach Not Ourselves*.

24. So Pickett, *The Cross in Corinth*, 41–42.

25. According to Timothy Savage, "Paul is distancing himself from arrogant speech as well as abusive speech . . . he is rejecting the vulgar rhetoric of his day and not the classical speech of the intellectual elite" (*Power Through Weakness*, 70–73).

26. Wan, *Power in Weakness*, 13; cf. Williams, *Enemies of the Cross of Christ*, 35–37.

competing assertions of his own would, in effect, concede the grounds on which their arguments are based.

> Paul resolved this dilemma by stressing that authentic Christian ministry is in fact not characterized by power and strength but by weakness and suffering, specifically the weakness and suffering of Christ.... A corollary of such an identification with Christ is that Paul's powerlessness paradoxically demonstrates the energy of God's grace in authentic life and ministry. Just as Christ's humiliation in death unleashes the power of resurrection, so too Paul's weakness brings into sharp relief a ministry of glory.[27]

But it is not as if all styles of ministry—in this case, all styles of preaching—are for Paul equally legitimate, so long as they are somehow validated by grace. On the contrary, the apostle draws a sharp contrast between preaching that is open to the power of God and preaching that appears to replace divine power with wisdom and eloquence of its own:

> My speech and my proclamation were not with plausible words of wisdom, but with a demonstration of the Spirit and of power, so that your faith might rest not on human wisdom but on the power of God.
>
> (1 Cor 2:4–5)

At one point Paul goes so far as to imply that no form of human speech has much value in itself: "The kingdom of God is not a matter of talk [λόγῳ]," he insists, "but of power" (1 Cor 4:2 TNIV). Admittedly, certain kinds of wisdom and utterance are gifts of God's Spirit (1 Cor 12:8), even as Paul himself engages rhetorical conventions in compiling his correspondence.[28] Yet the Corinthians evidently equate eloquence with inspiration, so that clever preaching becomes a mark of authority, even spiritual superiority.[29] For the apostle, whose vision is informed—and transformed—by "Jesus Christ, and him crucified" (1 Cor 2:2), the very opposite is true:

> What his opponents regard as worthy of praise—competitive boasting and aggressive behaviour—he condemns. What they deplore as ignoble and base—he esteems. In Paul's thinking,

---

27. Wan, *Power in Weakness*, 14; cf. 34–35.

28. On Pauline wisdom and rhetoric, see Barrett, "Christianity at Corinth," in *Essays on Paul*, 7–12.

29. Pickett, *The Cross in Corinth*, 53–57, citing the work of H. D. Betz in particular.

> their error arises from a false understanding of the cross. They
> have ignored its offensiveness and bypassed its shame.³⁰

He expands on this argument in the opening verses of 2 Corinthians, again drawing a direct parallel between his own suffering and consolation on the one hand, and that of Christ on the other:

> Blessed be the God and Father of our Lord Jesus Christ, the Father of mercies and the God of all consolation, who consoles us in all our affliction, so that we may be able to console those who are in any affliction with the consolation with which we ourselves are consoled by God. For just as the sufferings of Christ are abundant for us, so also our consolation is abundant through Christ.... We do not want you to be unaware, brothers and sisters, of the affliction we experienced in Asia; for we were so utterly, unbearably crushed that we despaired of life itself. Indeed, we felt that we had received the sentence of death so that we would rely not on ourselves but on God who raises the dead.
>
> (2 Cor 1:3-5, 8-9)

That affliction and consolation are a recurring pattern in the apostle's life is abundantly clear from the several catalogues of experience that Paul himself provides:

> We are afflicted in every way, but not crushed; perplexed, but not driven to despair; persecuted, but not forsaken; struck down, but not destroyed; always carrying in the body the death of Jesus, *so that* the life of Jesus may also be made visible in our bodies. For while we live, we are always being given up to death for Jesus' sake, *so that* the life of Jesus may be made visible in our mortal flesh.
>
> (2 Cor 4:8-11)³¹

Here it is striking that Paul twice repeats his interpretation of these events: not only do they correspond in principle to the model of Jesus' death and resurrected life, but identification with the former constitutes an essential precondition for participation in the latter. His suffering serves as a countercultural example of life "in Christ":

> Paul and others who are weak in terms of the dominant value system nevertheless do powerful things—for example, they

---

30. Savage, *Power Through Weakness*, 157.

31. Similarly 1 Cor 4:10-13; 2 Cor 6:4-10, 11:23-27, 12:7-10. On this passage, see further Savage, *Power Through Weakness*, 169-73.

survive despite the most extraordinary pressures and afflictions—and therefore this power must be not their own, but God's.[32]

But even more important is its theological character: Paul specifies that he finds himself "bearing" and "being given up to" death in imitation of Jesus "*so that* [ἵνα]" the life and power of Jesus may be manifested in him. While conscious that his experience of suffering is, like Christ's, intended for the benefit of the church (so Col 1:24), its more basic function is to deepen his own reliance on God. Only then does it become exemplary. To quote from A. B. Simpson, founder of the Christian and Missionary Alliance,

> This is Paul's physical experience, constant peril, infirmity and physical suffering, probably by persecution and even violence, in order that the healing, restoring, and sustaining power and life of Jesus might be manifested in his very body for the encouragement of suffering saints . . .[33]

Paul's language may be open to misconstrual, on at least two fronts. The first is that he goes on to counsel his readers, "Be imitators of me, as I am of Christ" (1 Cor 4:16; cf. 7:7, 11:1). Might this simply indicate a reinscription of power, an assertion of authority and demand for obedience that potentially justifies similar abuses of power on the part of preachers who take their cue from Paul? So it might seem to modern—even more so, postmodern—eyes.[34] But to read him in this manner overlooks the genuine shame and humiliation of which the apostle speaks (which is why his own converts view him with contempt), as well as the repugnant and terrifying character of crucifixion itself.[35] Cicero (106–43 BCE) speaks of crucifixion as "that most cruel and disgusting penalty [*crudellisimi taeterrimique supplicii*]," "that plague [*istam pestem*]" (*Verr.* 5.162, 165); for Philo it is a "supreme punishment [ἔφεδρα τιμορί]" (*Flacc.* 72); Josephus (ca. 37–100 CE) calls it "the most pitiable of deaths [θανάτων τὸν οἰκτίστον]" (*War* 7.203). Christian apologists concede the point: Paul admits that the Christian message

---

32. Meeks, *The First Urban Christians*, 183.

33. Simpson, *The Gospel of Healing*, 27–28; cited in Cosgrove, *The Cross and the Spirit*, 171.

34. So Castelli, *Imitating Paul*, esp. 97–115. For a more extensive response to Castelli, also from the perspective of cruciform theology, see Gorman, *Cruciformity*, 293–98.

35. Extensive evidence regarding the abhorrent character of crucifixion in the Greco-Roman world and its function as a sadistic pageantry of humiliation is found in Hengel, *Crucifixion in the Ancient World*, passim, followed by Shi, *Paul's Message of the Cross*, 21–52.

sounds like "nonsense [μωρία]" (1 Cor 1:18); Justin Martyr (ca. 100–165 CE) reports the accusation of "madness [μάνια]" (*Apol.* 1.13.4); Minucius Felix, writing some time around 200 CE, has his pagan opponent speak of "sick delusions [*figmenta mala sanae opinionis*]" (*Oct.* 11.9). To an unknown translator of Origen (ca. 185–254 CE) we owe the Latin phrase *mors turpissima crucis*: "the utterly vile death of the cross" (*Comm. Matt.* 27:22).[36] Since "the Roman world was largely unanimous that crucifixion was a horrific, disgusting business," no contemporary could possibly hear Paul's call for cruciform imitation as a strategy for domination on his part.[37] His invitation is for readers to experience the very nadir of futility and impotence, the complete abandonment of authority rather than its unjust appropriation.

Second, and somewhat more subtly, many Western Christians think of discipleship as a lifestyle choice, a condition freely chosen in the interests of personal salvation and the future of one's soul. For Paul to speak of being "fools for the sake of Christ" (1 Cor 4:10), "slaves for Jesus' sake" (2 Cor 4:5), or even "being given up to death for Jesus' sake" (2 Cor 4:11) makes it sound as though each of these is also a matter of volition, something chosen "for the sake of" one's Savior.[38] But this is not at all what he has in mind: in all three passages the same Greek phrase (διὰ Ἰησοῦν) might be better translated "because of, on account of Jesus," as it is in the NRSV rendering of Philippians 3:7 (which uses the same grammatical construction), "Whatever gains I had, these I have come to regard as loss *because of* Christ."[39] Paul's language implies loss and lack of personal volition, particularly so a few verses later when he writes of "being made conformable [συμμορφιζόμενος]" to the death of Christ (Phil 3:10)—a rare instance in which the KJV conveys the proper theological nuance of the original (even if its grammar is ambiguous).[40] As Paul explains a chapter further on in

---

36. References and (with the exception of Josephus [Thackeray, LCL]) translations are from Hengel, *Crucifixion in the Ancient World*, xi, 1, 3, 8 n.15, 27 n.19, 33 n.1, 37.

37. Ibid., 37.

38. Although the NRSV is cited here, with the sole exception of 1 Corinthians 4:10 NIV/TNIV ("fools for Christ"), NASB, NEB, NIV, RSV, and TEV all use the same language in each of these passages.

39. So also RSV, NEB; but NASB, NIV, TEV, TNIV "for the sake of." Cf. κατὰ Ἰησοῦν in Romans 15:5, Colossians 2:8, and Savage, *Power Through Weakness*, 153.

40. Harrisville (*Fracture*, 119) refers to the wording "becoming like him in his death" (common to NIV, NRSV, RSV, and TNIV) as "the clumsy translation of a phrase completely at odds with the notion of adopting a likeness at will." The grammatical issue at stake is whether the participle is in the middle or passive voice (since the form is the same in either case). Gorman (*Cruciformity*, 29 and n.25) makes a similar comment regarding KJV Philippians 3:12, "apprehended by Christ."

Second Corinthians, his idea is that "one has died for all; *therefore all have died*" (2 Cor 5:14). Hence the folly, slavery, and death of which Paul speaks are less matters of personal choice than of deadly imposition on the part of Christ who is truly "Lord." It is not so much that Christ commands allegiance (as would Caesar, "Lord" of Rome); rather, he has taken preemptive action on our behalf, ensnaring humanity in the conditions of his death. This is the implication of the tiny adverb "ἔτι"—"yet" or "still"—in Romans 5:8: "While we were *still* sinners, Christ died for us" (TNIV). Coming to a similar conclusion on the subject of "being given up to death on account of Jesus" (2 Cor 4:11), Cousar observes that "Jesus' way is the way of the cross, and identifying with him means that afflictions are simply part and parcel of the apostolic experience."[41] Not only as a disciple but even more so as a "minister of Christ Jesus" (Rom 15:16), Paul finds that crucifixion dictates the terms of his conduct: "necessity" is laid upon him, binding him to the will of another (1 Cor 9:16–17).[42]

Holy Dependent Ministry

In terms of practical implications, Paul's unusual defense and self-description recall the messianic vine and its wholly dependent branches. Both imply that ministry in the name and power of Christ first requires humility, self-emptying (along the lines implied by Philippians 2), and reliance on something other than oneself:

> True ministers thus denude their native strengths and empty their own claims. Authentic ministry is at heart kenotic ministry.... An authentic apostle is characterized not by his impressive credentials and spiritual endowments but by the presence of God's power which shines through his human fragility.[43]

Ministry is thus essentially cruciform, for it conforms to the precedent of Jesus' crucifixion. Paul indicates as much to his disgruntled congregants. Seeing that they are so concerned with questions of competence and confidence, he offers a distinctively theological explanation of the proper qualifications for ministry, including his own:

> Such is the confidence that we have through Christ toward God. Not that we are competent of ourselves to claim anything as

---

41. Cousar, *A Theology of the Cross*, 152.

42. See further Knowles, *We Preach Not Ourselves*, 76–82, on 2 Corinthians 2:14–17.

43. Wan, *Power in Weakness*, 15, 39.

> coming from us; our competence is from God, who has made us competent to be ministers of a new covenant, not of letter but of spirit; for the letter kills, but the Spirit gives life.
>
> (2 Cor 3:4–6)

For preachers to focus on themselves as the primary instruments of apostolic proclamation would be to rely on something already dead (2 Cor 5:14; Gal 2:19–20; Col 3:3, etc.), and therefore quite powerless to effect life-giving change in their hearers. The eminent Puritan apologist and preacher Richard Baxter (1615–1691), reflecting on the difficulties of frequent ill health and what he calls "a life still near to death," describes his early ministry in closely similar terms:

> I Preach'd, as never sure to Preach again,
> And as a dying man to dying men![44]

If such language seems too strong, that of the apostle is hardly more felicitous: "What we preach is not ourselves, but Jesus Christ as Lord, with ourselves as your slaves because of Jesus" (2 Cor 4:5). At least as he applies it to himself, the corollary of Christ's lordship is not glory and coregency for those who submit to his rule, but slavery instead, hardly an enviable position for any preacher either ancient or modern.

Limitations and inadequacies on the part of those who proclaim the gospel thus offer an obvious contrast to the transformative power of the gospel itself. Sometimes, as in Paul's case, actual physical suffering is in view: "We have this treasure," he says, "in clay jars, so that [ἵνα] it may be made clear that this extraordinary power belongs to God and does not come from us" (2 Cor 4:7). This much might have been clear from their first encounter with him, for, he recalls, "I came to you in weakness and in fear and in much trembling" (1 Cor 2:3).[45] Or, as Paul explains in the verses immediately following, the preacher may simply refuse to adopt prevailing cultural standards and methods of persuasive communication (1 Cor 2:4–5, cited above). In any event, the resolution to human weakness consists of unqualified reliance on the life-giving power of God:

> While authentic ministry does involve power and might, they are *God's*, not the minister's. An authentic minister of the gospel

---

44. "Love Breathing Thanks and Praise," Part 2, in Baxter, *Poetical Fragments*, 38, 40. Much like Paul, Baxter describes his trials as a "cross" that he must bear.

45. On the (uncertain) meaning of this reference, see Shi, *Paul's Message*, 162–68.

is characterized, ironically, not by power but by weakness—weakness that makes it necessary for one to rely totally on God.[46]

As Fred Craddock observes, "To offer up one's own words in the service of the Word is an act of full trust in God, whose power is made perfect in weakness."[47] This is not an excuse for pastoral incompetence, laziness, or a cavalier approach to ministerial responsibility. Paul himself can hardly be accused of laxity: the level of rigor he commends in 1 Corinthians 9:24–27 is proof enough of his high standards. He is simply acknowledging the limitations of human agency in spiritual affairs:

> Paul's theology of ministry in 2 Corinthians . . . [is] predicated on a profound awareness that whatever he does or says, it is God who converts and brings people to Christ, not Paul; it is God who comforts and blesses, not Paul; it is Christ in whom we live and through whom we come in worship to the Father, not Paul's programmatic or liturgical or homiletical giftedness. Thus the emphasis is on God's power, and with this the humbled awareness of Paul's human weakness to accomplish anything of value for God's kingdom.[48]

The apostle goes so far as to insist, again stressing the cause-and-effect relationship of human impotence and divine empowerment, that the very failings and frailties of which the Corinthians complain are in fact the primary source of his authority as an apostle of Christ:

> I will boast all the more gladly of my weaknesses, *so that* [ἵνα] the power of Christ may dwell in me. Therefore I am content with weaknesses, insults, hardships, persecutions, and calamities for the sake of Christ; for whenever I am weak, then I am strong.
>
> (2 Cor 12:9–10)

This, then, is spiritual authority that arises out of human insufficiency, an authority Paul will later assert by claiming a direct parallel between his own situation and that of the crucified *and risen* Lord: "For to be sure, he was crucified in weakness, yet he lives by God's power. Likewise, we are weak in him, yet by God's power we will live with him in dealing with you" (2 Cor 13:4 TNIV).

What Paul has in mind is clarified when we compare his notion of theological mortality with apparently similar assertions by one of Paul's

---

46. Wan, *Power in Weakness*, 57–58; cf. 84.
47. Craddock, *As One Without Authority*, 78.
48. Purves, *Reconstructing Pastoral Theology*, 206–7.

contemporaries, the Roman Stoic Seneca the Younger (ca. 4 BCE–65 CE). In response to a denial of resurrection on the part of some in Corinth (1 Cor 15:12), Paul protests that the hope of resurrection is what gives him courage in the face of mortal danger: "As for us, why do we endanger ourselves every hour? I face death every day—yes, just as surely as I boast about you in Christ Jesus our Lord" (1 Cor 15:30-31 TNIV). His assertion is categorical, literally, "I die daily [καθ' ἡμέραν ἀποθνῄσκω]." Seneca concurs that death is ever-present, although for him it is a natural event, and naturally to be expected:

> We do not suddenly fall on death, but advance towards it by slight degrees; we die every day [*cotidie morimur*]. For every day a little of our life is taken from us.[49]

Despite the similarity of expression, this is altogether different from Paul's characterization of death as an "enemy" that—notwithstanding its soteriological usefulness in the short term—is nonetheless destined for dismantlement, even destruction (1 Cor 15:26).[50] Moreover, according to Seneca, one who is upright and wise will not be dismayed by suffering:

> What element of evil is there in torture and in the other things which we call hardships? It seems to me that there is this evil—that the mind sags, and bends, and collapses. But none of these things can happen to the sage: he stands erect under any load. Nothing can subdue him; nothing that must be endured annoys him. For he does not complain that he has been struck by that which can strike any man. He knows his own strength; he knows that he was born to carry burdens.[51]

Paul, by contrast, confesses of himself and his fellow sufferers, "we were so utterly, unbearably crushed that we despaired of life itself" (2 Cor 1:8). "But that," he quickly adds, "was to make us rely not on ourselves but on God who raises the dead" (2 Cor 1:9 RSV). As Roy Harrisville rightly observes, "For Paul such 'extraordinary power' belongs to God alone."[52]

Embracing weakness, affliction, and death—even as a metaphor for spiritual experience—might today seem distinctly macabre, perhaps the sign of an unbalanced mind. Preachers and pulpit committees do not list

---

49. *Moral Epistles* 24.19-20 (Gummere, LCL), cited in Harrisville, *Fracture*, 88.

50. See further Lowe, "Death Dismantled," 184-86, 192-94; cf. 207-21.

51. *Moral Epistles* 71.26-27, cited in Harrisville, *Fracture*, 88-89.

52. Harrisville, *Fracture*, 89. Shi's observation (*Paul's Message*, 262) is equally apropos: "The weak apostle hardly fits into Cicero's ideal of the brave and wise: '. . . when the Wise Man is suffering torments of pain, he will say "How pleasant this is! How little I mind!"' (*Fin.* 5.27.80)!"

personal inadequacies or ministerial incompetence among their preferred aptitudes and job skills. Yet if our reading of John's gospel is in any way accurate; if the example of Jesus is anything to go by (above all in his death and resurrection); if Paul's theology and experience have any bearing on our own, then we will be forced to reckon, first, with our own fundamental inability to effect the kinds of spiritual change for which we and our congregations long; second, with the need to embrace this inability as an inescapable condition of Christian ministry; and third, with a corollary need for reliance on the unconstrained and uncontrollable power of God. As Paul demands so pointedly, "Who is sufficient for these things?"

Holding Fast the Word of Life: Ministry as Resurrection

Just as physical affliction, lack of eloquence or verbal force, an unimposing personal presence, and reversal of his social prominence as a Roman citizen correspond to "crucifixion," so Paul claims the power of Christ's resurrection as the basis for his ministry within the church. No doubt this entails direct charismatic authority: Paul implies as much in warning that the consequences of his return to Corinth are likely to be unpleasant for some (2 Cor 13:10). But even beyond specific matters of congregational discipline, says the apostle, the divine gift of life that has been unleashed by Christ's resurrection serves in principle to validate faithful proclamation of the gospel. Admittedly, its manifestation may be paradoxical and not easily discerned, for when it comes to matters of the spirit, things are not always what they seem. Hence believers must sometimes distinguish between troubling outward appearances and the glorious inner reality that they mask: "Even though our outer nature is wasting away," he explains, "Our inner nature is being renewed day by day" (2 Cor 4:16). Evidence of "glory" may be less persuasive or overwhelming than he and his congregants might prefer, as Paul indicates in a passage already cited earlier:

> We are afflicted in every way, but not crushed;
> perplexed, but not driven to despair;
> persecuted, but not forsaken;
> struck down, but not destroyed;
> always carrying in the body the death of Jesus,
> so that the life of Jesus may also be made visible in our bodies.
>
> (2 Cor 4:8–10)

Surely a list of ministerial successes would have been more impressive, the recitation of heroic achievements more immediately persuasive, but Paul offers nothing of the sort.⁵³ Accordingly, a hermeneutic of resurrection sometimes requires onlookers to discern an otherwise hidden reality: "We look not to the things that are seen but to the things that are unseen; for the things that are seen are transient, but the things that are unseen are eternal" (2 Cor 4:18 RSV).

That having been said, the transformation of which Paul speaks is nonetheless substantive, characterized by deliverance and "freedom" from all other forms of spiritual dominion on the one hand, and gradual conformity to Christ on the other:

> Now the Lord is the Spirit, and where the Spirit of the Lord is, there is freedom. And all of us, with unveiled faces, seeing the glory of the Lord as though reflected in a mirror, are being transformed into the same image from one degree of glory to another; for this comes from the Lord, the Spirit.
>
> (2 Cor 3:17–18)

Paul cites the same transformation in defense of his own ministry: he needs no letters of recommendation because the Corinthians themselves, having been converted under his ministry, offer more than sufficient proof of the power of his preaching:

> You yourselves are our letter, written on our [or: your] hearts, to be known and read by all; and you show that you are a letter of Christ, prepared by us, written not with ink but with the Spirit of the living God, not on tablets of stone but on tablets of human hearts.
>
> (2 Cor 3:2–3)⁵⁴

Whatever "glory" they perceive in themselves—Paul implies that they are not modest in this regard—is therefore because of, not despite, his ministry among them, no matter what his detractors might have to say on the issue.

As both of these passages imply, the gift of new life in Christ is a work of God's Spirit: faithful preaching of the gospel, which proclaims the death and resurrection of Jesus, draws hearers into that death while at the same time announcing the manifestation of God's power in the transformation of human identity. Paul illustrates one half of this equation from personal experience, with a manifesto that could be echoed by all who hear and receive the "word of the cross": "I have been crucified with Christ; it is no longer I who live, but Christ who lives in me" (Gal 2:19–20 RSV). The remaining implications of this twofold movement emerge only a few verses later, in an

---

53. Cf. Cousar, *A Theology of the Cross*, 154.
54. See further Knowles, *We Preach Not Ourselves*, 114–17.

exasperated outburst occasioned by his converts having turned away from the gospel they once trusted:

> You foolish Galatians! Who has bewitched you? It was before your eyes that Jesus Christ was publicly exhibited as crucified! The only thing I want to learn from you is this: Did you receive the Spirit by doing the works of the law or by believing what you heard? Are you so foolish? Having started with the Spirit, are you now ending with the flesh? Did you experience so much for nothing?—if it really was for nothing. Well then, does God supply you with the Spirit and work miracles among you by your doing the works of the law, or by your believing what you heard?
>
> (Gal 3:1–5)

Here Paul is clearly referring to his own preaching, with its open declaration of the Messiah's death.[55] But he also recalls for his readers the most elemental outcome of such proclamation, first in verses 2 and 3 then more fully in verse 5: corresponding to the preacher's announcement of the gospel is the manifestation of divine power, both in God's inward gift of the Holy Spirit and by means of outward signs and "miracles."[56] Certainly this was the case in Corinth, as Paul will recall in another defense of his ministry: "the signs of a true apostle were performed among you . . . signs and wonders and mighty works" (2 Cor 12:12).

In fact, "signs and wonders" appear to be an essential characteristic of Paul's apostolic ministry:

> For I will not venture to speak of anything except what Christ has accomplished through me to win obedience from the Gentiles,
> by word and deed,
> by the power of signs and wonders,
> by the power of the Spirit of God,
> so that from Jerusalem and as far around as Illyricum I have fully proclaimed the good news of Christ.
>
> (Rom 15:18–19)

---

55. Longenecker, *Galatians*, 100–101.

56. Paul likely intends a temporal distinction between the two sets of questions. One set refers to the past: "Did you receive [ἐλάβετε] the Spirit [i.e. upon first hearing the gospel] . . . ?" (v. 2; similarly v. 4: "Did you experience [ἐπάθετε] . . . ?"), while the other describes present experience: "Does he who supplies [ἐπιχορηγῶν] the Spirit to you and works [ἐνεργῶν] miracles among you . . . ?" (v. 5, in keeping with his later exhortations to "walk by the Spirit" [5:16–25]); so Cosgrove, *The Cross and the Spirit*, 39–49; cf. 163–67. But this distinction does not obviate the more basic correspondence between the gift of the Spirit and the resurrection of Christ.

To be sure, the "words" and "deeds" in question are, in one sense, Paul's own (cf. Rom 10:14). But his point—underscored by the parallel structure of these clauses—is that their effect and the attendant manifestations of the Spirit are not at all his own doing. Rather, the power of the gospel that he preaches is a matter of Christ and the Spirit working through him:

> What Paul has done as a λειτουργός [servant, minister] of Christ Jesus has not only been a subordinate service subsidiary to Christ's own priestly work, it has also been something which Christ has actually Himself effected, working through His minister.[57]

Such evidences have a specific function: "My speech and my proclamation were not with plausible words of wisdom," he tells the Corinthians, "but with a demonstration [ἀποδείξει] of the Spirit and of power" (1 Cor 2:4). As Timothy Lim explains, ἀπόδειξις is "a technical term in rhetoric which means a demonstration or cogent proof of argument from commonly agreed premises."[58] Thus Paul means to say that in place of clever words, convincing arguments, or generally accepted truths, apostolic preaching relies directly on God. According to Wilson, "The preacher mouths the words, but they are breathed out and infused with the Spirit, who carries them with power into the world."[59] But much as we wish that our words might unfailingly convey such authority, experience often indicates otherwise. Works of power (δυνάμεις) constitute a divine testimony to the resurrection by reproducing its potency not in the life of the proclaimer, necessarily, or the act of proclamation itself, but in the experience of the hearers themselves: "These are works of *life* for the community, performed by the life-giving Spirit of the one who raised Jesus from the dead (see Rom 8:11)."[60]

Accordingly, we cannot speak of the validation of apostolic ministry without exploring the work of the Spirit within the Christian community. Gorman describes the manifestation of Christ's "power-in-weakness" in

---

57. Cranfield, *Epistle to the Romans*, 2:758.

58. Lim, "'Not in Persuasive Words of Wisdom,'" 147, followed by Shi, *Paul's Message*, 170–71.

59. Wilson, *Setting Words on Fire*, 93.

60. Cosgrove, *The Cross and the Spirit*, 175 (emphasis original). Referring on the basis of Romans 1:16 to the message preached by Paul and others, Gorman argues that "the gospel as word of God is not just *about* God's saving power, it *is* God's power. . . . The word has 'performed' salvation" (*Cruciformity*, 275). But resurrection and the life of God cannot be reduced to the act of preaching itself. As Gorman subsequently acknowledges, "The power of the gospel message depends ultimately on the odd power of the act to which the message bears witness" (*Cruciformity*, 276).

terms of ethical transformation, transcendence of "gender, class, and racial boundaries (Gal 3:28)," the ability to endure suffering, and willingness to care for the poor and weak.[61] The consistent source and inspiration for all such responses is a uniquely divine empowerment that corresponds in principle to the superhuman, supernatural character of resurrection. This is equally true in the apostles' own life: once more compelled to explain the basis for his discipleship and ministry, Paul cites an admonition that comes, appropriately, from the risen Christ: "He has said to me, 'My grace is enough for you; for power comes to perfection in weakness'" (2 Cor 12:9).[62] Later copyists felt it necessary to clarify the text, adding a personal pronoun: "*My power is made perfect in weakness.*"[63] Yet even without such editorial assistance, the power that makes Christian life possible is, by definition, clearly divine.

At the conclusion of a difficult pastoral letter to the church in Galatia, Paul sums up his argument by declaring the full consequences of participation in Christ's death.[64] This is no simple matter of pastoral methodology or personal lifestyle. On the contrary, it entails the very basis and nature of human identity, that which gives life its purpose and meaning:

> May I never boast except in the cross of our Lord Jesus Christ, through which the world has been crucified to me, and I to the world. Neither circumcision nor uncircumcision means anything; what counts is the new creation.
>
> (Gal 6:14–15 TNIV)

That "the κόσμος has been crucified to me, and I to the κόσμος" is not simply an extravagant way of saying that Christian conviction is radical or all-encompassing, although its universal scope is certainly implied. In the theology of Second Temple Judaism, obedience to Torah was understood to bring adherents into harmony with a divinely ordered cosmos both ethically and in terms of observing hours of prayer and seasonal festivals (cf. Gal 4:9–10, Col 2:16–17).[65] Crucifixion, says the apostle, marks a decisive

---

61. Gorman, *Cruciformity*, 298–303 (with the quotation from 300). Gorman expands this argument in *Inhabiting the Cruciform God*, 105–28.

62. This felicitous translation comes from Barrett, *Second Epistle to the Corinthians*, 305–306; cf. 316–17.

63. See discussion in Thrall, *Second Epistle to the Corinthians*, 2:822–25, and n.413.

64. Here following Cosgrove, *The Cross and the Spirit*, 177–85.

65. So ibid., 76–77, 92–93, 182–83. For Josephus, "everything [in the law] has a disposition in harmony with the nature of the universe" (*Ant.* 1.24); as Philo explains, obedience to Torah therefore brings one into accord with the order of the cosmos (e.g. *On the Creation of the World* 3); see further Najman, "The Law of Nature," 55–73, esp.

end to such observances, since aligning oneself with the created order no longer constitutes the basis for a divinely ordered human existence. To press the point further, being "crucified together with Christ" (Gal 2:20), which anticipates the eventual, eschatological dissolution of the old order, is therefore the sole point of entry into God's "new creation" (so also 2 Cor 5:17).

What makes this relevant in principle to discipleship, ministry, and preaching in particular is that it applies not only "once for all" at the point of conversion, but also as an ongoing condition for continued participation in the life of Christ and empowerment conveyed by the Spirit of God:

> For life in the Spirit begins with death to the cosmos. Nevertheless, the matter is not quite so simple, inasmuch as those who have died to the world continue to live in it and are called to do so in ethically responsible ways by the power of the Spirit. . . . Hence, the very condition that appears in the first instance to exclude every conceivable earthly activity or obedience as requisite for ongoing reception of the Spirit turns out to have worldly implications of its own. That is, the fact that crucifixion with Christ extends itself into the world as existential participation in the cross would seem to imply that obedient participation in the suffering of Christ is a fundamental condition for life in the Spirit.[66]

Here, then, is yet a third explanation for the way in which Paul repeatedly speaks of sharing the conditions of crucifixion *so that* he may also experience the life and power of God. As we have seen, there is (first) a functional correspondence between human weakness and divine strength, whereby God accomplishes in and through the followers of Jesus what they themselves cannot. By modeling intentional dependence, even weakness and dishonor, Paul and his fellow apostles serve (second) as examples of "life-in-Christ" both to the church and to society at large. They are living illustrations of Christ's resurrection both in the general sense that God sustains them amidst affliction and in the more particular sense that they exercise ministries attended by the life-giving power of God. But in so doing (third), they minister at a point of intersection between God's first creation and the new order that is to take its place:

57–65; and Najman, "A Written Copy of the Law of Nature," 51–56. Conformity to cosmological cycles appears prominently in the worship of Qumran: see, e.g., Nitzan, *Qumran Prayer and Religious Poetry*, 61; Chazon, "Human and Angelic Prayer," 36–38.

66. Cosgrove, *The Cross and the Spirit*, 184; followed by Gorman, *Cruciformity*, 57–61.

> The great irony is that it is precisely in submitting to the suffering meted out by the powers of the old age that Paul is able to repulse those very powers.... Living as he does at the intersection of two ages he endures the "dyings" of the old in order to receive the "life" of the new.[67]

This explains how Paul can describe himself and other "servants of God ... as dying, yet behold, we are living" (2 Cor 6:4, 9).[68]

This sense of living at the overlap of old and new accounts for Paul's otherwise incongruous juxtaposition in 1 Thessalonians of imitating Christ and experiencing affliction on the one hand, with joy and spiritual empowerment, and on the other: "You became imitators of us and of the Lord, for you welcomed the message in the midst of severe suffering with the joy given by the Holy Spirit" (1 Thess 1:7).[69] Again when the apostle speaks to the church at Philippi of having personally "suffered the loss of all things ... *in order* that [he] may gain Christ" and of "becoming like him in his death, that if possible [he] may attain the resurrection from the dead" (Phil 3:8, 10–11 RSV), his point is that "cocrucifixion" with Christ constitutes the sole means of access to the life of God:

> These who are united by faith with the risen Christ experience his resurrection power. But if there is any share in the power of Christ's resurrection in present experience, that power comes through participation in his sufferings.[70]

Even apart from these cosmological implications, knowing Christ cannot therefore be reduced to a matter of intellectual apprehension, esoteric knowledge, or mystical experience, even if Paul's language contains hints of each.[71] Rather—and this is critical for preaching—it represents an integrative apprehension of Jesus in the whole of his identity, at once crucified and risen. Integration of experience on the part of the believer, whereby joy and affliction, weakness and empowerment, are equally intrinsic to discipleship, corresponds to an appreciation of Jesus' identity and accomplishment as a similarly integrated whole: "*the living Messiah remains continuous with the crucified Jesus.*"[72]

---

67. Savage, *Power Through Weakness*, 176.
68. This translation is borrowed from ibid., 177.
69. Cosgrove, *The Cross and the Spirit*, 185.
70. Williams, *Enemies of the Cross of Christ*, 188.
71. So Cousar, *A Theology of the Cross*, 159–61; cf. 161.
72. Gorman, *Cruciformity*, 19 (emphasis original). "As Käsemann famously said, 'The cross is the signature of the one who is risen'" (Gorman, *Inhabiting the Cruciform*

In Romans (generally thought to be as close as Paul comes to a programmatic summary of his theology), participation in suffering once more constitutes a necessary precondition for the exaltation yet to be experienced in full:

> Now if we are children, then we are heirs—heirs of God and co-heirs with Christ, if indeed we share in his sufferings in order that we may also share in his glory.
>
> (Rom 8:17 TNIV)

The remainder of this passage provides the context for proper interpretation, as Paul goes on to speak of the entire creation groaning while it waits to be set free from bondage to futility and decay (Rom 8:19–22). The implication is that even if individual Christians should manage to avoid persecution or physical affliction, we nonetheless still share the anguish of a broken creation.[73] Whether, then, in a broader or more narrow sense, the weakness and folly of the cross will apply as much to preachers and preaching as to their audiences: participation in crucifixion—whatever form that may take for the individual believer—is the sole and enduring means of access to empowerment by the Spirit of God, apart from which preaching consists of little more than well-intentioned words sprinkled over weary listeners.

The apostle's logic suggests the correlation of divine and human responsibilities, with inelegant proclamation of a shameful human death by rhetorically ineffectual and culturally dislocated preachers transformed by the bestowal of new life, glory, and power in the outpouring of God's Spirit upon the hearers. Because it is ruled by the cross, preaching as much as hearing must be an act of faith, relying for its validation on a gift that only God can bestow. Preaching is essentially an act of human weakness, unable to accomplish that of which it speaks, yet it is vindicated when God repeats in present experience something akin to resurrection by granting life to those who hear and believe.

Cross and Resurrection in Context

Attending to the manifestation of divine power in apostolic ministry highlights a puzzling anomaly in Paul's way of talking about himself in comparison to other members of the church at Corinth. Paul does not, by and large, claim transformation for himself, as though he has been made mighty

---

God, 71).

73. Cousar, *A Theology of the Cross*, 173.

and glorious by his association with the resurrected Christ and the power of the Holy Spirit. Instead, he claims such transformation for his converts. Christian experience, we noted earlier, can appear weighted in the direction of imitating Jesus' death. Yet when he compares his own experience to that of the congregation, Paul suggests the opposite: "Death is at work in us," he tells them, "but life in you" (2 Cor 4:12). Perhaps his comment is ironic, a continuation from the previous letter of the beleaguered apostle's mock self-deprecation: "We are weak, but you are strong. You are held in honor, but we in disrepute" (1 Cor 4:10). Likewise, as we have seen, there are strong rhetorical and strategic reasons for Paul not to claim too much "glory" for himself. It may even be that Paul has in mind the idea of apostolic service on behalf of others.[74]

The experiential disparity between the apostle and his converts when it comes to identifying with Christ may also reflect their respective social locations.[75] While a few members appear to be of higher social standing, the majority of the congregation is not:

> Consider your own call, brothers and sisters: not many of you were wise by human standards, not many were powerful, not many were of noble birth. But God chose what is foolish in the world to shame the wise; God chose what is weak in the world to shame the strong; God chose what is low and despised in the world, things that are not, to reduce to nothing things that are, so that no one might boast in the presence of God. He is the source of your life in Christ Jesus, who became for us wisdom from God, and righteousness and sanctification and redemption . . .
>
> (1 Cor 1:26–30)

Here the fuller context of his comments is all-important. Paul is not concerned with social description for its own sake: rather, his unflattering portrayal implies that the Corinthians will perhaps identify most readily with the abasement of Christ. Nonetheless, Christian faith has evidently provided these socially disadvantaged congregants with a kind of theological status reversal, so that from a theological perspective Paul's sarcastic description of them is quite accurate: "Already you have all you want! Already you have become rich! Quite apart from us you have become kings!" (1 Cor

---

74. So Pickett, *The Cross in Corinth*, 142–49; cf. especially 2 Corinthians 4:5: "ourselves as your slaves because of Jesus."

75. On the social location of Paul's converts and its implications for their sense of identity, see especially Shi, *Paul's Message*, 103–6, and Meeks, *First Urban Christians*, 47–72, with important qualifications offered by Longenecker, "Socio-Economic Profiling," 36–59.

4:8). Not unreasonably, perhaps, they intend to translate this theological gain into socially relevant terms, hence their approval of Apollos and the "super-apostles."[76] As a result, Paul's task is as difficult as it is delicate: although he cannot afford to crush their theological hope, he must nonetheless distinguish between soteriology and social expectation. Christ's gift of new life is not to be employed as a means of personal advancement or civic self-promotion. On the contrary, it is their lack of prestige according to prevailing social standards that allows the power of God at work in their midst to be seen in its proper light.

Similarly in his letter to the Philippian church, Paul appeals to the example of the cross in order to counteract what he describes as—notwithstanding the suffering and persecution that they also experience (Phil 1:28–30)—"selfish ambition," "conceit," and lack of "humility" (Phil 2:3). Whatever the identity of Paul's opponents in this letter, it appears that here too he is concerned to remedy a sense of privilege and exaltation on the part of some.[77] Indeed, the language of the pivotal "Christ hymn" may imply that the problem stems from certain members of the congregation (as in Corinth) overemphasizing the consequences of resurrection. This he counterbalances by appeal to crucifixion:

> Let the same mind be in you that was in Christ Jesus,
> who, though he was in the form of God,
> did not regard *equality with God* as something to be exploited,
> but emptied himself, taking the form of a slave . . .
> to the point of death, even death on a cross.
>
> (Phil 2:5–6, 8)

Whereas the Colossian believers must be reminded of their exaltation with Christ (Col 3:10), the Philippians need, as it were, to be brought back down to earth: their own "equality with God," a consequence of Christ's enfranchisement of them, provides no grounds for vaunting. This passage assumes its proper dimensions in contrast to social customs and expectations of the day:

> The narrative of 2:6–8 has rightly been described as one of "downward mobility." Joseph Hellerman rightly argues that it is a *"cursus pudorum,"* or downward-bound succession of ignominies, constructed in contrast to Rome's *cursus honorum*, the

---

76. So Savage, *Power Through Weakness*, 160.

77. Williams, *Enemies of the Cross of Christ*, 128–33.

elite's upward-bound race for honors, imitated in various ways throughout the provinces and colonies.[78]

The social and political dimensions of this corrective are further reflected in Paul's references to Christian "citizenship" (Phil 1:27, 3:20), the point of which is to distinguish Christian identity from modes of engagement in Greco-Roman society, with its very different system of values.[79] It is therefore no accident that Paul speaks of himself and Timothy as "slaves of Christ Jesus" (Phil 1:1) and, as in his letters to Corinth, describes his afflictions as an expression of his life in Christ (e.g. Phil 1:12–14, 20–21).[80] In both letters, he stresses his own abasement (in contrast to self-promotion on the part of others), while—particularly so in 2 Corinthians—emphasizing the congregants' transformation *in accordance with Christ*. Even though death and resurrection are soteriologically inseparable categories, Paul applies the least obvious aspect to himself and his congregants, respectively: "Death is at work in us, but life in you." Given that Western culture today has an especially high view of personal agency, and that ordained ministry typically emphasizes formal professional qualifications, Paul's example invites us as minsters of the gospel to consider ways in which we too are constitutionally incapable of creating divine life in ourselves, much less dispensing it to others.

In the final analysis, the validation of apostolic ministry (as of preaching generally) consists of the participants' conformity to the whole testimony of Christ. In the case of the Corinthians, Paul intends neither that they remain socially excluded, in a state of perpetual humiliation, nor that they pursue social advancement or emulate the self-promotion of the "super-apostles." Rather, just as the wisdom of God is "a secret and hidden wisdom" (1 Cor 2:7) and the "word of the cross" is about "power . . . in weakness" (2 Cor 12:9), so proclaiming Christ imposes the conditions of death and resurrection on the preacher, while the proof of such preaching lies in the hearers being conformed to Christ in their turn, in weakness and glory alike. Whether in defense of his own ministry or as a more general principle, then, Paul is categorical: faithful preaching of Christ's shameful death and glorious resurrection bears fruit by reproducing the same paradoxical

---

78. Gorman, *Inhabiting the Cruciform God*, 16–17, citing Hellerman, *Reconstructing Honor*, 130.

79. Williams, *Enemies of the Cross of Christ*, 115–17, 145–46; cf. 229–31.

80. Similarly for Epaphroditus who, says Paul, "came close to death *for the work of Christ*" (Phil 2:30). Compare also Paul's insistence in Philippians 3:11–12 that he himself has not yet attained resurrection or been made "perfect," which is likewise meant to guide the readers' estimation of their own status in Christ (3:12).

conditions in all concerned. Imperfect fruit, perhaps—the apostle and his converts would each see this as a fair assessment of the other—but fruit nonetheless in the form of "life-out-of-death," "new creation" in a world that lives by old rules, and a human identity transformed by the cross of Jesus.

As stated at the outset, what concerns us in this study is less the theological *content* of preaching—how, for instance, to preach about crucifixion or the doctrine of the atonement—than its theological *method*. As Nancy Lammers Gross insists, our task is not (or not simply) to preach precisely *what* Paul preached, but to preach the *way* Paul preached.[81] And that is something different altogether. Accordingly, Paul's operational theology of the cross introduces an important qualification to our understanding of the world view that underlies Jesus' agricultural parables. His extended metaphor of the messianic vine and its wholly dependent branches affirms that Jesus himself is, at least for disciples, the proximate source of the divine life and vitality of which such parables speak. But in addition, whatever meaning it may have had for those who first heard it, Jesus' insistence that "Apart from me you can do nothing" cannot now be interpreted apart from his cross. When he says, "Where I am, there will my servant be also" (John 12:26), being "with" Jesus will necessarily entail participation in the whole of his saving work: it means that the road to resurrection will always, by necessity, pass by way of the cross.[82] Certainly this is Paul's view of things. For him as for Luther, the divine life and power that is at the heart of the Christian gospel cannot be reduced to a simple "nature" theology or "Creation spirituality," as might otherwise be inferred from Jesus' parables concerning the natural world. Rather, even when it is mediated through creation, the vitality in question remains located within its divine source, and therefore can only be conveyed by God. This critical distinction is only sharpened by Paul's declaration of a *new* creation and the experiential categories of death and resurrection that accompany it. Whether we take our cue from Synoptic agricultural parables, from the Johannine vine and branches, or from a Pauline theology of the cross, the underlying premise is the same: that life in God's kingdom comes from God alone.

---

81. As stated in the epigraph of her study, "If you cannot preach like Paul then do what Paul did; don't just say what Paul said" (Gross, *If You Cannot Preach*, i) For Gross this means that "We must bring Paul's words, as Scripture, into conversation with our contemporary world in such a way that a fresh word is brought to life" (*If You Cannot Preach*, 128).

82. For Luther's exposition of this principle, see von Loewenich, *Luther's Theology of the Cross*, 117–23.

"THEOLOGY OF THE CROSS" AND THE MINISTRY OF PROCLAMATION

The paradox of Jesus' crucifixion—implying life in the face of death, strength amidst weakness, wisdom in folly, and revelation of God in human degradation—points to what Martin Luther first called a *theologia crucis*, or "theology of the cross."[83] Luther coined this term around 1518 in distinction to what he called a "theology of glory," referring not to Christ's resurrection (as we might expect in the context of our present discussion) but to a way of knowing God by appeal to scholastic speculation and the evidence of the natural world:

> The *theologia crucis* is a theology of revelation, which stands in sharp contrast to speculation. Those who speculate on the created order ... have, in effect, forfeited their right to be called 'theologians.'[84]

More to the point, a "theology of glory" constitutes an abuse of power by appeal to religion: it "eschews weakness and vulnerability and instead seeks dominion and success in the name of God."[85] Contemporary equivalents today would include a wide range of practices and outlooks, from "positive confession" and the so-called "prosperity gospel" to ecclesiastical triumphalism in its many manifestations and the co-opting of religious ideology in the service of military or state power. For Luther the way of glory and the way of crucifixion are irreconcilable opposites, since in his view God is truly revealed "only in suffering and the cross."[86] Indeed, for Luther, the cross and all that it represents is the touchstone of properly "Christian" theology, with the paradoxical scandal, weakness, and horror of crucifixion revealing an otherwise hidden, unknowable God. Contemplated in the cross, God turns out to be the very opposite of what one might otherwise expect:

> When the crucified Jesus is called the "image of the invisible God," the meaning is that *this* is God, and God is like *this*. God is not greater than he is in this humiliation. God is not more glorious than he is in this self-surrender. God is not more powerful

---

83. The classic treatment of Luther's *theologia crucis* is that of von Loewenich, *Luther's Theology of the Cross*; especially relevant to the present discussion are 17–31, 112–32; for a review of Luther's impact on the interpretation of Paul, see Williams, *Enemies of the Cross of Christ*, 10–25.

84. McGrath, *Luther's Theology of the Cross*, 148–53; here, 149.

85. Brown, *Cross Talk*, 22.

86. Pelikan and Lehmann, *Luther's Works*, 31:53.

than he is in this helplessness. God is not more divine than he is in this humanity.[87]

Jesus' crucifixion therefore establishes firm boundaries for the Christian perception of God. Gorman's comment on Philippians 2:6–11 is characteristic: "Here we must emphasize that the cross is not just one theophany among many; it is the *definitive* theophany."[88] Or as Luther observes more simply in his commentary on the Psalms: "*Crux sola est nostra theologia* (The cross alone is our theology)."[89]

There is no small irony in the fact that our own study began by reviewing Jesus' appeal to God's self-revelation in creation, since this perspective would seem incompatible with a *theologia crucis*, at least as Luther conceived of it. Yet here our concern is less with theological epistemology—how or where God may be discerned—than with methodology, and homiletical methodology in particular. Since, for Jesus, both the history of God's saving acts (recorded in the Scriptures of Israel) and the world of nature reveal a beneficent and gracious Creator, these categories encompass all possible sources of divine knowledge. They also incorporate the Christian canon as it testifies to the completion of God's saving work. Thus the questions for today's preacher are more practical and operational: given that God is revealed somewhat generally in creation, with historical specificity in Jesus of Nazareth, and most immediately via the testimony of Scripture and the Holy Spirit, how may we speak of this God in a manner that is effectual or transformative in its own right? How do the spiritual realities to which we bear witness become "real" in the lives of our listeners? In what sense or by what means does preaching "the message of the cross" convey meaning that the listener does not already possess? A "theology of the cross" suggests that the terms and conditions explored in the present chapter remain in force for preachers today—to the extent, that is, that we are willing to be informed by Jesus' own experience of God. For to be governed by that experience is to encounter the life and power of God no longer in the world of nature alone, nor simply by appealing to the testimony of Hebrew Scripture, but above all through the manifestation of God's "new creation" in the resurrection of Jesus from death.

Still, this raises an important question. Sally Brown describes the concern many contemporary preachers have with ideologies of the cross: in practice, they can reinforce inequity, supporting strategies of domination, enforced submission, and oppression. She and others tell stories of women

---

87. Moltmann, *The Crucified God*, 205 (emphasis original).
88. Gorman, *Inhabiting the Cruciform God*, 34 (emphasis original).
89. Quoted in Forde, *On Being a Theologian of the Cross*, 81.

having been counseled by their male pastors to submit to domestic abuse as a means of identifying with Jesus and his cross, and she relates the warning of postcolonial theologians that emphasis on Jesus' suffering can encourage political passivity on the part of the oppressed.[90] Might not the line of reasoning proposed in this study be subject to the same critique? Might not talk of "new creation" at the expense of the "old," or of participation in suffering, crucifixion, and death reinforce unhealthy, even dangerous forms of injustice or exploitation? Can a violent cross, in short, beget anything other than violence?

Affirming the theological value of Jesus' crucifixion neither excuses his murder nor provides a blanket justification for suffering in general. On the contrary, insofar as his death amounts to an outrageous injustice, it highlights the moral evil of which humanity is capable, and in principle names unjust suffering for what it truly is:

> As Karl Theodor Kleinknecht says, the Pauline texts neither give flat theological justification to sufferings nor speak of "God's reconciliation with misery." Rather, because they reflect on suffering from the perspective of the relationship to Christ—and link its sense to that relationship—what results is a battle against suffering and death.[91]

Moreover, my own experience suggests that a theology of the cross, particularly as Luther explained it, makes most sense to the truly powerless. My own discovery has been one of grace, hope, and sustaining power at moments of utter weakness and despair. To be sure, rescue is better than words of comfort, and healing would be preferable to a gift of strength simply to endure affliction, but some situations are for the moment either partly or wholly irreversible due to the oppressive differentials of power that remain characteristic of a fallen humanity, together with the legacy of multigenerational brokenness and systemic dysfunction that such inequity produces. Those who are powerless to help themselves find sustenance and encouragement at the cross of Jesus precisely when their own resources are at an end. That this may sound politically incorrect or offensive to some does not make it any less true in practice.

In this regard, it is especially important that we attend to Paul's nuanced application of this theological model, particularly so at Corinth and

---

90. Brown, *Cross Talk*, 16–18, 53–54; similarly Heim, *Saved from Sacrifice*, 23–29. At the same time, Heim offers powerful narrative corroboration of the transformative power of Jesus' solidarity with those who suffer (*Saved from Sacrifice*, 29–31).

91. Harrisville, *Fracture*, 124, quoting from Kleinknecht, *Der leidende Gerechtfertigte*, 386.

Philippi, for he is concerned in each case to apply the dynamic of crucifixion and resurrection in a manner appropriate to the social location and theological outlook of a specific group of believers. A careful reading of his correspondence suggests that in each situation he is seeking to redress a theological balance rather than endorsing either tribulation or exaltation for their own sake. The apostle's own circumstances provide a case in point:

> If anyone else has reason to be confident in the flesh, I have more: circumcised on the eighth day, a member of the people of Israel, of the tribe of Benjamin, a Hebrew born of Hebrews; as to the law, a Pharisee; as to zeal, a persecutor of the church; as to righteousness under the law, blameless.
>
> (Phil 3:4–6)

Were this not enough, Luke quotes him as saying that he is "from Tarsus in Cilicia, a citizen of no ordinary city" (Acts 21:39 NIV; cf. 22:3), and, more importantly, a Roman citizen by birth (Acts 22:25–29). The latter in particular made him one of a privileged few: "The possession of Roman citizenship was a high social distinction in the Near East."[92] Still, even this coveted status is included in his general renunciation of honor and entitlement for the sake of Christ:

> Yet whatever gains I had, these I have come to regard as loss because of Christ. More than that, I regard everything as loss because of the surpassing value of knowing Christ Jesus my Lord. For his sake I have suffered the loss of all things, and I regard them as rubbish, in order that I may gain Christ.
>
> (Phil 3:7–8)

This example, specifically embodying a theology of the cross, is relevant to preachers not for the encouragement of self-loathing or morbid self-denial, but because Paul, both a Roman citizen and a faithful Jew, comes to this strategy from a position of enviable power and social prestige. Its relevance for us lies in the fact that preachers, too, tend to be powerful, both in the sense that most of us enjoy the legal protections, physical safety, and relative financial security afforded citizens of Western democracies, and in the more specific ecclesiastical sense that preaching gives us a pulpit and forces congregants to attend our words when they would otherwise have no conceivable reason for doing so. These social factors are compounded by psychological considerations: as Michael Quicke observes, "Hubris plagues

---

92. Bruce, "Citizenship," *ABD* 1:1048. Recent discussion of Paul's social status is summarized by Shi, *Paul's Message*, 253.

the act of preaching; rightly convinced of preaching's importance, preachers can wrongly become self-important."[93] At least as practiced by Paul, a theology of the cross is a strategy whereby he disabuses (the term is apt) himself of claims to power, *in order that* God's power may take precedence. His logic, in fact, is strikingly similar to that of John the Baptist in relation to Jesus: "He must increase; I must diminish" (John 3:30). Thus when he encourages his converts and congregants to imitate Christ, it is not as if he is imposing a discipline from afar, or from some great height. Rather, he leads by example and invites them to share the conditions of his own discipleship: he admonishes them to imitate him (1 Cor 4:16) as he imitates Christ (1 Cor 11:1), in fellowship with other unjustly suffering believers (1 Thess 1:6).

Even so, social and structural considerations do not address the most critical implication of Paul's theology of the cross, which applies to all preachers and disciples without exception. It is that crucifixion represents the death of well-intentioned religious endeavor. The cross of Jesus exposes the hard truth that in pursuit of piety we go so far as to murder God's emissaries (the Messiah foremost among them). This conviction is not unique to Christianity, for it is already deeply rooted in Jewish prophetic tradition.[94] It is a pessimistic assessment, to be sure, but one that Paul himself would have surely endorsed. Having aspired to utmost faithfulness in the service of God, he succeeds only in persecuting the disciples of the Messiah, becoming complicit in the death of the church's first martyr. Even should our own experience prove less grim, we are nonetheless incapable either of elevating ourselves into the divine presence (as Paul admits in Romans 3:23) or of bestowing life on others (the essence of his explanation in 2 Corinthians 3:5–6). Sober reflection on personal history would persuade most of us that we are singularly unfit to serve as representatives or spokespersons for a holy God (no matter how much preachers like to think of themselves as such). The cross reminds us that all "glory, majesty, power, and authority, before all time and now and forever" (Jude 1:25) belong to God alone, no matter what pleasant illusions we, our churches, or certain elements of our society may entertain about gaining power or accruing glory for ourselves.

Notwithstanding Paul's repeated emphasis on identifying with and imitating Christ, it remains the case that Jesus' death and resurrection accomplish for us what we cannot achieve for ourselves. Even if Paul claims

---

93. Quicke, *Preaching As Worship*, 28.

94. This "Deuteronomistic" perspective is reflected in a wide range of biblical texts and "in almost all writings that have survived from Palestinian Judaism between 200 bce and 100 ce," as well as in later rabbinic literature (so Steck, *Israel und das gewaltsame Geschick der Propheten*, 189, with further discussion in Knowles, *Jeremiah in Matthew*, 96–109; the quotation is from 101).

that his personal suffering complements that of Christ (Col 1:24), any attempt at imitation will be partial and limited, never fully measuring up to or matching, much less replacing, his saving work on our behalf. Of course, Christ having suffered for and instead of us obviates any *soteriological* need for us to suffer in turn. But the implications for ministry are equally important: Paul's experiential theology, however powerful, should not be taken to imply that the effectiveness of one's ministry depends on one's ability to model Christ. For that would be to cast the preacher as a necessary instrument and agent of divine power, precisely what participation in "crucifixion" denies.[95] At its best, as Andrew Purves again reminds us, the church's ministry simply reflects and participates in Jesus' completed ministry on our behalf. In this respect, soteriology and ecclesiology, the life of faith and the faithful service that is its expression operate by the same, not different. christological principles:

> First, Jesus Christ is himself both God's saving Word of address to humankind, *and* the human response of hearing and receiving that Word and acting in perfect obedience toward God. . . . Second, Christian faith and life in general, and Christian ministry in particular, are our participation through the Holy Spirit in this twofold ministry of Jesus Christ, where the Word of God is spoken, heard, obeyed, and given back to God in its fullness in fulfillment of its purpose.[96]

All of this leaves the preacher in a strange dilemma. Preaching "the whole counsel of God" (Acts 20:27 RSV) means first, at the level of rhetoric and persuasion, confessing that we are unable to convince our hearers of the truth of which we speak. Indeed, persuasion itself must be renounced to the extent that it seeks to exercise power over one's hearers. Although I have already quoted Charles Campbell on this point twice in print,[97] I have yet to find anyone else who explains the principle better, and so will do so here once more. Taking his cue from Hans Frei's 1975 study, *The Identity of Jesus Christ: The Hermeneutical Bases of Dogmatic Theology*, Campbell draws out the homiletical implications of a theology of the cross. According to Frei, Jesus intentionally embraces powerlessness when he turns his face toward Jerusalem, refuses to resist his opponents, and willingly submits to crucifixion:

---

95. So Cousar: "The archetype is Christ, not Paul. Paul becomes simply an example of what union with Christ entails and only in this sense does his experience function as a paradigm for others" (*A Theology of the Cross*, 169).

96. Purves, *Reconstructing Pastoral Theology*, 44–45 (emphasis original).

97. Knowles, *We Preach Not Ourselves*, 64; Knowles, "Sowing Seeds," 62–63.

> Jesus intentionally rejects the way of violence and coercion, for the purposes of God cannot be fulfilled by violent means. In obedience to God Jesus makes a transition from ministry to crucifixion, from authoritative power to helplessness.[98]

What Frei calls a "pattern of exchange," Campbell offers as a model for preaching:

> As a form of discipleship shaped by the identity of Jesus Christ, preaching is not primarily storytelling or narrative artistry, but rather an act of moral obedience.... Not only is the preacher's *message* shaped by the story of Jesus ... but the very *act* of preaching itself is a performance of Scripture, an embodiment of God's reign after the pattern of Jesus.[99]

This does not imply passivity, weakness, or lack of conviction on the part of the preacher: on the contrary, it requires great courage not to fall back on familiar and psychologically effective tactics of rhetorical manipulation (by means of guilt and shaming in particular), haranguing one's listeners, or appealing to ecclesiastical authority. David J. Lose refers to this kind of preaching as "kenotic rhetoric," by which he means

> one that proclaims Christ by following his lead through the darkness of Good Friday to the dawn of the new day at Easter. In short, preachers of the cross must be prepared to empty themselves and risk the rejection of the "weak" word of the gospel in terms of both the content and form of their confession.[100]

Just so, Stanley Hauerwas notes the irony of balancing the strength of his convictions with a commitment to pacifism: "I do think that Christians should disavow war, but because I am committed to nonviolence I cannot use the sermon as a stick to beat those who do not believe war is incompatible with the worship of Jesus into submission."[101] It is an amusing illustration, to

---

98. Campbell, *Preaching Jesus*, 214.

99. Ibid., 216 (emphasis original). Campbell pursues this thesis further in *The Word Before the Powers*: "Preaching enacts a concrete ethical performance of Jesus' third way—the way of active, nonviolent resistance to and engagement with the principalities and powers of the world.... The faithful preacher does not remain silent but witnesses boldly, announcing the coming of God's reign in Jesus Christ, exposing the deadly, idolatrous ways of the powers, and envisioning an alternative world—the new creation" (79–80).

100. Lose, *Confessing Jesus Christ*, 206.

101. Hauerwas, *A Cross-Shattered Church*, 13.

be sure, yet the same is true of all Christian proclamation: appealing to Jesus implies a commitment to the way of God that he embodies.

> As disciples of Jesus ... faithful preachers not only reject passivity, but also refuse to coerce belief or resort to violent domination, even in the face of conflict, disbelief, and rejection. Preachers accept a strange kind of powerlessness, which finally relies on God to make effective not only individual sermons, but the very practice of preaching itself; like the Word made flesh, the preacher's words must be "redeemed by God" to be effective.[102]

This should make us reluctant to speak of preaching as "performative utterance," as though well-intentioned religious language were somehow capable in itself of effecting spiritual transformation among its hearers. We need to remember that coming under the shadow of the cross means initially falling silent, for at his death silence is enforced even upon Jesus, the incarnate Word.

Beyond more formal considerations of rhetoric or language, preachers submit to the conditions of the cross by confessing the futility (even the idolatry) of their own religious aspirations. Far from being worthy to serve as spokespersons for God, much less Χριστιανοί—"little Christs" (Acts 11:26)—preachers acknowledge their own moral complicity in the death of the Messiah. As such, they are first and foremost recipients of mercy rather than gatekeepers or dispensers of it. Jesus alone—not the preacher—now holds the keys to death and life (cf. Rev 1:18). We are reliant on Christ, that is, not merely to make our language effective, but to raise us and our hearers alike from well-deserved death.

From a certain perspective, then, it would appear that the rhetorically unconvincing and spiritually ineffectual preacher now has nothing left to do: preaching itself would seem futile and vain. But precisely at this point, Campbell's insistence on the manner in which Jesus bears witness to the reign of God brings the task of the preacher at last into clearer focus:

> In the practice of preaching, the preacher enacts the way of Jesus in the world—the way of nonviolent engagement with the powers. Apart from all the words spoken, the practice itself proclaims that the church does not resort to violence in the name of truth, but rather witnesses.... Indeed, in the act of witnessing to Jesus, the church is reminded that a resort to violence would be a contradiction of the One who is preached.[103]

---

102. Campbell, *Preaching Jesus*, 216.
103. Ibid., 216–17.

As Richard Bauckham explains, such an approach is not only theologically consistent with the conditions of the cross, but also eminently suited to the circumstances of postmodernism:

> The image the Bible itself often suggests for the way its truth is to be claimed is that of witness. This is an extremely valuable image with which to meet the postmodern suspicion of all metanarratives as oppressive. Witness is non-coercive. It has no power but the convincingness of the truth to which it witnesses. Witnesses are not expected, like lawyers, to persuade by the rhetorical power of their speeches, but simply to testify to the truth for which they are qualified to give evidence. But to [bear] adequate witness to the truth of God and the world, [this] must be a lived witness involving the whole of life and even death.[104]

The suggestion that preaching take the form of enacted testimony or "lived witness" has been taken up by a number of writers, with promising results. Characterizing the sermon as a kind of noncoercive testimony that respects divine prerogatives while acknowledging the church's responsibility for ministry offers a helpful model for proclaiming the life of God in its paradoxical manifestation via the crucifixion and resurrection of Jesus. We turn now to a more detailed consideration of this proposal.

---

104. Bauckham, *Bible and Mission*, 98–99.

Part Three

GOD'S WORD

Chapter 5

"We Speak of What We Know and Testify to What We Have Seen"

Homiletics as Testimony

> Some things are to be enjoyed, others to be used, and there are others which are to be enjoyed and used. Those things which are to be enjoyed make us blessed. Those things which are to be used help and, as it were, sustain us as we move toward blessedness in order that we may gain and cling to those things which make us blessed.
>
> —Augustine of Hippo (354–430 CE)[1]

AUGUSTINE OF HIPPO: MEANS, ENDS, AND THE PURPOSE OF PREACHING

Although it seems a very strange way to start a handbook on preaching, Saint Augustine begins his widely influential *De Doctrina Christiana* by discussing the difference, first, between things in themselves and the signs that point to them, and second, between that which we may enjoy for its

---

1. Augustine, *On Christian Doctrine* 1.3, 9.

own sake and that which is merely useful in moving us toward blessedness.[2] According to Augustine, only the Father, Son, and Holy Spirit can truly be enjoyed for their own sake:

> Thus in this life, wandering from God, if we wish to return to our native country where we can be blessed, we should use this world and not enjoy it, so that the "invisible things" of God "being understood by the things that are made" [Rom 1:20] may be seen, that is, so that by means of corporal and temporal things we may comprehend the eternal and spiritual.[3]

His earlier study, *Concerning True Religion*, explained how all the wonders of the universe, even though they come from the hand of God, provide a case in point. In a manner reminiscent of Jesus' parables about growth and fruitfulness in nature, Augustine argues that the true purpose of creation is to direct our attention toward the Creator:

> We should not vainly behold the beauty of the sky, the order of the stars, the brightness of light, the alternations of day and night, the monthly courses of the moon, the fourfold seasons of the year, the meeting of the four elements, the life-force of seeds begetting forms and numbers, and all things that keep their nature and their appropriate measure each in its own kind. In considering these things there should be no exercise of vain and perishing curiosity, but a step should be taken towards immortal things that abide forever.[4]

All these things are meant to point beyond themselves. But Augustine is not a frowning killjoy, refusing to enjoy the simple pleasures of life. His argument—like that of Jesus before him—is simply that God, not God's creation, is the true source of life. To be satisfied with God's works, rather than the source of those works, is to settle for second best, to mistake means for ends, and thus to fall short of the true source of our own life.

The same distinction, he says, applies to preaching. Human language, especially when it seeks to delight and persuade, illustrates the tendency of fallen creatures to mistake means for ends. Here Augustine addresses his complaint to divine Wisdom:

---

2. See Bonner, "Augustine as Biblical Scholar," 547–49, and more extensively, Fish, *Self-Consuming Artifacts*, 21–43, on which the following discussion is based.

3. Augustine, *On Christian Doctrine* 1.4, 10.

4. *De Vera Religione* 29.52; cf. 42.79; from Burleigh, *Of True Religion*, 49, quoted in part by Fish, *Self-Consuming Artifacts*, 25.

> Those who love the things you make instead of yourself are like [those] who listen to the eloquence of a wise man. In their overeagerness to hear his beautiful voice and the skillful cadence of his words, they neglect the primary importance of his thoughts for which the spoken words were to serve as signs. Woe to those who turn away from your light and are delighted to cling to their own darkness![5]

Although (or because) Augustine is trained in classical rhetoric, he wants to distinguish between words, which point beyond themselves, and the realities to which those words should direct us, above all the reality of God. Human words are ultimately useful, he contends, only to the extent that they lead us to the life of God. Yet paradoxically, this is something words themselves cannot accomplish. To explain what he means, Augustine compares preaching to medicine: both, he insists, can only succeed by the power of God. His initial proof is drawn from 1 Corinthians 3:7:

> For "neither he that planteth is anything nor he that watereth; but God that giveth the increase." Whence it happens that even with the assistance of holy men, or even if the holy angels themselves take part, no one rightly learns those things which pertain to life with God unless he is made by God docile to God. ... Medicines for the body which are administered to men by men do not help them unless health is conferred by God, who can cure without them; yet they are nevertheless applied even though they are useless without His aid.[6]

Preaching and teaching are thus means to a blessed end, not ends in themselves; they are not to be enjoyed for their own sake, but rather to be used for the sake of something greater. Even if preachers hope to lead their hearers to God, eloquence and human artistry cannot accomplish this task on their own, for the necessary power comes from God alone. Accordingly, for Augustine, more valuable by far than eloquence in preaching is preaching marked by the wisdom of Scripture:

> For a man speaks more or less wisely to the extent that he has become more or less proficient in the Holy Scriptures.... For one who wishes to speak wisely... even though he cannot speak

---

5. *De Libero Arbitrio* 2.16.43, from Augustine, *The Teacher*, 153; cf. *On Christian Doctrine* 3.9.13: "He is a slave to a sign who uses or worships a significant thing without knowing what it signifies. But he who uses or venerates a useful sign divinely instituted whose signifying force he understands does not venerate what he sees ... but rather that to which all such things are to be referred" (86–87).

6. Augustine, *On Christian Doctrine* 4.16.33, 142.

eloquently, it is above all necessary to remember the words of Scripture.[7]

Notwithstanding this devaluing of rhetoric, Augustine spends the remainder of his book analyzing the rhetoric of Scripture, then applying "biblical" styles to different kinds of preaching![8]

What, then, is the function of words; of rhetoric generally and well-crafted preaching in particular? Clearly they are not ends in themselves, but if Augustine is to be taken at *his* word, it is not even clear how they may serve as means. According to literary critic Stanley Fish, the limited usefulness of human language calls preaching itself into question:

> In the context of Christian assumptions, only God persuades, and He persuades independently of the vessel He chooses as a means, whether it be a man or a sermon.... The practical result of this, as we have seen, is to make practical nonsense of the lessons rhetorical manuals usually teach; and the result of that result is the raising of a question: why write sermons at all?[9]

For Fish, Augustine's description of the task makes Christian preaching a "self-consuming artifact," a literary device that "signifies most successfully when it fails, when it points *away* from itself to something its forms cannot capture."[10] His analysis of Augustine seeks to uncover various levels of semantic contradiction, which need not concern us directly, yet Fish offers a telling insight into the kind of preaching that Augustine seems to have had in mind:

> Such a sermon ... will be continually pointing away from itself, calling attention to what it is not doing (and indeed could not do), proclaiming not only its own insufficiency, but the insufficiency of the frame of reference from which it issues, the human frame of reference its hearers inhabit.
>
> ... And therefore, a sermon that is true to Augustine's *ars praedicandi* [i.e., art of preaching] will in the end give itself over to God, just as it will give over to God the selves of its charges.[11]

To be sure, this is a delicate balance: preachers must employ words, even artful words, all the while acknowledging the limitations of those words,

---

7. Augustine, *On Christian Doctrine* 4.5.7–8, 122.

8. For a helpful summary and application of Augustine's rhetorical categories, see Wilson, *Setting Words on Fire*, 103–9.

9. Fish, *Self-Consuming Artifacts*, 39.

10. Ibid., 4 (quoted in the Introduction, above; emphasis original).

11. Ibid., 42.

and thereby referring hearers to the sole prerogative of God as the one who bestows the life and healing of which the preacher speaks.

As a more recent example of this odd tension, African American preaching is unquestionably the most artful of our day, informed by a long tradition of rhetorical styles and conventions:

> One of the most notable characteristics of African American preaching is the skillful use of oral language as a prized communicative tool. How best to convey the gospel through formal, crafted speech continues to be a studied and highly sought-after art among young and old black preachers alike.[12]

Yet the same tradition is more aware than most that rhetoric alone does not create an effective sermon. Originally addressed to the powerless and oppressed by preachers who themselves suffered the same constraints, African American preaching appeals to the power of a sovereign God as one of its most basic assumptions. Cleo LaRue explains:

> As a result of their historical marginalization, what became most important to blacks in their encounter with Christianity was an intimate relationship with a powerful God, who exhibited throughout scripture a willingness to side with the downtrodden in very concrete and practical ways.[13]

Turning to God is what makes preaching possible in the first place: preparation cannot proceed without what LaRue calls "*A sense of divine encounter*" to spark the process of wrestling with the biblical text.[14] Preachers in this tradition—as in many others—come to the Bible in full expectation that it will speak of divine grace and intervention: "The hermeneutic of God, the mighty sovereign who acts mightily on behalf of the powerless and oppressed, is the long-standing template blacks place on the scriptures as they begin the interpretive process." Thus, inevitably, such preaching testifies to the transforming power of God, manifested above all in the crucifixion and resurrection of Jesus, and therefore also at work in the life of the congregation: "The demonstration of God's power is the fundamental key to understanding what drives, motivates, and gives shape and life to the creation and organization of the black sermon."[15] LaRue does not claim that God's power is *a* key to black preaching, one of several: rather, it is *the* key, the one

---

12. LaRue, *I Believe I'll Testify*, 81.
13. LaRue, *The Heart of Black Preaching*, 114.
14. LaRue, ed., *Power in the Pulpit*, 6 (emphasis original); cf. LaRue, ed., *More Power in the Pulpit*, 4.
15. LaRue, *The Heart of Black Preaching*, 112–13; cf. 25–27.

most basic principle to which this tradition appeals. As with Augustine's comparison of preaching to medicine and physical healing, or even Jesus' use of provocative stories about the abundance of nature, the narrative and rhetorical form of preaching are ultimately subservient—perhaps even incidental—to theological purpose and agency. What the parables of Jesus, Augustine's classical rhetoric, and African American oratory all have in common is the fact that they function theologically as forms of testimony to divine power. To see how this insight applies to preaching generally will require a more detailed foray into some of the many dimensions of Christian witness.

If (as in Jesus' parables) the gift of life to which preaching attests comes from God alone; if the power of transformation rests with God rather than the preacher; if preachers themselves participate in the conditions of the cross; and if words alone are incapable of effecting deep spiritual change in their hearers, then we will need to reexamine some of our cultural assumptions about the role of preaching in relation to congregational change. Because of its essentially passive, nonutilitarian character, "testimony" or "witness" provides the most appropriate category—both theologically and practically—for understanding this ministry. Karl Barth characterizes Christian life generally as a form of testimony to the sufficiency of God, while Walter Brueggemann discusses the testimony of Israel as recorded in Hebrew Scripture. Both illustrate their arguments by appealing to the law court, but the potential of this analogy is most fully developed by Paul Ricoeur, whose insights have been popularized and applied to preaching by Tom Long and Anna Carter Florence (amongst others). The contributions of each writer will be evaluated and refined with reference to the evidence of the New Testament, which offers a number of important qualifications and further developments for understanding this concept.

KARL BARTH: CHRISTIAN LIFE AS WITNESS

In seeking to define the essential nature of Christian identity, and of the distinctively Christian vocation that flows from it, Karl Barth (1886–1968) looks for an answer that corresponds to the person of Christ as Lord; that is, a human identity and vocation wholly derived from and dependent upon the identity and accomplishment of Christ himself. For Barth, even personal appropriation of divine salvation is secondary to the fact that, in receiving this gift, Christians bear witness to a saving initiative that precedes any human response. Faith does not bear witness, first and foremost, to a particular act of reception, but to the primacy of divine action on behalf of humanity that makes reception possible. Characteristically *Christian* witness, of course, derives from God's prior testimony in the person of Jesus, "the eternal Word of the Father who speaks from all eternity."[16] Randi Rashkover explains that, in Barth's view, human knowledge of God proceeds from the fact of Jesus' incarnation: "Through the incarnation God proclaims or testifies to himself through the creaturely reality of the man Jesus. Jesus' creaturely reality becomes the site of positive testimony to God."[17] Thus from Jesus' definitive testimony *to* and *by* God—in the form of the Word of God made flesh—proceeds the possibility of language *about* God: divine self-testimony generates human testimony by way of response.

Only once the source and content of Christian testimony are established does the role of the individual witness emerge more clearly. By turning to God in repentance and trust, recipients of God's Word join their own lives and voices to God's self-articulation in the person of Jesus of Nazareth. To cite the Apostle Paul, "In him [Jesus] every one of God's promises is a 'Yes.' For this reason it is through him that we say the 'Amen,' to the glory of God" (2 Cor 1:20). In Christ, that is, God provides the initial testimony to his own faithfulness and grace; believers then respond by declaring "Amen"—"So be it, it is true!" This suggests that Christian testimony is both passive and active: we first receive God's testimony by beholding and yielding to it, then declare to others what we have experienced as true:

> [The Christian] is in fact a witness in the twofold sense that [one] has seen and heard the acts of God, or in the New Testament His one consummating and conclusive act . . . and that [one] is called to the work of declaration . . . addressing, imparting and proclaiming to others that which [one] has seen as God's act and heard as His Word.[18]

Expanding on this idea, Barth appeals to the analogy of the law court:

> They are made His witnesses: not idle spectators merely watching and considering . . . but witnesses who can and must declare what they have seen and heard [1 John 1:3] like witnesses in a law-suit. Their calling embraces not only the fact that God gives them knowledge concerning Himself and the doing of His will,

---

16. *CD* I.1, 436, quoted in Rashkover, *Revelation and Theopolitics*, 155.
17. Rashkover, *Revelation and Theopolitics*, 155.
18. *CD* IV.3.2, 593.

and that He calls them to this knowledge, but also the fact that He summons and equips them to declare what He has given them to know. In other words, their calling means both that He reveals Himself in His action and also that He summons them into the witness-box as those who know.[19]

Thus ministry in all its many aspects entails bearing witness to the ways of God, not in some abstract or impersonal sense, but because those who minister are caught up personally and corporately in the *missio Dei*. For Barth, this does not reduce ministry—preaching in particular—to a perpetual recitation of contemporary spiritual experience. Certainly testimony to personal experience of God can be helpful within a particular sermon.[20] Yet the reality to which one ultimately bears witness remains the definitive, ongoing action of God in Christ, which always takes precedence over any individual experience or imitation of it.[21] This implies that conversion and ministry—for instance the preaching of repentance and the act of repentance that responds to such preaching—are morally and theologically identical, in that both confess the righteousness of God and the insufficiency of human existence apart from God.[22] Thus the penitential gesture of turning from self to God in Christ (which is the most basic form of Christian confession) and the preacher's act of relying on God in the course of inviting listeners to do the same are both forms of testimony to the true character of the divine-human relationship. All forms of Christian testimony, then, from conversion to discipleship, ministry, and mission, bear witness to the sufficiency of God, revealed in Jesus of Nazareth, as the source of all life.[23]

Barth's insistence on the primacy of divine testimony significantly limits the theological function of the sermon, along the lines already suggested by Augustine's distinction between divine and human agency, or Luther's

---

19. Ibid., 576.

20. Wilson (*Setting Words on Fire*, 149–64) offers a thoughtful exploration of this approach.

21. "The action, work or activity of Christ unconditionally precedes that of the [one] called by Him" (*CD* IV.3.2, 598); similarly, "The personal liberation of the Christian can and should fit him for this ministry of witness. But it cannot and should not become the content of his witness. The servant has to proclaim his Lord and His work and Word, not himself or the processes by which he has become His servant nor the privileges which he has come to share as such" (ibid., 676).

22. Cf. Rashkover, *Revelation and Theopolitics*, 130–31.

23. Along the same lines, Charles Wood proposes that all aspects of Christian faith and theological inquiry can be unified under the category of "witness," and that a prime criterion for the authenticity of this witness is its specific testimony to Jesus Christ (*Vision and Discernment*, esp. 37–42).

theology of the cross. Preaching too is a theologically derivative activity, a response to divine action rather than its necessary instrument, much less a means of somehow prompting God to act. The preacher as witness cannot mediate between God and humanity:

> Preaching must conform to revelation. First this means negatively that in preaching we are not to repeat or transmit the revelation of God by what we do. Precisely because the point of the event of preaching is God's own speaking... there can be no question of our doing the revealing in any way. In all circumstances we must respect the fact that God *has* revealed himself and he will reveal himself as the one who comes again.[24]

Barth appeals to what he calls the "unconditional 'whence'" and "unconditional 'whither'" of Christian proclamation: "whence" is the "once for all" (ἐφάπαξ; Heb 10:10) of Christ's accomplishment; "whither" is the eschatological imperative of Christ's victorious return.[25] Accordingly, he declares, "the thrust of the sermon is always downhill, not uphill to a goal. Everything has already taken place."[26] Far from assuming responsibility for the work of God's kingdom, "preaching cannot try to be a proof of the truth of God" either by means of logical arguments or through the use of rhetoric. Because it is only testimony, and dependent on the unsubstitutable primacy of revelation, "preaching may not try to create the reality of God."[27]

WALTER BRUEGGEMANN: THE TESTIMONY OF ISRAEL

For Walter Brueggemann, on the other hand, the testimony of faith is rooted and reflected primarily in the nature of the biblical text. Appealing to categories articulated by Ricoeur (to whom we will return more fully in due course), Brueggemann contends that the Hebrew canon represents the particular testimony of Israel, arising out of its encounter with God. Brueggemann too employs the metaphor of the trial and law court, although the implications he adduces are considerably more radical than was the case for Barth. As Brueggemann sees it, the witness is free to choose any one of many possible renderings of the events in question; whichever construal is chosen, "the testimony is a public presentation that shapes, enjoins, or constitutes reality. In this sense, the testimony is *originary*: it causes to be,

---

24. Barth, *Homiletics*, 47 (emphasis original).
25. Ibid., 51–54.
26. Ibid., 53.
27. Ibid., 47–48.

in the courtroom, what was not until this utterance." Thus the decision of the court—acceptance of such testimony on the part of the reader or faith community—establishes the truth, the reality of the situation. In theological terms, as applied to Hebrew Scripture, this means that "testimony becomes revelation."[28] As Brueggemann sees it, "for Old Testament faith, *the utterance is everything.*"[29]

Israel's testimony typically takes the form of thanksgiving, especially for the manifestation of God's righteousness and sovereign power, whether in the act of creation, in deliverance out of bondage, or in giving shape to the life of those who call on his name.[30] Likewise Israel celebrates the divine character that these acts reveal, bearing witness that God is ever and always "gracious and merciful, slow to anger, and abounding in steadfast love and faithfulness" (Exod 34:6).[31] But at the same time, the testimony of Hebrew Scripture is characteristically "disjunctive": God may (to borrow the language of Jeremiah 1:10) "build and plant," but the same sovereign is liable to "pluck up and pull down, destroy and overthrow" (Jer 1:10). Indeed, Brueggemann argues that Israel's experience as a whole is essentially disjunctive, for over against claims for the presence and sustaining power of God is a rich tradition of lamentation that complains of divine absence, unwillingness, or inability to intervene in situations of human need. Over and over the faithful cry out, "How long, O Lord?" or "Why?" or "Where is God?"[32] Amidst testimony to the fidelity of God runs this bold countertestimony and cross-examination of such claims. Job offers a signal illustration of this perspective, although it is also widely present among the Psalms, and especially in the book of Jeremiah. Citing many of the same texts, Samuel Terrien likewise speaks of a "hidden God," or more precisely of

---

28. Brueggemann, *Theology of the Old Testament*, 121. In a brief reflection written some fifteen years after the publication of this study ("*Theology of the Old Testament: Testimony, Dispute, Advocacy* Revisited," 28–38), Brueggemann concedes that its language is hyperbolic, at times unhelpfully so. While not denying the possibility of historical reference, he indicates that his purpose had been to distance himself from historical positivism at either extreme of scepticism or fideism; as to his assertion that the God of Israel is found in the biblical text and "nowhere else," he argues that this claim maintains the irreducible character of Scripture as "testimony." Quoting also from Brueggemann's treatment of preaching, the ensuing discussion addresses the second of these issues.

29. Brueggemann, *Theology of the Old Testament*, 122 (emphasis original).

30. On these categories of thanksgiving, see ibid., 126–212.

31. Ibid., 215–24.

32. Ibid., 319–21.

Deus absconditus atque praesens, God simultaneously hidden and present.[33] This leads him to describe biblical theology, in both Testaments, in terms of a *"theologia crucis* which haunts the heart of the Hebraic as well as the Christian commitment to proclaim the name" of God.[34] Brueggemann too acknowledges the disjunctive tension, or dialectic, in Christian testimony to the events of Good Friday and Easter Sunday, which balances the "now" of present faith against the "not yet" of eschatological hope.[35] Thus for Judaism and Christianity alike, he says, whether exemplified by the events of Israel's exile and return or by the revolutionary paradigm of Jesus' death and resurrection, "The core narrative of human life and human destiny is 'into the Pit' of trouble and 'out of the Pit' by the power of Yahweh."[36]

Brueggemann's description of Christian preaching is of a piece with this theological perspective, both in the sense that it valorizes the sense of dislocation and lament typical of postmodern "exile," and with respect to the nature of Christian speech. In his view, preaching gives voice to pain and alienation, while at the same time imagining a more hopeful future of the sort described by the promises of Scripture.[37] Accordingly, preaching is an act of sacred "imagination" whose only interest is that of inviting the hearers to act out the possibilities of which it speaks. Such preaching, says Brueggemann, is specifically disinterested in metaphysical realities; indeed, "the preacher, in the drama of the sermon, must thus 'undo' much of the metaphysical preoccupation of the church tradition."[38] But this is a homiletic of the powerful, and of the spiritually able: it assumes that hearers have the wherewithal to rescue themselves from their social exile and spiritual desolation, if only they put their minds to it. A homiletic of the cross, by contrast, is blessed with no such confidence: echoing the cry of Paul, "We despaired of life itself" (2 Cor 1:8), it lacks even the ability to imagine a better future, and is instead wholly dependent on the actual, concrete intervention of a metaphysical God. Against Brueggemann's claim that *"Yahweh is a product and consequence of Israel's testimony,"*[39] a cruciform homiletic bears witness that God's people are themselves the product and consequence of God's life-giving power, and this is what inspires their testimony. In both

---

33. Terrien, *The Elusive Presence*, 321, 470.

34. Ibid., 474.

35. Brueggemann, *Theology of the Old Testament*, 311–12, 401–2.

36. Ibid., 483; cf. 555, 563–64.

37. Brueggemann explores these motifs in a number of studies, among them *Finally Comes the Poet*; *Cadences of Home*; and *Deep Memory, Exuberant Hope*.

38. Brueggemann, *Cadences of Home*, 33.

39. Ibid., 45 (emphasis original).

testaments we find the declaration, "You are my witnesses" (Isa 43:10, Acts 1:8, etc.), which is indeed a fair characterization of preaching. And there is no question that especially in a skeptical, postmodern world, preaching is more of a deprivileged "bid for assent" than an authoritative declaration or command.[40] But it is not as if "The truth of God rides on the testimony of the witnesses," as Brueggemann claims;[41] rather, the testimony of the witnesses rides on the truth—the enduring fidelity and utter reliability (*'emûnah*)—of God, without which their testimony would be both empty and false. Likewise in the Gospels, while it is certainly true that "Telling parables was one of Jesus' revolutionary activities, for parables are subversive reimaginings of reality,"[42] our examination of those same parables reveals their testimony to "the Scriptures [and] the power of God" as the source and basis for Jesus' imaginative vision of divinely-ordered reality.

Moreover, Hebrew Scripture is not simply the testimony of Israel in any straightforward fashion, for this text also claims to record what Barth rightly calls the "self-testimony" of God. The faithful of Israel are frequently said to "call on," "proclaim," or "name" the God in whom they place their trust. But in two pivotal passages from the book of Exodus, the critical verb (*qr'* [קרא]) occurs not on human lips, but in the mouth of God:[43]

> And [God] said, "I will make all my goodness pass before you, and will *proclaim* before you the name, 'The Lord'; and I will be gracious to whom I will be gracious, and will show mercy on whom I will show mercy."
>
> (Exod 33:19)

> The Lord descended in the cloud and stood with him there, and *proclaimed* the name, "The Lord." The Lord passed before him, and *proclaimed*, "The Lord, the Lord, a God merciful and gracious, slow to anger, and abounding in steadfast love and faithfulness, keeping steadfast love for the thousandth generation, forgiving iniquity and transgression and sin, yet by no means clearing the guilty, but visiting the iniquity of the parents upon the children and the children's children, to the third and the fourth generation."
>
> (Exod 34:5–7)

---

40. Brueggemann, *Deep Memory*, 19–20.
41. Brueggemann, *Cadences of Home*, 47.
42. Brueggemann, *Deep Memory*, 73.
43. So Moberly, *At the Mountain of God*, 77.

"We Speak of What We Know and Testify to What We Have Seen"

The second passage in particular offers the single most comprehensive and influential description of Israel's God in the entire Hebrew Bible.[44] Granted, as Brueggemann argues, "Historical criticism has seen that all utterance in the Old Testament about God, even utterance placed in the mouth of God, has a human speaker or writer as its source."[45] Yet even if its *proximate* source is human, the assertion of a more ultimate and definitive source cannot be lightly dismissed. The claim of Scripture is that even as human worshipers cling tenaciously to the task of fashioning gods in their own image (verbally and otherwise), God no less faithfully bears witness to the divine character both in word and, perhaps more persuasively, by consistently rescuing his people from various disasters, many of their own making. God's verbal self-testimony is thus borne out and repeatedly validated by the calling and formation of a community whose very existence is shaped by the divine character that these passages (and many others like it) proclaim. However partial, imperfect, or lamented may be various individual and particular experiences of God (all faithfully incorporated within the biblical record), the broader trajectory of Israel's experience consistently affirms the mercy, grace, and especially the fidelity of God. In this larger perspective, God's words and God's saving deeds each interpret and affirm the other.

According to Brueggemann, Israel in effect calls God to account, testifying in the face of God's failure to rescue or answer when called upon. Certainly the importance of questioning and lament—whether historically, theologically, or psychologically—cannot be underestimated. Yet within the Hebrew canon these motifs stand alongside another, equally important tradition in which it is God who calls *Israel* to account on the matter of fidelity. The so-called "prophetic lawsuit" (*rîb* [ריב]) envisages God summoning his people to acknowledge—testify, even—that it is they, not he, who have failed to keep faith:

> The Lord rises *to argue his case*; he stands to judge the peoples.
> The Lord enters into judgment with the elders and princes of his people...
>
> (Isa 3:13–14)

> Hear the word of the Lord, O people of Israel;
> for the Lord has an *indictment* against the inhabitants of the land.

---

44. For an extended exploration of this language in Jewish, Christian, and Islamic devotion, see Knowles, *The Unfolding Mystery of the Divine Name*.

45. Brueggemann, *Theology of the Old Testament*, 121–22.

> There is no faithfulness or loyalty, and no knowledge of God in the land.
>
> (Hos 4:1)

> Hear what the Lord says: Rise, plead your *case* before the mountains, and let the hills hear your voice.
> Hear, you mountains, the *controversy* of the Lord ... for the Lord has a *controversy* with his people, and he will contend with Israel.
> O my people, what have I done to you? In what have I wearied you? Answer me!
>
> (Mic 6:1–3)

Whether these texts share enough characteristics to be considered a genre of their own remains a matter of scholarly contention, but the language of legal proceedings and the appeal to testimony are unmistakable.[46] Again, it is God who takes the initiative in soliciting testimony: if God's ways do not speak for themselves, then God's people are more than welcome to examine them. The prophets do not lack confidence as to whose conduct is better able to withstand scrutiny.

Citing evidence from Exodus, Augustine of Hippo, Pseudo-Dionysius, and agnostic philosopher Jacques Derrida—one could hardly imagine more unusual allies—Janet Martin Soskice contends that only "the gift of God's self-disclosure in history" provides us language with which we may speak of God:

> To be a theologian, we might say, is always to stand under the primacy of the signified over the signifier (an exact reversal of what Derrida thinks to be the case for language in general) but at the same time to know that the signified can only be named through gift.[47]

---

46. Ringgren, *s.v.* ריב *rîḇ*; מריבה *mᵉrîḇâ*, TDOT 13:477–78.

47. Soskice, "The Gift of the Name," 231–46; here, 245–46. In fact it is Derrida himself who first quotes Pseudo-Dionysius: "At the end of the *Divine Names*, the very possibility of speaking of the divine names and of speaking of them in a correct manner returns to God, 'to That One who is the Cause of all good, to Him who has first given us the gift to speak and, then, to speak well' [*Divine Names* 13.981c].... This is what God's name always names, before and beyond other names: the trace of the singular event that will have rendered speech possible even before it turns itself back toward—in order to respond to—this first or last reference" (Derrida, "How to Avoid Speaking: Denials," in Coward and Foshan, eds., *Derrida and Negative Theology*, 98).

To be a preacher, we might say, and thus to bear faithful witness to the God who keeps faith with us, is always to stand under the primacy of God's own testimony. Here we may expand on Barth's understanding of the twofold character of Christian witness: as God bears witness to the divine character in word and deed, so the objects of that saving initiative witness its life-giving power, and attest in turn to what they have seen and heard. Testimony by God creates the possibility of testimony concerning God. It is from this dynamic that preaching proceeds.

"BEHOLD THE LAMB OF GOD": PAUL RICOEUR AND THE PREACHER AS WITNESS

Two contemporary theorists who have done much to popularize the idea of preaching as a form of testimony are Tom Long, whose best-selling *The Witness of Preaching* is currently in its second edition, and Anna Carter Florence, for whom *Preaching As Testimony* reclaims the marginalized voices of women over many centuries.[48] Like Brueggemann, both take their cue from the work of Paul Ricoeur, in particular an essay first published in French in 1972 entitled "The Hermeneutics of Testimony."[49] Ricoeur is a nuanced and demanding thinker, so in assessing his ideas we must proceed with caution. What follows is no more than a brief sketch, an initial foray into the world of his thought rather than a comprehensive accounting, yet one that will prove amply rewarding even for so concrete and practical a task as the preparation of next Sunday's sermon. Ricoeur explores the philosophical basis on which finite humans, and finite human language, may speak of "the absolute" (that is, God). According to Florence,

> What Ricoeur argues is this: Christian hermeneutics, or Christian interpretation, is not based in facts. It is based in testimony, which is an entirely different interpretive framework.[50]

---

48. Long, *The Witness of Preaching*; Florence, *Preaching as Testimony*. Florence's study is a revision of her doctoral dissertation, completed in 2000 at Princeton Theological Seminary, where she studied under Long. Separately, in *Testimony*, Long discusses the nature of testimony as constitutive of Christian identity.

49. Ricoeur, "The Hermeneutics of Testimony," in *Essays on Biblical Interpretation*, 119–54; originally published as "L'herméneutique du témoignage," 35–61. In discussing Hebrew Scripture as testimony, Brueggemann comments simply, "Here I am much informed by an essay of Paul Ricoeur" (*Theology of the Old Testament*, 119–20 and n.7).

50. Florence, *Preaching as Testimony*, 61.

But this overstates Ricoeur's position, or at least is liable to be misunderstood as implying that Ricoeur thinks Christian belief to be somehow nonfactual or less than fully true.[51] Although he has considerably more to say about the nature of religious language as a species of metaphorical or poetic discourse, one way of approaching Ricoeur is to distinguish between scientific, objective knowledge (or knowledge of objects in and of themselves) on the one hand, and religious knowledge that entails personal engagement and commitment on the other. Oversimplifying considerably, knowledge *about* God implies and requires a personal response *to* God, in a way that impersonal objects do not.

Ricoeur makes an important distinction between religious and nonreligious forms of testimony, although similar conditions apply in each case. Nonreligious testimony requires, first, a witness who beholds something firsthand; second, a recipient who hears and receives this testimony; and third, the need for adjudication as to whether such testimony should ultimately be accepted. This situation is analogous to a legal trial at which the facts of a particular case are in dispute; where indeed, "we cannot claim to have certainty but only probability, and the probable is only pursued through a struggle of opinion."[52] As in a trial that calls for judicial decision, testimony implies argumentation: "Testimony is thus caught in the network of proof and persuasion."[53] In this context the character of the witness is all-important because the witness must be relied on to tell the truth. And it is no accident, in Ricoeur's view, that the language of "martyrdom" arises out of the Greek terms that refer to bearing witness, because when truth is at stake, "The witness is capable of suffering and dying for what he [sic] believes."[54] For the one who bears witness in this manner, nonreligious testimony has three internal dimensions, which correspond in some measure to the three external components outlined above. First comes the "testimony of the senses," our beholding of some specific event, followed (second) by the words of testimony to which such beholding gives rise. Then third, according to Ricoeur, the words themselves reflect an interior "testimony of

---

51. For Ricoeur, testimony is "quasi-empirical," by which he means that "testimony is not perception itself but the report, that is, the story, the narration of the event. . . . Testimony as story is thus found in an intermediary position between a statement made by a person and a belief assumed by another on the faith of the testimony of the first" ("Hermeneutics of Testimony," in *Essays on Biblical Interpretation*, 123; I am grateful to Dustin Boreland for pointing out this important distinction).

52. Ibid., 125.

53. Ibid., 127.

54. Ibid., 129.

conscience," the testimony of personal conviction and commitment from which verbal confession proceeds.⁵⁵

Although similar conditions apply to the human dimensions of specifically religious testimony, the latter is nonetheless set apart by the nature and universal significance of its subject matter. In this connection Ricoeur quotes Isaiah 43:8–10 ("'You are my witnesses,' says the Lord, 'and my servants whom I have chosen'" [v. 10]), from which he derives four key inferences:

1. "The witness is not just anyone who comes forward and gives testimony, but the one who is sent in order to testify. Originally, testimony comes from somewhere else."

2. The testimony in question does not concern isolated facts but "the radical, global meaning of human experience. It is Yahweh himself who is witnessed to in the testimony."

3. "The testimony is oriented toward proclamation" on behalf of all people.

4. "This profession implies a total engagement not only of words but of acts and, in the extreme, in the sacrifice of a life."⁵⁶

Ricoeur is careful to point out that here too the giving of testimony implies a dispute that calls for decision, and that bearing witness is frequently a matter of life and death, especially for the prophets of Israel. But in this case it is God who initiates and calls for deliberation; moreover, the testimony in question concerns God's own character and saving action, and the decision to be made requires a choice between truth and falsehood, God and idolatry. Accordingly:

> What separates this new meaning of testimony from all its uses in ordinary language is that the testimony does not belong to the witness. It proceeds from an absolute initiative as to its origin and its content.⁵⁷

In order for the people of Israel to render their decision, God calls forth witnesses on both sides of the dispute. Again Ricoeur quotes the words of Isaiah, this time from another passage belonging to the "prophetic lawsuit" tradition:

---

55. Ibid., 130.

56. Ibid., 131; cf. Long, *Witness of Preaching*, 46; Florence, *Preaching as Testimony*, 63.

57. Ricoeur, "Hermeneutics of Testimony," in *Essays on Biblical Interpretation*, 130.

> "Who is like me? Let him proclaim it, let him declare and set it forth before me.... And you are my witnesses! Is there a God besides me?.... All who make idols are nothing, and the things they delight in do not profit; their witnesses neither see nor know, that they may be put to shame."
>
> (Isa 44:7–9)

Notwithstanding the interior dimensions of testimony and the need for deliberation, Ricoeur insists that prophetic testimony—testimony to the objective presence and power of God—cannot be reduced to a matter of personal conviction. On the contrary, it concerns the reality of God's saving work in human history:

> It is not possible to testify *for* a meaning without testifying *that* something has happened which signifies this meaning.... There is therefore no witness of the absolute who is not a witness of historic signs, no confessor of absolute meaning who is not a narrator of the acts of deliverance.[58]

Reflecting on Deuteronomy 26:5b–10b, considered the core historical confession of Israel's identity, Ricoeur observes,

> What is essential in the case of narrative discourse is the emphasis on the founding event or events as the imprint, mark, or trace of God's act. Confession takes place through narration... *God's mark is in history before being in speech.* It is only secondarily in speech inasmuch as this history itself is brought to language in the speech-act of narration.[59]

The same principles apply to the New Testament, which "Ricoeur, in his own way, takes... for what it claims to be: 'testimony' to the transforming power of the Resurrection."[60] Here too God calls and sends witnesses to provide "eyewitness testimony" concerning the life, passion, and resurrection of Jesus of Nazareth: "The confession that Jesus is the Christ constitutes testimony par excellence."[61] For Ricoeur there is no disjunction "between the eyewitness testimonies of the life of Jesus and the encounter with the Resurrected One," including that of Paul on the Damascus road, notwithstand-

---

58. Ibid., 133–34 (emphasis original).

59. Ricoeur, "Toward a Hermeneutic of the Idea of Revelation," in *Essays on Biblical Interpretation*, 79 (emphasis added).

60. Lewis S. Mudge, "Paul Ricoeur on Biblical Interpretation," in Ricoeur, *Essays on Biblical Interpretation*, 2.

61. Ricoeur, "Hermeneutics of Testimony," in *Essays on Biblical Interpretation*, 134.

ing different emphases on the part of the evangelists between testimony as confession of faith and testimony as narration of events.[62] Again, he insists, "There is no separation between the Jesus of History and the Christ of faith. This unity is written: Jesus-Christ."[63] With particular reference to Johannine literature, Ricoeur traces the continuity between God's sending of the Son, the Son's testimony to the Father, the eyewitness testimony of the disciples (including John the Baptist), and testimony borne by the Holy Spirit.[64] Divine initiative comes once more to the fore: "The *exegesis* of God and the *testimony* of the Son are the same thing;"[65] it is from this dynamic that the disciples' subsequent testimony proceeds. Then, in turn, as their testimony is recorded in Scripture, the content and convictions of Christian faith come to be transmitted increasingly by preaching based on the biblical text.[66]

Ricoeur's delicate balancing of divine initiative and human responsibility effectively preserves the human freedom to choose on the one hand, while acknowledging the historical reality of divine self-revelation on the other. Of particular relevance to preaching is his understanding of biblical exegesis:

> The concept of testimony such as is drawn out by biblical exegesis, is hermeneutical in a double sense. In the first sense it *gives* to interpretation a content to be interpreted. In the second sense it *calls for* an interpretation.
>
> Testimony *gives* something to be interpreted.... The absolute declares itself here and now.[67]

Thus the conviction that the biblical narrative bears faithful witness to God's self-revelation in history is what makes scriptural interpretation—and preaching—possible. Were it not for the divine self-manifestation that provides something worth interpreting, religious conviction—and preaching—would be no more than an endless series of speculations about human opinion:

---

62. The quotation, from 135, has been corrected: against the Stewart/Reagan translation, "the encounter with the resurrection Lord [*sic*]," the original text refers to "la rencontre du Ressuscité" (*Le Témoignage*, 47).

63. Ricoeur, "Hermeneutics of Testimony," in *Essays on Biblical Interpretation*, 145.

64. Cf. ibid., 136–41.

65. Ibid., 137 (emphasis original).

66. Ibid., 136. For a more nuanced account of the implications, both for Ricoeur and for preaching, of the shift from eyewitness testimony to the testimony of the text, see Gross, *If You Cannot Preach*, 60–63.

67. Ricoeur, "Hermeneutics of Testimony," in *Essays on Biblical Interpretation*, 143–44 (emphasis original).

> A hermeneutic without testimony is condemned to an infinite regress in perspectivism with neither beginning nor end.... For the self-manifestation of the absolute here and now indicates the end of the infinite regress of reflection. The absolute shows itself.[68]

Ricoeur articulates something akin to a hermeneutic of the cross. He speaks repeatedly of "divestment" ([se] *dépouiller, dépouillement*)—meaning variously dispossession, divestiture, or stripping away—on the part both of God and of the human witness. God draws back from coercing assent by submitting to the conditions of history and human testimony; we in turn admit the limitations of our human understanding, and therefore acknowledge the need to weigh not only the testimony of others but also our own responsibility for discernment and decision in matters of divine truth.[69] Ricoeur calls this "a double humility."[70] Kevin Vanhoozer explains the human responsibility for "divestment" as follows:

> The question that apparently demarcates true from false testimony is this: does this testimony not only express but occasion new experiences of the absolute? Confronted with true testimony to the absolute, we too confess, "Yes, here is the source of my being and its meaning." In the face of testimony to the absolute, we relinquish our own paltry attempts to justify or constitute our existence and recognize or discover that our existence is illumined and transformed by the testimony.[71]

A hermeneutic of the cross entails considerably more than this, to be sure, but it is nonetheless central to Ricoeur's understanding of human identity in the presence of God: "The biblical theme of dying to self becomes in Ricoeur's philosophy the idea of the subject's abandoning all pretensions to justify and give meaning to [one's] own existence."[72] In other words, to be a witness is to acknowledge that the source of human identity and signifi-

---

68. Ibid., 144.

69. For Ricoeur, this principle is characteristic of preaching in particular: "For the philosopher, to listen to Christian preaching is first of all to let go (*se dépouiller*)" (Ricoeur, "Naming God," 223; quoted in Pape, *A Ricoeurian Revision*, 130; published as *The Scandal of Having Something to Say*).

70. Ricoeur, "Hermeneutics of Testimony," in *Essays on Biblical Interpretation*, 150–51.

71. Vanhoozer, *Biblical Narrative*, 260.

72. Ibid., 261. Cf. Pape, *A Ricoeurian Revision*, 170: "Ricoeur's is a thoroughly theological hermeneutical disposition that waits and listens for a transforming voice not its own."

cance lies outside oneself, in the event or events to which one testifies, rather than in the role of bearing witness itself.

But Vanhoozer is skeptical about the historical character of testimony, at least according to Ricoeur: "It should now be apparent that what Ricoeur means by testimony is far removed from the testimony with which historians work." Ricoeur, it would appear, is more interested in "consciousness and self-understanding" than in matters of historicity per se:

> As in art, so too with biblical narrative the "truth" of the text may be had apart from the events it narrates actually having happened. Testimony speaks not of the literal but [of] the spiritual event of recognition. We recognize essential truths through contingent testimonies. It is not the truths that are contingent, but the testimonies. Accordingly, "testimony" in Ricoeur's thought more properly relates to the reader's historicity (the manner of his being-in-the-world) than to "the deeds of men in the past."[73]

If this is the case, then it would seem that the power of Christian testimony is reduced to the preacher's ability to persuade, if only by recourse to the appeal of personal conviction, as Florence contends:

> A sermon in the testimony tradition is not an autobiography but a very particular kind of proclamation: the preacher tells what she has seen and heard *in the biblical text and in life*, and then confesses what she believes about it. Furthermore—and this is the troublesome part for preachers—there is no proof for testimony other than the engagement of a witness, and no proof for a sermon other than the engagement of the preacher. It is impossible to prove whether a sermon is true or false. One can only believe it or reject it.[74]

Yet Ricoeur himself suggests the opposite: "The attempt to bracket reference and to keep sense, i.e., to raise only questions of meaning and to drop questions about historical reality, fails somewhere, because it runs against my main contention that even fictions are about a world."[75] For Ricoeur, texts have the power to disclose the reality of which they speak—they offer the possibility of new coherence or meaning—which is true above all of the biblical text, whose testimony the sermon conveys. This being the case, the

---

73. Vanhoozer, *Biblical Narrative*, 262–63.
74. Florence, *Preaching as Testimony*, xiii (emphasis original); similarly xviii.
75. Ricoeur, "Reply to Lewis S. Mudge," in Ricoeur, *Essays on Biblical Interpretation*, 44.

purpose of faithful interpretation, one form of which is Christian preaching, is to bear witness to what Ricoeur calls the "world of the text":

> Thus, above and beyond emotions, disposition, belief, or nonbelief, is the proposition of a world which in the biblical language is called a new world, a new covenant, the kingdom of God, a new birth. These are the realities unfolded before the text, which are certainly for us, but which begin from the text. This is what one might call the "objectivity" of the new being projected by the text.[76]

In this manner, biblical testimony concerning God corresponds to the reality of which it speaks—it does not simply bear witness to the convictions or identity or "being-in-the-world" of those who speak, but invokes a divine reality, disclosed by God, that is not limited by the scope of human language alone. This principle applies above all to Christian proclamation:

> It is the function of the preaching of the Cross and Resurrection to give to the word "God" a *density* which the word "being" [alone] does not possess. In its meaning is contained the notion of *its* relation to us as gracious, and of *our* relation to it as "ultimately concerned" and as fully "re-cognizant" of it.[77]

As Ricoeur astutely observes, "To understand the word 'God' is to follow the direction of the meaning of the word."[78] In other words, preaching of the cross and resurrection, proceeding as it does from what Ricoeur takes to be a divine self-declaration and self-definition, creates the possibility of this gracious reality coming to expression in the experience of the hearer.

Still, all this seems a very long way from the Sunday morning sermon, or anything else very concrete or practical. Yet it need not be so, for Ricoeur is wrestling with concerns that are central both to God's proclamation of the "Word"—in the person of Jesus—and to our own. Like Barth, Ricoeur repeatedly insists that God speaks and acts in human history; above all, in the person of Jesus, God offers testimony to himself. But humanity has the ability to reject God, God's Son, and God's word alike, whatever form they may take. We retain an inalienable right to decide for ourselves whether or

---

76. Ricoeur, "Philosophy and Religious Language," 81. On Ricoeur's understanding of the disclosive power of texts, see further Porter and Robinson, *Hermeneutics*, 122–24, and, more comprehensively, chapters 3 ("Paul Ricoeur and the World of the Text") and 4 ("A Ricoeurian Revision of Postliberal Homiletics") of Pape, *A Ricoeurian Revision*, 78–180.

77. Ricoeur, "Philosophy and Religious Language," 46 (emphasis original).

78. Ibid., 83.

not to accept such testimony. Preachers know this every time they mount the pulpit steps. In good faith they bear witness to what they have seen and heard, adding their voices to the testimony of Scripture and the collective testimony of the saints ever since. But not everyone will take their word for it: congregants can—and do!—reject such evidence out of hand. At this point the conditions of the cross become especially critical, for the church must confess its faith in the same humble manner as God chooses to reveal himself: in paradox, mystery, and partial hiddenness. Whereas Paul and Luther focus on the implications of Jesus' crucifixion, Ricoeur looks to Moses at the burning bush, where the name that God utters—"I am who I am" (Exod 3:14)—simultaneously reveals and conceals the divine identity. The implications of this self-utterance are of profound significance for preaching:

> To the extent that to know God's name is to have power over him through an invocation whereby the god invoked becomes a manipulatable thing, the name confided to Moses is that of a being whom human beings cannot really name; that is, hold within the discretion of their language.[79]

As Lance Pape rightly observes,

> God is not grasped or made available by the Bible. Even biblical narrative with its bold bid to trace God's movements amidst the contingencies of human history acknowledges this limit: God is disclosed through story as hidden and untamable. In these texts we are encountered by the One we cannot name, summon, or control.[80]

Preachers know this too: no matter how important they think themselves to be, no matter how prestigious a pulpit they occupy or how impressive their professional credentials, God does not simply "show up" when summoned. Simply speaking the right words—however eloquently—does not make God "happen" for the hearers. Human language, even inspired language, does no more than bear witness to a divine reality that cannot be controlled or otherwise manipulated by mere words. The assent of faith can therefore never be coerced, whether by sacred texts, the church as an institution, or its preachers, any more than God coerces assent by means of the burning bush or the cross of Christ. Accordingly, Ricoeur characterizes revelation itself as

---

79. Ricoeur, "Toward a Hermeneutic of the Idea of Revelation," in *Essays on Biblical Interpretation*, 93–94.

80. Pape, *A Ricoeurian Revision*, 130.

"nonviolent appeal."[81] In Ricoeur's philosophy as in a theology of the cross, to speak of God requires us to speak in the same manner as God speaks, by bearing witness in a manner that respects the absolute freedom of every hearer to decide for themselves, as well as God's own absolute freedom to employ such speech in bestowing life.

Still, even though we each retain the power to determine our own response, it is not as if in preaching and hearing sermons we can pronounce a final sentence with regard to the things of God, as though the very "reality" of God were dependent on the decision of the hearers or even the authenticity of those who testify. It may appear so on the surface, or from a merely subjective point of view: "Works and signs are open to judgment. The absolute itself is on trial."[82] Yet hearers are not called to adjudicate between equally valid alternatives: as Ricoeur puts it, "It is always necessary to choose between the false witness and the true witness, between the father of lies and the faithful witness."[83]

Ricoeur's emphasis on divine initiative, divine self-reference, the objective character of divine revelation, and God's calling of humanity to decide between truth and idols, means that in the process of making our decision we reveal *ourselves* for who we really are. In weighing testimony that concerns God, we judge ourselves, and find ourselves judged. This is the ultimate significance and profound responsibility of Christian proclamation, for preachers and hearers alike. John Webster explains further:

> Setting aside darkness and turning to the light are not within the competence of readers (theories of readerly virtue usually trip at this point). To discern the light of God is to discern that which itself gives the possibility of its own discernment. We see light in God's light. Interpretation of the clear word of God is not therefore first of all an act of clarification but the event of being clarified. Reading, therefore, always includes a humbling of the reader, a breaking of the will in which there is acted out the struggle to detach our apprehension of the text from the idolatrous schemas that we inevitably take to it, and by which we seek to command or suppress it or render it convenient to us.[84]

The decision facing those who receive this testimony to the saving work of God—whether in the history of Israel or Jesus of Nazareth—concerns more

---

81. Ricoeur, "Toward a Hermeneutic of the Idea of Revelation," in *Essays on Biblical Interpretation*, 95.

82. Ricoeur, "Hermeneutics of Testimony," 146.

83. Ibid., Ricoeur, "Philosophy and Religious Language," 81.

84. Webster, "Biblical Theology and the Clarity of Scripture," 379.

than the object of our worship, a choice between the God of Abraham and various idolatrous alternatives. As Ricoeur indicates, what is at stake is the idolatry of our own discernment, which entails a choice between defining the world we inhabit on our own terms or submitting instead to life, human identity, even discernment itself, as defined and given by God.

In this respect the content of such testimony again determines not only the manner in which it is given (respecting the absolute freedom of the recipient) but also the conditions of its reception (requiring renunciation of the idolatry of autonomous human existence). In other words, preaching that bears witness to God's gift of new life will only be understood by those who are willing to receive that life on its own terms, as a gift that replaces all other accounts of human existence and turns absolutely toward God. Likewise, if it is faithful to the source and content of its own testimony, preaching that bears witness to God as the source of life will do so humbly and graciously, knowing that its own words are *no more than testimony*. Preaching that bears witness to the life of God will acknowledge God—not preachers or preaching—to be the only source of that life.

For this reason we are wise to be cautious about any assertion of homiletical "authority." According to Long,

> The witness image emphasizes the authority of the preacher in a new way. The preacher as witness is not authoritative because of rank or power but because of what the preacher has seen and heard.[85]

Florence concurs:

> Preaching in the tradition of testimony shifts the locus of authority away from the ministerial office and places it with the one who testifies: that is, the one who has seen and believed the liberating power of God's Word, and who then risks proclaiming the truth of the gospel.[86]

But as we have seen, there is an important difference between finding authority in "the word of the cross" and attributing authority to the one who proclaims it. If we are to have authority in the pulpit, it will be all the authority of a naked, broken, would-be Messiah, one slowly gasping out his last breath while soldiers mock and gamble to pass the time. "What the preacher has seen and heard" is in fact a spectacle so "low and despised" as to bring all things to nothing—preachers and sermons included—"so that no one might boast in the presence of God" (1 Cor 1:28–29). This being so, the

85. Long, *The Witness of Preaching*, 47.
86. Florence, *Preaching as Testimony*, xxvi.

specifically cruciform dimensions of Christian testimony will require more detailed examination.

"GOD IS MY WITNESS": TESTIMONY AND DIVINE CORROBORATION IN CHRISTIAN PREACHING

For all the complexity of Ricoeur's thought (to say nothing of Augustine and Barth), the argument to this point may be summarized in comparatively simple terms: preaching that bears faithful witness to the life of God is itself conditioned by the nature of that life. In this all three thinkers concur: the content, manner, method, even the reception of human testimony concerning God all necessarily engage the human witnesses in the reality they behold, and of which they speak. Human testimony concerning God responds and therefore corresponds to divine self-testimony, which provides both language and narrative in the record of Scripture, thereby making it possible for us to speak about God. Christians testify that God's ultimate self-testimony comes in the person of Jesus of Nazareth, whom John calls the Λόγος, the incarnate "Word" who provides the key to the meaning of all things. Christian preaching in particular must therefore conform to the testimony of Jesus, whether in the details of his teaching about the reign and "kingdom" of God, or in the pattern of experience indicated by his death and resurrection. Just as Jesus' parables bear witness to "the Scriptures [and] the power of God," so the preacher's testimony to the life of God is both inspired and given shape by divine self-testimony in the person of the one with whom the parables originate. Above all, because of the cross, this means that we can pray for, point to, and proclaim the transforming power that comes from God, but we ourselves simply cannot (with apologies to Patrick Stewart's Captain Picard) "make it so."

Compounding the necessary powerlessness—spiritual impotence, even—of the preacher is the problem of historical distance. This is not only a matter of historical distance between the modern reader and an ancient text, but also one of separation between the original events and every subsequent audience, a separation implied by the need for witnesses. Likewise drawing on Ricoeur, Nancy Lammers Gross puts it this way:

> The situation with which we are faced is that "the Gospel itself has become a text, a letter. As a text, it expresses a difference and a distance, however minimal, from the event that it proclaims." Put simply, Scripture is not the Christ event. Scripture is the witness to the Christ event.[87]

As Ricoeur explains, "We ourselves are no longer those witnesses who have seen. We are the hearers who listen to the witnesses: *fides ex auditu*."[88] The text he quotes in Latin is from Romans 10:17 ("So *faith comes from what is heard*, and what is heard comes through the word of Christ"), where the apostle has in mind a preached or spoken word ($\dot{\rho}\tilde{\eta}\mu\alpha$), in this case the message preached by the messengers of Christ. Whether, then, we take our cue from Paul of Tarsus or Paul Ricoeur, it would appear that, in effect, the testimony of Scripture—and all the more so preaching—stands between us and Christ; indeed that we receive the revelation of God's incarnate Word only second or third hand, at one remove or more from the real thing. This would seem to require of us not only faith in Christ himself, but faith in the biblical writers who bear witness to Christ, faith also in those who expound and preach the Scriptures, in an ever-extending sequence throughout the history of the church that increasingly separates us from the source and object of our faith. Rather than serving as the sole mediator between God and humanity (1 Tim 2:5), it would appear that Christ himself must be endlessly mediated.

Yet this view of testimony contradicts not only a fundamental component of Christian soteriology, but also the nature of the Christian message itself. For as Ricoeur himself acknowledges, "The kerygma is not first of all the interpretation of a text; it is the announcement of a person. In this sense, the word of God is, not the Bible, but Jesus Christ."[89] Whereas preaching concerns the testimony of Scripture, the gospel message concerns Jesus of Nazareth; as William Willimon astutely notes, "God's Word became a person before God's words became a book."[90] Ricoeur's own resolution of this dilemma is characteristically nuanced:

> To decipher Scripture is to decipher the witness of the apostolic community. We are related to the object of its faith through the confession of its faith. Hence, by understanding its witness, I

---

87. Gross, *If You Cannot Preach*, 62, quoting Ricoeur, "Preface to Bultmann," 56.
88. Ricoeur, "Preface to Bultmann," 54; quoted in Gross, *If You Cannot Preach*, 62.
89. Ibid.
90. Willimon, *Undone By Easter*, 17.

receive equally, in its witness, what is summons, kerygma, "the good news."[91]

In this sense, he says, the significance of the biblical text far exceeds the literal meaning of the words it contains. Should Scripture and preaching seem to stand between us and the historical experience to which they bear witness, the fact that they function as *testimony*, as a proclamation of the "good news," nonetheless summons and directs us parabolically beyond the words themselves to the object of that testimony, to Christ himself. As Lammers Gross notes (with considerable finesse), the implication of Ricoeur's proposal is that preaching and hearing sermons is about far more than the interpretation of Scripture, narrowly understood. Because the testimony of the text bears witness to something greater than itself,

> *the text has the potential and power to disclose to the interpreter a world of its own.* . . . *The text literally means more than it says, and points beyond itself to the world to which it refers. The text has the potential to open up to us this new world.*[92]

Leaving all the philosophers, theologians, and theorists behind, the shorthand version of this conviction could be stated in the basic assertion that "God speaks to us through Scripture in the power of the Holy Spirit."[93] Indeed, closer examination of the preaching of the earliest church as a model for all Christian preaching suggests that the active testimony of God's Spirit does not come to an end with the closing of the biblical canon.

"YOU ARE WITNESSES OF THESE THINGS": TESTIMONY IN THE NEW TESTAMENT

> The Church's witness will always be subordinate to the Spirit's. It is less that we do the witnessing and He confirms our testimony, than that He bears the witness and we corroborate His.[94]

Read in too narrow a sense, the idea of preaching as testimony suggests that for the present moment, between the definitive self-testimony of Jesus' life, death, and resurrection, and the final vindication of that testimony in

---

91. Ricoeur, "Preface to Bultmann," 56; quoted by Gross, *If You Cannot Preach*, 62–63.

92. Gross, *If You Cannot Preach*, 101–2 (emphasis original).

93. Ibid., 102.

94. Stott, *Our Guilty Silence*, 57. This quotation was brought to my attention by Matt Lowe.

"We Speak of What We Know and Testify to What We Have Seen"

eschatological triumph, preachers are more or less on their own. They may look back in faith and forward in hope—possibly also upwards in prayer—but that is all. Although the following survey offers only a partial account of "testimony" as a theological theme in the New Testament, the Gospel of John, the book of Acts, the Epistles of Paul, and the Letter to the Hebrews all suggest that something more is underway in the preaching moment.[95] The testimony of the apostles suggests that preachers also do well to look around, in expectation of God at work even now in their midst, for they are not left to their own devices in bearing witness to the power of divine life.

The Book of Acts

According to Luke, the disciples' testimony to Jesus is a characteristically postresurrection activity. During his lifetime, Jesus sends out his closest followers "to proclaim the kingdom of God and to heal" (Luke 9:2), but the only "testimony" Luke mentions refers to the dust they must shake off their feet as they leave any village that rejects them (Luke 9:5 // Mark 6:11). Luke likewise shares with the other synoptic evangelists Jesus' prediction that the coming persecution will provide the disciples with "opportunity to testify" (Matt 10:18 // Mark 13:9 // Luke 21:13). Both prospects and contexts are altogether negative. But this changes in the final chapter of his Gospel, where Luke recounts Jesus' explanation of how the testimony of "the law of Moses, the prophets, and the psalms" concerning him has now been fulfilled, and that the disciples' task is henceforth to proclaim forgiveness in his name, beginning from Jerusalem. "You are witnesses [μάρτυρες] of these things," he declares (Luke 24:44–48). The Acts of the Apostles opens on a similar note, with Jesus' final words prior to him being taken from their sight: "'You will receive power when the Holy Spirit has come upon you; and you will be my witnesses [καὶ ἔσεσθέ μου μάρτυρες] in Jerusalem, in all Judea and Samaria, and to the ends of the earth'" (Acts 1:8). Although Pauline theology (e.g., 1 Cor 6:20, 7:23) might encourage reading a possessive genitive here, an objective genitive is more likely: it is not that they "belong" to him but rather that the risen Messiah is the object of their testimony (as later in the case of Jesus' words to Paul, Acts 22:18, 23:11: περὶ ἐμοῦ).

Throughout Acts, language that concerns "attestation," "testifying," and "testimony" (διαμαρτύρεσθαι, μαρτυρεῖν, μαρτυρία, μάρτυς) sometimes entails juridical intent, in particular with regard to Paul's several trials and

---

95. One significant omission is any discussion of "testimony" in the book of Revelation, on which see, e.g., the summary in Osborne, *Revelation*, 56–57; or, for a more theological analysis, Finamore, *God, Order, and Chaos*, 135–40.

speeches in self-defense (so Acts 20:26, 22:5, 26:5; cf. Luke 22:71, Acts 6:13, 7:58). But more typically it applies to the apostolic proclamation concerning God's vindication of the crucified Messiah, as is clear already from the qualifications required for a disciple to replace Judas: "'One of these must become a *witness* with us to his resurrection'" (Acts 1:22). Just so, testimony to the resurrection is a consistent keynote of the preaching of the apostles, beginning with Peter's first sermon on the day of Pentecost:

> "David spoke of the resurrection of the Messiah, saying, 'He was not abandoned to Hades, nor did his flesh experience corruption' [Ps 16:10]. This Jesus God raised up, and of that *all of us are witnesses*. Being therefore exalted at the right hand of God, and having received from the Father the promise of the Holy Spirit, he has poured out this that you both see and hear.... Therefore let the entire house of Israel know with certainty that God has made him both Lord and Messiah, this Jesus whom you crucified."
>
> (Acts 2:31–33, 36)

This exposition of events links three broad considerations: first, that God has vindicated the crucified Jesus by raising him to new life, in fulfillment of Scripture; second, that the Spirit of God is poured out as an expression and outcome of this vindication; third, that the apostles are witnesses (μάρτυρες) of and to the resurrection. More comprehensively, the concept of "witness" applies to this passage in at least seven different ways: 1) Scripture testifies in advance to the vindication of the Messiah; 2) the Father in turn bears witness by raising Jesus from death; 3) Jesus himself gives evidence of his exaltation and authority by pouring out the gift of the Spirit; 4) the apostles witness Jesus alive once more and 5) receive experiential testimony to this fact in the form of the Spirit resting upon and empowering them; 6) crowds of devout onlookers witness (but misunderstand) this unexpected outpouring; as a result of which 7) Peter (and soon other apostles with him) bear verbal witness to the true meaning of all that has transpired in their midst.

Thus the apostles are not alone in bearing witness to the resurrection of the Messiah. Even when Luke writes of the apostles testifying on the basis of personal experience, they do so as part of a larger theological and narrative whole, as in the case of Peter's sermon to the assembly at Caesarea:

> "God anointed Jesus of Nazareth with the Holy Spirit and with power ... he went about doing good and healing all who were

> oppressed by the devil, for God was with him. *We are witnesses* [μάρτυρες] to all that he did both in Judea and in Jerusalem. They put him to death by hanging him on a tree; but God raised him on the third day and allowed him to appear, not to all the people but to us who were *chosen by God as witnesses* [μάρτυρες], and who ate and drank with him after he rose from the dead. He commanded us to preach to the people and *to testify* [διαμαρτύρασθαι] that he is the one ordained by God as judge of the living and the dead. All the prophets *testify* [μαρτυροῦσιν] about him that everyone who believes in him receives forgiveness of sins through his name." While Peter was still speaking, the Holy Spirit fell upon all who heard the word.
>
> (Acts 10:38–44)

In this passage, first, the apostles are said to be witnesses both of Jesus' preresurrection ministry and, by virtue of divine election, to his resurrection (10:39, 41). Second, juridical language once more establishes a parallel between the role of Scripture (the prophets in particular, 10:43) and that of the apostles (10:42) in testifying to the work of the Messiah, even though the content of that testimony is not quite the same in each case. Third, the cognates μαρτυρ (both forms meaning to testify, serve as a witness) and διαμαρτύρεσθαι (to attest, solemnly declare) are used in parallel and as virtual synonyms (similarly Acts 23:11, 26:22–23).[96] Fourth, just as "the Holy Spirit and . . . power" accompany the ministry of Jesus, so Peter's preaching is confirmed in similar fashion: "the Holy Spirit fell upon all who heard the word" (10:44). This divine attestation creates new testimony in its wake, as the narrative juxtaposes "Gentiles" on one side, in whom the power of the Spirit is manifested, with "circumcised believers" on the other, whose role is to hear, observe, and thereby confirm—even with astonishment—this surprising attestation:

> The circumcised believers who had come with Peter were astounded that the gift of the Holy Spirit had been poured out even on the Gentiles, for they heard them speaking in tongues and extolling God.
>
> (Acts 10:45–46)

Because this is once more a matter of divine initiative, Peter's Jewish-Christian companions find that they must conform their own testimony to the testimony of the Spirit. This is the force of Peter's rhetorical question:

---

96. On the overlapping semantic domains of these terms, see L&N §33.223, 262–63.

"Can anyone *withhold* water for baptizing these people who have received the Holy Spirit just as we have?" (10:47). As with every work of the Holy Spirit from the day of Pentecost onwards, these witnesses, far from having the freedom to craft convincing arguments of their own, find themselves constrained by the divine initiative that has overtaken them.

The apostles "testify" (διαμαρτύρεσθαι; Acts 2:40; 8:25; 18:5; 20:21, 24) and "exhort" (παρεκάλεῖν; 2:40); they "speak the word of the Lord" and "proclaim the good news" (εὐηγγελίζειν; 8:25 cf. 18:5); they are "witnesses" (μάρτυρες; 3:15, 13:31) to Jesus' resurrection by virtue of firsthand experience: the various terms overlap to a large extent. Not infrequently their preaching takes the form of biblical exposition, appealing to the testimony of the prophets (10:43, 15:15) or, in Paul's case, the law of Moses and the prophets alike (28:23).[97] Paul too testifies concerning Jesus' messianic identity (18:5) and "the kingdom of God" (28:23), bearing witness to "the good news of God's grace" (20:24). But having encountered the Risen Lord for himself, he can present eyewitness testimony of his own. Defending himself before the hostile crowds in Jerusalem, the apostle reports Ananias' words to him soon after his conversion:

> "The God of our ancestors has chosen you to know his will, to see the Righteous One and to hear his own voice; for you will be his witness [μάρτυς] to all the world of *what you have seen and heard.*"
>
> (Acts 22:14–15)

In the same context, the apostle recounts having confessed to the risen Messiah his own complicity in "the blood of your witness [τοῦ μάρτυρός σου] Stephen" (Acts 22:20). Here the choice between objective and possessive genitives is less clear, as both senses seem fitting. But even more important is the designation of Stephen as a "witness." Notwithstanding the fact that Stephen is "full of faith and the Holy Spirit" (Acts 6:5), and preaches the longest sermon by far in the entire book (Acts 7:2–53), he never actually mentions the resurrection of Jesus. His testimony is not like that of disciples who knew Jesus' earthly ministry or "ate and drank with him after he rose from the dead" (Acts 10:40), but more immediately visionary:

> Filled with the Holy Spirit, he gazed into heaven and saw the glory of God and Jesus standing at the right hand of God. "Look," he said, "I see the heavens opened and the Son of Man standing at the right hand of God!"

---

97. Trites, *The New Testament Concept of Witness*, 147–48.

(Acts 7:55-56)

In other words, he is a "witness" in precisely the same sense as is Paul, one whose experience of Jesus, while personal, is nonetheless entirely mystical and eschatological.[98]

Paul offers King Agrippa an even more detailed account of his conversion:

> I asked, "Who are you, Lord?" The Lord answered, "I am Jesus whom you are persecuting. But get up and stand on your feet; for *I have appeared to you* for this purpose, to appoint you to serve and testify to the things *in which you have seen me* and to those *in which I will appear to you*."

(Acts 26:15-16)

On such a view, apostolic testimony to resurrection concerns not only the forty days of Acts 1:3 but—unless the experience of Paul and Stephen is assumed to be unique—an ongoing series of encounters with the risen Lord. Luke's introduction to the second of his two volumes implies as much: "In my former book, Theophilus, I wrote about all that Jesus *began* to do and to teach, until the day he was taken up to heaven" (Acts 1:1–2). That is, the words and deeds of the Messiah do not cease at the conclusion of his earthly ministry.[99] At least in the book of Acts, then, the church's testimony *to* Jesus arises from their ongoing experience *of* Jesus, of being encountered *by* Jesus.

Summarizing the argument to this point, Barth and Ricoeur agree that human testimony to the works of God is initiated by the testimony of the works themselves, which constitutes divine self-testimony. Moreover, as the definitive record of the testimony of God, Scripture provides both language and conceptual categories that make it possible for us to speak faithfully about God. In terms of human responsibility for preaching, Augustine and the African American homiletical tradition concur that our language about God is empty without divine anointing and empowerment. But the biblical record further indicates that after all human testimony falls silent, God has the last word. This is so not just with respect to the eschatological completion of all things, but also in the more immediate sense that having first initiated a human witness to the ways of God, God acts once more to confirm it. Luke's editorial summary in Acts 4:33 implies as much: "With *great power* [δυνάμει μεγάλῃ] the apostles give their testimony [μαρτύριον] to the resurrection of the Lord Jesus, and great grace was upon them all." Throughout

---

98. Similarly ibid., 132.
99. Longenecker, *Acts*, 253.

the book of Acts, "power" consistently refers to the work of God, and in particular that of the Holy Spirit. Jesus—"a man attested . . . by God with deeds of power [δυνάμεσι], wonders, and signs that God did through him" (2:22; similarly 10:38)—thus tells the disciples, "You will receive power [δύναμιν] when the Holy Spirit has come upon you" (1:8). Signs and works of "power" subsequently accompany the ministries of Stephen (6:8), Philip (8:13), and Paul (19:11). Both "power" and "grace" are categories that indicate immediate divine affirmation of the message that they preach.

Luke refers more specifically to the confirming agency of the Holy Spirit, as in the case of Peter preaching before the Sanhedrin:

> "The God of our ancestors raised up Jesus, whom you had killed by hanging him on a tree. God exalted him at his right hand as Leader and Savior that he might give repentance to Israel and forgiveness of sins. And we are witnesses to these things, *and so is the Holy Spirit whom God has given to those who obey him.*"
>
> (Acts 5:30–32)

This passage juxtaposes the role of the Spirit with that of the apostles. Although Peter does not specify the content or manner of either testimony, the same role for both may imply a concrete set of actions on the part of the Spirit that would match the apostles' verbal proclamation. Later, in Peter's address to the Jerusalem council, God's gift of the Spirit itself constitutes the substance of the divine witness:

> After there had been much debate, Peter stood up and said to them, "My brothers, you know that in the early days God made a choice among you, that I should be the one through whom the Gentiles would hear the message of the good news and become believers. And God, who knows the human heart, testified [ἐμαρτύρησεν] to them *by giving them the Holy Spirit,* just as he did to us . . ."
>
> (Acts 15:7–8)

In yet another passage, this time a summary of the ministry of Paul and Barnabas at Iconium, the testimony of signs and wonders is identified as a work not of the Holy Spirit, but of the risen Lord:

> So they remained for a long time, speaking boldly for the Lord, who testified [τῷ μαρτυροῦντι] to the word of his grace by granting signs and wonders to be done through them.
>
> (Acts 14:3)

Thus, according to the Acts of the Apostles, the Father testifies to the authenticity of the church's preaching by bestowing the gift of the Spirit; the Son testifies by granting signs and wonders; the Holy Spirit testifies by works of "power," all thereby confirming the apostolic testimony that Jesus' resurrection has initiated. To set apostolic preaching within its most comprehensive theological context, God bears self-witness first in the history of Israel, then in the sending and empowering of the Son, above all by raising him from inglorious death; the church bears witness to this vindication in its proclamation of Christ; thereupon God affirms the church's witness both in the gift of the Holy Spirit and by works of healing and power that the Spirit accomplishes in its midst. With this final confirmation, divine self-testimony comes full circle.

The Gospel of John

Characterizing the divine gift of salvation and life on the one hand, and the human ministry that it inaugurates on the other, as complementary forms of testimony is by no means unique to Luke or the theology of Acts. The theology of testimony is also central, for example, to the Gospel of John.[100] The previous chapter of our study began with a discussion of Jesus' dependence on the will of the Father in the fourth Gospel. Among the passages considered in that earlier context was John 5:30, where the RSV inserts a reference to Jesus' "authority" even though there is no equivalent term in the original Greek: "'I can do nothing on my own *authority*; as I hear, I judge; and my judgment is just, because I seek not my own will but the will of him who sent me.'"[101] In fact, Jesus goes on to speak not of authority but of the "testimony" (μαρτυρία) that validates his ministry. Such testimony, he says, takes three different forms, each originating with a different source:

> "If I testify about myself, my testimony is not true. There is another who testifies on my behalf, and I know that his testimony to me is true. You sent messengers to John, and he testified to the truth. Not that I accept such human testimony, but I say these things so that you may be saved. . . . But I have a testimony greater than John's. The works that the Father has given me to complete, the very works that I am doing, testify on my behalf

---

100. According to Trites, "The idea of witness in John's Gospel is both very prominent and thoroughly juridical, and is to be understood in terms of Old Testament legal language" (*New Testament Concept of Witness*, 80; argued in detail 78–124).

101. Compare GNT: "I can do nothing on my own authority"; NASB: "I can do nothing on My own initiative."

> that the Father has sent me. And the Father who sent me has himself testified on my behalf.... You search the scriptures because you think that in them you have eternal life; and it is they that testify on my behalf."
>
> (John 5:31–34, 36–37, 39)

Preceding his ministry in one form, he says, is the testimony of Scripture (cf. 1:45, 5:46, 12:41), in another that of John the Baptist, who was sent by the Father (1:6) and "came as a *witness* to testify to the light, so that all might believe through him. He himself was not the light, but he came to *testify* to the light" (John 1:7–8; cf. 1:15, 32–34). Likewise Jesus' works of healing, insofar as they relied on and demonstrated the power of God, represent another form of divine testimony; as he subsequently reiterates, "The works that I do in my Father's name testify to me" (John 10:25; cf. 14:11). And it is at least possible that verse 37—"the Father who sent me has himself testified on my behalf"—represents yet a fourth kind of witness, as Brown contends, whether the testimony of the Father refers to the events of Sinai or those of Jesus' baptism (cf. 1:32–34), or to an internal testimony of the Spirit. In any event, as Brown observes, "It is important to stress that the four witnesses are, in Jesus' mind, only four different aspects of the witness of 'Another,' that is, the Father, on his behalf."[102]

Later Jesus will essentially contradict himself by offering testimony on his own behalf, even though this reversal elicits condemnation from his opponents (John 8:13). His reason for doing so, he explains, is self-knowledge, as well as his knowledge of the Father:

> Jesus answered, "Even if I testify on my own behalf, my testimony is valid because I know where I have come from and where I am going, but you do not know where I come from or where I am going."
>
> (John 8:14; cf. 3:32)

In what manner does Jesus bear witness to his own identity? Most likely in the seven declarations of his messianic character ("I am the living bread," "I am the light of the world," "I am the vine," etc.), as well as by using the construction ἐγώ εἰμι in a more absolute sense (e.g., John 8:58: "Before Abraham was, I am").[103] In this regard he simply adds his testimony to that of the Father: as he responds to those who challenge him, "'In your own Law it is

---

102. Brown, *John I–XII*, 227–28.
103. On these references, see ibid., 533–38 and Beasley-Murray, *John*, 89–90.

written that the testimony of two witnesses is true. I am one who testifies for myself; my other witness is the Father, who sent me'" (John 8:17–18 TNIV).

As much in this Gospel as in the book of Acts, therefore, the ability to bear witness concerning Jesus' true identity is based on personal experience. Jesus explains to Nicodemus, "We speak of what we know and testify to what we have seen" (John 3:11). Why he employs the first person plural remains a matter of debate (is Jesus referring to the Father, or to his disciples?),[104] but however it was originally intended, this declaration expresses a principle that is basic to all forms of "testimony" in John. At least implicit here is the mutual knowledge of Father and Son, as of the Messiah and his disciples: "I know my own and my own know me, just as the Father knows me and I know the Father" (John 10:14–15). That the witness of the Spirit arises out of similar intimacy is underscored by Jesus' reiteration, immediately following, of the basis for the disciples' testimony:

> "When the Advocate comes, whom I will send to you from the Father, the Spirit of truth who comes from the Father, he will testify on my behalf. You also are to testify *because you have been with me from the beginning.*"
>
> (John 15:26–27)

The title "Advocate" or "Counselor" (παράκλητος) can sometimes have the sense of "legal advisor," although in John's gospel the role of the Spirit is more one of consolation and confirmation. But these various senses are not exclusive of one another; according to Brown,

> The Paraclete is a *witness* in defense of Jesus and a *spokesman* for him in the context of his trial by his enemies; the Paraclete is a *consoler* of the disciples for he takes Jesus' place among them; the Paraclete is a teacher and guide of the disciples and thus their *helper*.[105]

As distinct from the testimony of Jesus' own words and works, the Paraclete bears witness initially by teaching the disciples and recalling Jesus' instructions: "The Advocate, the Holy Spirit, whom the Father will send in my name, will teach you everything, and remind you of all that I have said to you" (John 14:26; cf. 16:13–15). But in addition, the discourse in chapter 15 concerns testimony directed outwards, toward a hostile and unreceptive "world" that is unlikely to be persuaded by the words of the disciples alone. Here both in content and in execution the testimony of the disciples

---

104. Brown, *John I-XII*, 132.
105. Brown, *John XIII-XXI*, 1135–43; here, 1137 (emphasis original).

depends on divine initiative, first in the sense that their message concerns Jesus (not themselves), and second in the fact that their witness follows and takes its cue from that of the Spirit: "the Spirit of truth . . . will testify on my behalf. You also are to testify." Lesslie Newbigin points out that according to this passage the testimony of the Spirit functions in a distinctly cruciform manner:

> It is important to note what is not said. It is not said that the Spirit will help the disciple to bear witness. That would make the action of the disciples primary and that of the Spirit auxiliary. What is said is that the Spirit will bear witness and that—secondarily—the disciples are witnesses. . . . What is promised here is that the Spirit will perform His own miracle in the hearts and consciences of people so that they are brought to recognize Jesus as the one he is. The words, the works, and—above all—the sufferings of the community will be the means by which the witness is borne, but the actual agent will be the Spirit who, because he is the Spirit of the Father, is the Spirit of truth. . . . The promise . . . made to the Church which shares in the tribulation and humiliation of Jesus . . . is that, exactly in this tribulation and humiliation, the mighty Spirit of God will bear his own witness to the crucified Jesus as Lord and Giver of life.[106]

The fourth Gospel thus shares with Acts a proto-Trinitarian understanding of divine testimony, as Father, Son, and Holy Spirit again concur in bearing witness to Jesus' messianic identity.[107] They also share a common emphasis on the witness of Scripture, and of Jesus' works of power. On the human side of the equation, just as John the Baptist prepared the way beforehand, so the Johannine disciples will add their voices to this multidimensional testimony, as does the writer of the Gospel in compiling his narrative (so John 19:35, 21:24). Indeed, to the extent that this Gospel emphasizes Jesus' divine identity, John the Evangelist bears witness of his own to the power and meaning of the resurrection. In contrast to Acts, however, the fourth Gospel lacks any mention of God offering testimony that confirms apostolic preaching. Yet this dynamic is once more operative both in Pauline theology (as emerged from our previous discussion of Galatians and the Corinthian correspondence) and in the letter to the Hebrews.

---

106. Newbigin, *The Light Has Come*, 206–8, quoted in Johnson, *The Glory of Preaching*, 242–43.

107. Again in 1 John 5:6–11, the Father bears witness by bestowing eternal life (v. 11), the Son "by water and blood" (vv. 6, 8), and the Spirit (apparently) by testifying to the truth (v. 7). However, this passage is extraordinarily complex and hence controverted: for full discussion see Brown, *The Epistles of John*, 573–99.

Paul and the Letter to the Hebrews

To recapitulate and expand the results of our previous investigation, divine affirmation of Paul's preaching in Galatia took the form of God pouring out the Holy Spirit, on the one hand, and working "miracles," on the other (Gal 3:5). Indeed, as Paul tells the Corinthians, "signs and wonders and mighty works" are "the signs of a true apostle" (2 Cor 12:12). This is nowhere clearer than in the summary of his ministry that Paul offers to the church at Rome (quoted earlier), according to which preaching of the gospel, "signs and wonders," and the power of the Holy Spirit all function in concert:

> I will not venture to speak of anything except what Christ has wrought through me ... by word and deed, by the power of signs and wonders, by the power of the Holy Spirit, so that from Jerusalem and as far round as Illyricum I have fully preached the gospel of Christ.
>
> (Rom 15:18–19 RSV)

Paul's appeal to ἀπόδειξις ("demonstration" or "proof") serves in much the same way: "My speech and my proclamation were not with plausible words of wisdom, but with a *demonstration* of the Spirit and of power" (1 Cor 2:4). The Corinthian believers, he says, having been converted under his ministry, are proof enough of this principle: "You show that you are a letter from Christ delivered by us, written not with ink but with the Spirit of the living God, not on tablets of stone but on tablets of human hearts" (2 Cor 3:3 RSV). Similarly, writing to the church at Thessalonica, Paul recalls how evidence of the Holy Spirit at work in his preaching confirmed both the truth of the gospel message and God's favor upon its hearers:

> For we know, brothers and sisters beloved by God, that he has chosen you, *because* [ὅτι] our message of the gospel came to you not in word only, but also in power and in the Holy Spirit and with full conviction.
>
> (1 Thess 1:4–5)

Still, the concept and language of "testimony" are not entirely absent from the letters of Paul. Like the Gospel of John and the apostles in Acts, he too speaks of preaching about Jesus' resurrection in the language of the law court:

> If Christ has not been raised, our preaching is useless and so is your faith. More than that, we are then found to be false

witnesses [ψευδομάρτυρες] about God, for we have testified [ἐμαρτυρήσαμεν] about God that he raised Christ from the dead.

(1 Cor 15:15 TNIV)

Just so, he summarizes the gospel that he preaches as "testimony [τὸ μαρτύριον]" that gives rise to faith (1 Thess 1:10; cf. 2 Tim 1:8). Likewise he describes the work of the Spirit as bearing internal witness to the work of new creation in the life of the believer: "When we cry, 'Abba! Father!' it is that very Spirit bearing witness [συμμαρτυρεῖ] with our spirit that we are children of God" (Rom 8:15-16; cf. 9:1). For Paul, then, both the internal testimony of the Spirit and evidence of divine "power" that attends apostolic preaching serve to confirm the message of new life made available through the death and resurrection of Jesus.

Warning against the dangers of apostasy, the letter to the Hebrews offers a closely similar account of the message of salvation:

> It was declared at first by the Lord, and it was attested to us by those who heard him, while God also *bore witness* [συνεπιμαρτυροῦντος] by signs and wonders and various miracles and by gifts of the Holy Spirit distributed according to his own will.
>
> (Heb 2:3-4 RSV)

Here, then, are three aspects or sources of testimony. First, the Lord Jesus testifies to the salvation that he brings (so Hebrews 1:2: "in these last days [God] has spoken to us by a Son"); second, those who witnessed this testimony firsthand verify what they have heard; third, God offers a confirmatory witness by means of miraculous acts, as well as by the gift and gifts of the Spirit. Ceslas Spicq suggests that rather than specifying different kinds of divine action, "signs," "wonders," and "miracles" in this passage represent in turn the manifestation, nature, and origin of such proofs.[108] But the distinction is not so clear cut: reference to "signs and wonders" (σημείοις . . . καὶ τέρασιν) indicates that the experiences in question point in principle beyond themselves (all the more so as this phrase alludes to Israel's deliverance from Egypt), while reference to "miracles" or "works of power" (δυνάμεις) denotes their supernatural origin and agency.[109] The text makes no direct mention of spiritual "gifts," but refers instead to "divisions/distributions of the Holy Spirit according to his [i.e., God's] will"

---

108. Spicq, *L'Épitre aux Hébreux*, 68.

109. So Rengstorf, *s.v.* σημεῖον κτλ, *TDNT* 7, 241-43 (with reference to Acts); 260 (for Hebrews); and Rengstorf, *s.v.* τέρας, *TDNT* 8, 125; cf. L&N 33.477, 480; 76.7.

"We Speak of What We Know and Testify to What We Have Seen" 175

(Heb 2:4). While particular charisms are no doubt intended, the passage as a whole indicates the multiplication and variety of forms of divine testimony: signs, wonders, miracles, and gifts or evidences of the Spirit together bear witness to the power of God.

Several chapters later, summarizing the argument of the book as a whole, Hebrews again cites the testimony of the Holy Spirit:

> For by a single offering he [Christ] has perfected for all time those who are sanctified. And *the Holy Spirit also bears witness* [μαρτυρεῖ] to us; for after saying, "This is the covenant that I will make with them after those days, says the Lord: I will put my laws in their hearts, and I will write them on their minds," then he adds, "I will remember their sins and their misdeeds no longer."
>
> (Heb 10:14-17 RSV)

In this case, the witness of the Spirit is recorded in Scripture, in the words of Jeremiah 31:33-34 in particular.[110] This second appeal to the Spirit reveals a theology of divine and human testimony as multifaceted as in Luke or Paul: as implied already by the opening lines ("Long ago God spoke to our ancestors . . . by the prophets, but in these last days he has spoken to us by a Son," Heb 1:1-2), first the Spirit at work in the prophets and the sacred text, then Christ himself bears witness; next comes apostolic proclamation, followed by preachers and teachers such as the writer to the Hebrews himself; their words are subsequently confirmed by an outpouring of "signs," "gifts," and other evidences of the Spirit of God.

Finally, testimony in the letter to the Hebrews includes an important eschatological dimension. For the encouragement of his readers, the author recounts a long list of those who have kept faith in the course of Israelite history, describing them as "a great cloud of witnesses" (12:1). This imagery is highly nuanced: having borne faithful witness in the past, these saints remain as onlookers, present to witness the church's faith even now. At the same time, notwithstanding an exhortation for readers to look to Jesus as the "pioneer and perfecter" of their faith (Heb 12:2), the fact that they have reached their goal and are at rest in God's presence is testimony in itself, a source of encouragement for those still on the way. Here for the purpose of exhortation rather than confirmation of the gospel, the testimony of Scripture thus incorporates past, present, and future dimensions alike.

---

110. Compare the citation of LXX Ps 8:5-7 with διεμαρτύρατο in Hebrews 2:6-8 and μαρτυρεῖται with LXX Psalm 110:4 in Hebrews 7:17 (similarly μαρτυρούμενος in 7:8), as noted by Trites, *New Testament Concept of Witness*, 217-18.

Although this brief summary by no means exhausts the New Testament evidence, and while it is important to acknowledge the distinctive theological perspectives of each document, there are nonetheless sufficient lines of continuity to suggest a broad theological trajectory with regard to the concept and language of "testimony" in the early church. Informed as well by our discussion of Augustine, Barth, Brueggemann, and Ricoeur in particular, the general contours of this perspective may be summarized as follows:

1. God is self-named and self-defined in the history of Israel; the Scriptures of Israel thus constitute a human record and witness to the self-testimony of God;

2. Definitive testimony to the reign and ways of God appears in the person of Jesus of Nazareth, whose messianic identity is attested in different ways by Hebrew Scripture, by John the Baptist, and by works of life-giving "power" that are characteristic of his ministry;

3. God offers climactic testimony to Jesus as Messiah by raising him from an ignominious death to new life;

4. The risen Jesus commissions his disciples to bear witness in turn to this vindication; whereupon,

5. Apostolic preaching testifies that God has indeed raised Jesus, making life and salvation available to all who entrust themselves to God's saving initiative;

6. The preaching of this "gospel" is attended by various forms of testimony to the power of the Holy Spirit, whether conversion itself, various "signs and wonders," or inner conviction and ongoing spiritual guidance for the benefit of believers.

In light of this summary, it is essential to recognize that the church's ministry of preaching is but a single aspect or moment within a much larger historical and theological trajectory. Preaching is not, in principle, self-initiated or self-authenticating, as though the power of the Christian message were dependent upon the abilities of those who proclaim it. Rather, the testimony that lies at the core of Christian preaching is itself initiated, sustained, and authenticated by God's ongoing attestation to the Messiah: whether in the history of Israel, the preaching of John the Baptist, the ministry of Jesus, the testimony of the resurrection itself, or in response to apostolic proclamation that bears witness to Christ. Indeed, just as every work of faithful witness stands between Jesus' first and second advent, between the inauguration of the kingdom and its glorious fulfillment, so as a microcosm of this larger theological movement preaching that testifies to his crucifixion and resurrection stands between divine testimony that initiates the church's proclamation and divine testimony that confirms it. This latter testimony takes the form of life-giving empowerment through the Holy Spirit, poured out as an eschatological pledge or guarantee (ἀρραβών; 2 Cor 1:22, 5:5; Eph 1:14) of still-greater fulfillment yet to come.

In sum, Christian testimony in general and the testimony of preaching in particular are only possible because they are first initiated and shaped by the divine testimony that precedes them, then corroborated and brought to completion by the divine testimony that ensues. How this principle governs the actual content and conduct of our own preaching will be the subject of the next and final chapter.

Chapter 6

"God's Field, God's Laborers"
Preaching as Parabolic Testimony to the Grace of God

> The secret of life is to have a task, something you devote your entire life to, something you bring everything to, every minute of the day for the rest of your life. And the most important thing is—it must be something you cannot possibly do!
>
> —Henry Moore (1898–1986)[1]

If Saint Anselm, second Norman Archbishop of Canterbury (ca. 1033–1109), comes up in discussion today, it will almost certainly be in connection with his famous treatise on the atonement, *Cur Deus Homo* (*Why God Became Human*), where he interprets Jesus' sacrifice in terms of penal substitution, as an offering that satisfies divine justice. Almost unknown is the last of his many works, *De Concordia*, or more fully, *On the Harmony of God's Foreknowledge, Predestination, and Grace with Free Choice*.[2] Anselm addresses

---

1. Quoted in Hall, *Life Work*, 54. This quotation came to my attention in Quicke, *Preaching as Worship*, 23, where the author recounts a personal meeting with Moore.

2. Subsequently quoted and noted in the text (unless otherwise indicated) from Saint Anselm, *Basic Writings*, by the abbreviated Latin title, followed by section, chapter, and page references to the translation volume. The following (simplified) account of Anselm's argument derives from Williams, "God Who Sows the Seed," 616–21.

the topics indicated by this title in three separate sections, the last of which concerns divine grace. Does it not seem, he wonders, that a passage such as John 15:5, "Without me you can do nothing," indicates grace to be essential, while other passages imply free will and freedom of choice (*De Concordia* 3.1 [374])? Since there is evidence for both in Scripture, he concludes, both must have a role to play in salvation. To explain how these two principles work together, Anselm offers an illustration from the natural world: just as the food that sustains us requires seeds and cultivation, so God sows the seeds of salvation in our hearts by means of Scripture, and cultivates them by the power of the Holy Spirit:

> So just as God in the beginning miraculously made grain and other things that sprang forth from the earth to nourish human beings, without a cultivator or seeds, so too did he wondrously make the hearts of the prophets and apostles, and indeed the Gospels, fertile with the seeds of salvation, without any human teaching. From those seeds we take whatever we sow wholesomely in "God's husbandry" [1 Cor 3:9] for the nourishment of our souls, just as what we grow for the nourishment of our bodies comes to us from the first seeds of the earth.
>
> (*De Concordia* 3.6 [381–82])

According to Anselm, we can only choose the salvation of which Scripture speaks once God has shown us the way: what grace provides, we can will to receive. Of course, for that seed to save us it must first be planted, and planting requires preachers: as Paul writes, "Faith comes by hearing, and hearing by the word of Christ" (Rom 10:17; *De Concordia* 3.6 [381]). Hearing certainly requires proper understanding, just as conversion calls for submission of the will, but these too are prompted by the Spirit of God, since—again Anselm quotes Paul—"Neither the one who plants nor the one who waters is anything, but God who gives the growth" (1 Cor 3:7; *De Concordia* 3.6 [381]).

Even though Anselm's main interest is in articulating a theology of the Holy Spirit, preaching offers a fitting example of the way in which God sows seeds of life in the human heart:

> Although God does not give growth to every seed, nevertheless our farmers do not cease to sow in the hope of some small harvest. Similarly, the soil of the human heart does not bring forth the fruit of faith and justice without the appropriate seeds. And although God does not cause all seeds of this kind to grow,

> nevertheless He commands His husbandmen to sow His word earnestly and in hope.[3]

Writing 900 years ago to a church and society vastly different from our own, the Archbishop of Canterbury speaks of preaching as an offer of divine life that relies for its power on the agency of God's Spirit in the lives of its hearers. For him the role of the Holy Spirit within the Trinity, the work of God in giving life to creation, and the transformation of human hearts by grace are all of a piece. At all three levels, in all three spheres, the power of the Spirit represents God's love, and life, in action. In the words of one interpreter,

> The same dynamism by which the Holy Spirit is life-giver within the Trinity also characterizes the Spirit's work in the economy of creation, redemption, and transformation. By planting supernatural seeds and giving them growth, the Holy Spirit vivifies all creation and thereby brings all things—but especially God's rational creatures—to their appointed end.[4]

In much the same way, our own study has sought to demonstrate that preaching concerns, above all, God's gift of life itself. Certainly this is true of Jesus' preaching in parables, for as Jesus himself explains, the key to his teaching lies in Scripture, with its testimony to God's ways, and in the recognition of God's power at work in the world. The "power" of which he speaks is not supernatural might for its own sake, but rather the life-giving vitality by which seeds sprout and vines bear rich fruit, the generous agency of grace by which God makes the sun rise and the rain fall on good and evil alike. Indeed, this same divine power is the true source of the life of God's people, from which the fertility of all their "seed"—their heritage and progeny—arises. This foundational theological premise has important implications for the way in which we interpret Jesus' teaching, his parables in particular. Rather than simply preaching *about* the parables (that is, explaining their content), preaching after the *manner and method* of Jesus' parables requires us to understand much more than the culture and society of which he spoke. Valuable and necessary as this background will be, the fact that Jesus' parables ultimately concern the "kingdom of God" directs our attention to the source of all life; the parables of growth in particular invite us to consider ways in which this life comes to expression in human experience. Clifton Black summarizes the implications of parable form for preaching better than I am able to:

---

3. *De Concordia* 3.6, quoted from Hopkins and Richardson, *Anselm of Canterbury*, 208–9.

4. Williams, "God Who Sows the Seed," 627.

> *Authentic Christian preaching may be construed as an intrinsically parabolic activity.* I do not urge that every sermon take as its text a parable, whether of Ezekiel or of Jesus. Neither am I suggesting that all preaching must create or adopt a parable, or be framed as a parabolic story, to make its point. Nor can Christian preaching be reduced to parables or to a parabolic template for homiletics. My point is not tactical but theological: namely, whatever else it may be, Christian preaching is nothing less than a life-giving encounter between human hunger and Godly nurturance.[5]

More specifically, Jesus' parables and the example of his life both testify to the same foundational principle: that life-giving vitality lies in the hand of God alone. The parables do this by speaking about strange transformations and unexpected growth, tantalizing hearers with the possibilities of God's reign. Jesus enacts the same principle, especially in John's gospel, by demonstrating a strange and profound spiritual passivity, refusing to initiate ministry or otherwise respond to the needs around him in order to wait upon the will of God, and thereby rely entirely upon God's unique empowerment when he does take action. Climactically, Jesus demonstrates his utter and unreserved dependence on the life that God gives by submitting to death, indeed a death so abased and unthinkable as to seem the very antithesis of all things divine.

What for Anselm is merely an illustration of how the Holy Spirit works within creation in some measure represents the essence of our own proposal: that the power of divine life operates in relation to preaching in the same way as seeds—animal, botanical, and human alike—were thought to function in the world of Jesus' day: we may sow, but only God can bestow the actual gift of life. More specifically, borrowing a point that Jesus and Paul both make with regard to this same gift (John 12:24, 1 Cor 15:36), preaching that intends to sow God's seeds of life must follow the pattern of Jesus' death and resurrection. Just as seeds must first be buried and "die" before they can bear fruit, so words sound lifeless and voices fall silent, even when they speak of God, apart from the divine gift of life. That preaching is a theologically "cruciform" undertaking makes "testimony" its most appropriate rhetorical form. The practical implications of this proposal will occupy the remainder of our study.

---

5. Black, "Four Stations En Route to a Parabolic Homiletic," 388 (emphasis original).

PREACHING AS PARABLE AND THE PATTERN OF THE CROSS

Our discussion began with the problem of preaching from the parables of Jesus, or rather, with three problems for preaching that the parables bring to light. The first of these is cultural or historical, concerning the social dynamics and intellectual setting of Second Temple Judaism and the ancient Mediterranean world. The second, more subtle difficulty concerns narrative and rhetoric: parables are works of metaphor and imagination, resisting our attempts at distilling from them moral principles or abstract concepts about God. In parables, nothing functions the way it should: while their settings and protagonists may seem real enough, the conclusion of these narratives is always outlandish, at times even outrageous. While the first difficulty may be overcome with only moderate effort, the second proves more challenging, for it points toward a third, explicitly theological consideration, which is the disruptive reality of God. For preachers, this insight emerges only as the product of long experience:

> Preaching on a parable is a novice preacher's dream but often an experienced preacher's nightmare. The beginning preacher walks into a parable with a confident gait, striding boldly over what appears to be familiar terrain. Parables seem so much more accessible, more "preacher friendly," than many other types of Scripture.... But the more we get to know the parables, the less confident we become of our understanding of them. As soon as we reach out to grasp a parable's seemingly obvious truth, a trapdoor opens and we fall through to a deeper and unexpected level of understanding.... The experienced preacher knows that the parables, so beguilingly simple on the surface, are, like a field with a hidden treasure, rich in meanings easily overlooked.[6]

As we have seen, the power of the parables has to do with the nature of their subject matter:

> I believe parables are powerful. They may be designed for a kind of group conversion. Parables usually begin rather tritely, depicting our everyday world in an everyday way, but then in most cases there is something surreal that disrupts our world and hints at a wider, more mysterious world—as well as a more astonishing God. Parables may well move us toward what Jesus called the "kingdom of God."[7]

6. Long, *Preaching and the Literary Forms of the Bible*, 87.
7. Buttrick, *Speaking Parables*, xiii.

While this is David Buttrick's formulation of the issue, the argument of the foregoing study has been that such transformative power is not limited to parables, indeed that it does not reside within the parables themselves or any other form of human communication in its own right. Power to transform the listener—whether for parables, preaching, or ministry in general—resides rather in God; hence good preaching (like the parables themselves) points away from itself and urges us toward God, challenging us with the unconstrainable reality of divine grace. To be fair, Buttrick himself intends much the same point, and does not mince words:

> A startling fact: We have not preached the realm of God. We have preached kingdom parables but in peculiar ways. We have turned them into pointed lessons in individual morality, or therapeutic advice for the living of life. But have we preached the kingdom of God as a sociopolitical image? Well no, not really.[8]

Yet Buttrick's critique does not go nearly far enough. The problem is not one of choosing between individual interests and those of society or culture as a whole; rather, the core issue is distinctly theological. Too much of our preaching is innocuous and tame; we do not seem to know the One of whom we speak. It seems easier—certainly less disruptive or countercultural—to turn aside from God's awesome refusal to be domesticated, trading the vision of God's presence and the terror of holiness for moral truisms, "family values," appeals for money, or bland assurances that things will work out fine in the end. Whether this is the result of ignorance, obstinacy, or outright rebellion on our part, the parables confront us—not with condemnation, necessarily, but by teasing us with hints of transcendence and provoking us to consider grace. Preaching should, surely, do the same. But in order to accomplish this impossible task, preachers will—paradoxically—have to give up trying, in order to allow God to do it for us. Even, against all expectation, through us.

To this end, Paul Simpson Duke offers the following advice:

> Like other biblical texts, a parable not only says something; it *does* something. A sermon should aim to do what the parable does. Each parable has its own distinctive function—to amaze at divine extravagance, to convict of our need for grace, to prompt obedience to divine command, to warn against naive impatience—but all of them function as well to invite or provoke us into active personal and communal engagement, reaction, reflection, and response. This is not merely the parables' method;

---

8. Ibid., 33.

> it is at the center of their gift. A parable sermon will follow this function.[9]

This explanation is both true in a limited sense and, at the same time, profoundly untrue. A sermon should, by all means, aim to do what the parable does, but this is only because by itself a parable ultimately achieves little or nothing apart from vexing its reader. If anything, a sermon should be an exercise in modesty, directing attention away from itself as an instrument of change and toward God, who alone can accomplish the rescue, restoration, and ultimate transformation of spiritually lost hearers. Returning to an image from the introduction, parables and sermons are effective when they function parabolically, serving to reflect and focus some external source of energy on an intended target. Just so with respect to light, mirrors are extremely useful, reflective parabolas even more so. But neither are much use in the dark. It is in this very sense that Paul can insist, "Neither the one who plants nor the one who waters is anything, but only God who gives the growth." On this point Martin Luther is characteristically blunt, and John Calvin no less so. First, Luther:

> It is easy enough for someone to preach the word to me, but only God can put it into my heart. He must speak it in my heart, or nothing at all will come of it. If God remains silent, the final effect is as though nothing had been said.[10]

Calvin is equally insistent on the need for divine intervention:

> The testimony of the Spirit is superior to reason. For as God alone can properly bear witness to his own words, so these words will not obtain full credit in the hearts of men, until they are sealed by the inward testimony of the Spirit. . . . For though [Scripture] in its own majesty has enough to command reverence, nevertheless, it then begins truly to touch us when it is sealed in our hearts by the Holy Spirit.[11]

Our argument has been that the theological content and rhetorical function of parables—their evocation of a divine power that, by definition, lies beyond human control—corresponds in principle to the pattern of Jesus' death and resurrection. Just as Jesus's teaching often (first) takes the form of parables that (second) function parabolically in the sense that they reflect

---

9. Duke, *The Parables*, 99 (emphasis original).

10. Cited in Paul Althaus, *The Theology of Martin Luther*, 39. I am grateful to David Courey for this reference.

11. *Institutes* 1:7, 4–5, quoted in J. Kent Edwards, "Deep Preaching," 83.

the power of God, so, in a third sense, his life and ministry generally may also be considered "parabolic." This observation originates with Harrisville, who points out how, in chapters 2 and 3 of Paul's letter to the Philippians, the experiential trajectories laid out by the Christ hymn and by the apostle's own autobiography both trace a parabolic curve.[12] Accordingly, the language of Phil 2:6–9 serves to plot the theological contours of Jesus' experience:

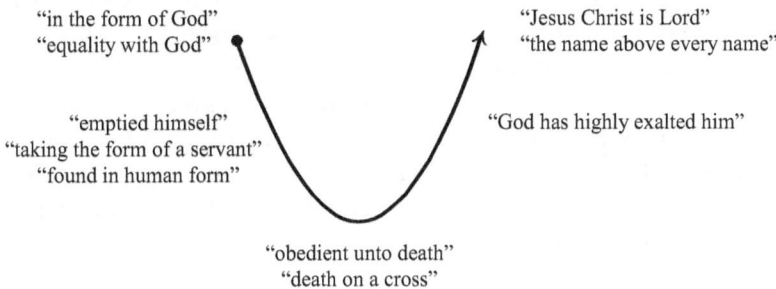

To this corresponds the shape of Paul's own experience, which he describes in similar terms (Phil 3:4–11):

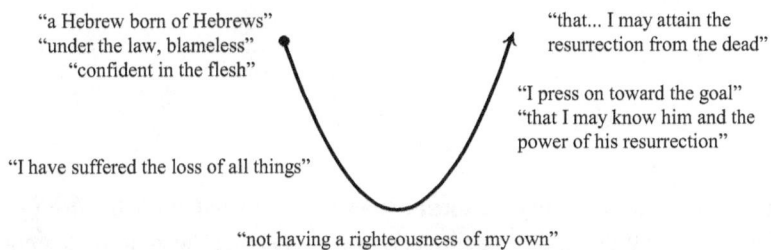

Much as his continued reliance on the life-giving power of God is *akin* to resurrection, Paul does not claim to have experienced it fully ("Not that I have already obtained this or have already reached the goal," Phil 3:12): for the moment it remains an expression of eschatological hope. In proposing this as the shape of Christian discipleship generally, he affirms the power of God amidst suffering while yet avoiding triumphalism:

---

12. Harrisville, *Fracture*, 114–17. The following discussion expands on Harrisville's treatment. Although not cited by Harrisville, literary critic Northrop Frye also plots the narrative of Jesus' life in terms of both U-shaped and circular trajectories; see *The Great Code*, 169–76.

Clearly, the acting subject of the hymn and of the autobiography is the same: Jesus Christ. And the mode of existence in both is the same: servanthood and suffering. It is the same because the earth remains the sphere of Christ's activity, whether in his humiliation or exaltation. Thus, while Paul lives, his existence is cruciform, for in this mode the crucified and risen Christ makes his appearance.[13]

For Paul, ministry—and the apostolic ministry of proclamation in particular—follows a similar trajectory: it is rooted in a sense of theological purpose and call, even obligation ("Woe to me," he confesses, "If I do not proclaim the gospel" [1 Cor 9:16]); is attended by weakness, self-effacement, and inability; yet as such is subject to the empowerment of God and the anointing of the Holy Spirit. Although no one passage describes this process in full, we may borrow from 1 Corinthians 9:16–17 and 2 Corinthians 4:1–7 to indicate its essentially cruciform dimensions:

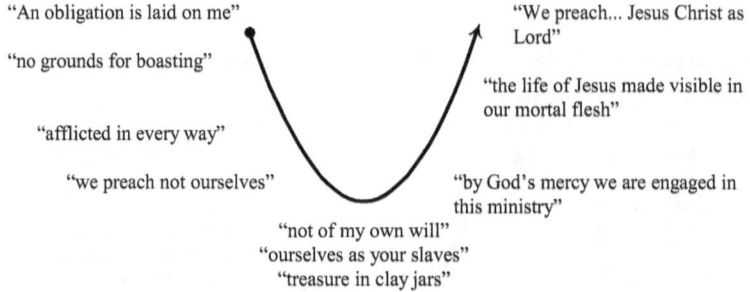

What distinguishes the cruciform dynamic of apostolic ministry from the biographical trajectories of both Jesus and Paul is that the various elements of this third description need not be chronologically sequential: they represent different aspects of a simultaneous reality. Paul's experience is one of "power *amidst* weakness," not power *after* or *replacing* weakness; of "dying yet behold, we live" (2 Cor 6:9 NASB); for "*whenever* I am weak," he insists, "*then* I am strong" (2 Cor 12:10 NRSV). Equally relevant on the "descending" side of this curve might be 1 Corinthians 4:9–13 ("God has exhibited us apostles as last of all . . . fools for the sake of Christ . . . weak . . . in disrepute . . . the rubbish of the world, the dregs of all things"), while on the other side would be indications of divine affirmation such as 1 Thessalonians 1:5 ("our gospel came to you . . . in power and in the Holy Spirit and with full conviction" [RSV]). Similar dynamics apply not only to his own ministry, but also to that of his companions and—if only by virtue of the universal

---

13. Harrisville, *Fracture*, 115–16.

import of Jesus' death and resurrection—to all ministers and preachers of the Christian gospel.[14]

Each in their own way—Jesus' agricultural parables, his ministry according to the Gospel of John, the pattern of his death and resurrection, Paul's experience as a preacher of the cross, and the basic dynamics of Christian ministry—bespeak a human weakness and inability that confesses its own limitations in order to rely instead on the transformative power of God. Bearing witness in the course of our own preaching to the divine gift of life will require that we yield to both aspects of this twofold dynamic: first crucifixion, then resurrection. Just as Jesus points beyond himself and thus bears witness to the life of God, so preachers and their sermons point beyond themselves to the sole sufficiency of God's life-giving power, so that the validation of their ministry relies neither on institutional authority nor on the convincing nature of their rhetoric, but on the manifestation of that same divine life in the lives of their congregants. The parabolic, cruciform dimensions of Jesus' teaching and experience thus call for a parabolic, cruciform kind of preaching that both reflects and gives rise to a parabolic, cruciform discipleship as preacher and congregation alike join Jesus at the cross, then find themselves alive with him on the other side of an empty tomb. To understand what this means in practice, it will be helpful to explore, first, the spiritual disciplines that express such an orientation in the life of the preacher, then, second, the corresponding characteristics that reflect a similar orientation on the part of the congregation.

"The Stench of Death": The Testimony of a Crucified Preacher

Apart from the general applicability of cross and resurrection as the most basic categories of Christian experience, embracing death seems particularly relevant for preachers in the contemporary West, above all if we are to understand our ministry as one of bearing witness to God's gift of life in Christ. In this cultural context, "embracing death" will mean acknowledging the limitations of our own ministries in a manner that will seem to contradict much that we commonly assume about human responsibility and the role of the pastor or preacher in the life of the church. Our assumption is

---

14. In this respect it is important to note Paul's consistent use of first-person plural language when describing his ministry: e.g., 1 Corinthians 1:23 ("*We* proclaim Christ crucified"), 2:6–7 ("*we* speak God's wisdom"), 3:9 ("*we* are God's servants, working together"); 2 Corinthians 1:9 ("Jesus Christ, whom *we* proclaimed among you, Silvanus and Timothy and I"), 4:1 ("it is by God's mercy that *we* are engaged in this ministry"), 4:5 (" For *we* do not proclaim ourselves; *we* proclaim Jesus Christ as Lord"), etc.; so Fee, *The First Epistle to the Corinthians*, 75 n.34.

that the purpose of ministry is to minister, to achieve the goals and accomplish the mission of a particular organization. On this view, the effectiveness of a given ministry can be measured in terms of its ability to achieve the goals in question. If this is the case, then our role is clear: preachers produce converts and augment the spiritual life (along with the size and social influence) of their congregations. We are agents of change; the instrument of change is the gospel; effective use of this instrument on the part of the agent brings about spiritual transformation, congregational growth, and passionate engagement in the work of God's kingdom. But the terrifying truth is that ministry doesn't always work like this. Unless we simply ignore all evidence to the contrary, or else conclude that the gospel itself is ultimately ineffectual, might it be that we have misunderstood our own role as agents of spiritual change? Might our obsession with spiritual productivity, numerical expansion, and the strategic importance of our own ministries reflect the fact that we have been misled by what Paul calls "another gospel" (Gal 1:7), a "different gospel" from that which Paul preached (2 Cor 11:4)? Might it be, in fact, that cruciformity and testimony alike are inconsistent with a view of human agency that we have taken for granted in Christian ministry?

In a little-known essay from 1972 entitled "Témoignage et Société Technicienne" ("Testimony and Technological Society"), French philosopher Jacques Ellul (1912–1994) argues that testimony is in principle incompatible with a culture such as ours that idolizes technology and technical expertise.[15] Technological society is concerned with "technique," with the use of means and instruments by which we order our world and thereby construct our sense of personal or social identity, as well as our understanding of the cosmos itself.[16] In a technological society, human identity is viewed as a product or consequence of the various means or "techniques" by which we choose to define ourselves. On such a view, identity is malleable because it is the product of reason and choice; even Christian discipleship is no longer a matter of acquiescence to a greater absolute, but is rather an instrument of sorts, a means of achieving a goal—in this case a more fulfilled human existence. This difficulty is compounded (especially, we might add, for those

---

15. Ellul, "Témoignage et Société Technicienne," 441–55 (not yet to my knowledge available in translation).

16. Ellul's classic formulation of this analysis is *The Technological Society*, first published in French in 1954 and anticipating by nearly four decades the similar, albeit nontheological, critique offered by Neil Postman in *Technopoly*. In contrast to Ellul, however, Postman considers "technique" largely benign: "The argument, in short, is not with technique. The argument is with the triumph of technique, with techniques that become sanctified and rule out the possibilities of other ones" (*Technopoly*, 142).

charged with communication of the Christian gospel) by the technology and techniques of mass media, which are concerned not with ultimate truth or "reality" but with *simulacra*, images and projections that mediate and thereby substitute for the things they depict.[17] On such a view, the image is everything (as the advent of visual technology in congregational worship amply demonstrates). By contrast, for Ellul as with Ricoeur, authentic Christian testimony concerns that which is fundamentally constitutive in its own right: it is not simply one more bit of information among many but rather it is groundbreaking, earth-shattering, requiring a choice between truth and idolatry. It concerns that to which we bear witness precisely because it offers a definition of our existence that is *not* subject to human control. But in a technological society, a society in which information technology offers us the ability to fashion our vision of the world, "testimony" is reduced to little more than personal conviction, or mere opinion.

Once testimony is reduced to opinion, it becomes akin to propaganda, another instrument by which we seek to engineer a desired outcome. Yahweh, for instance, becomes the "product" of Israel's testimony, just as the preacher becomes "instrumental" in the life of the congregation, the bearer of a vital word without which there would ostensibly be no life. But preaching as testimony in the sense that Ricoeur intends it (especially so preaching that testifies to crucifixion) succeeds by bearing witness to its own *noninstrumentality*, its own definitive *inability* to make happen that of which it speaks. It is not one means among many, a better opinion, a superior world view or more successful strategy by which to achieve a fulfilled (perhaps even eternal) life, no matter what certain preachers may claim. It is rather an exercise in nonutility, a renunciation of means, an attestation to the fact that only God, not words or human works, can raise the dead, especially so when the otherwise dead (or formerly dead) are ranged throughout the pews in front of the pulpit from which one speaks. And surely the same is true for every preacher of the cross, of whom it might be said, like Abel in the King James rendering of Hebrews 11:4, "he being dead yet speaketh"!

The nonagential character of testimony, says Ellul, is especially relevant when it comes to the question of Jesus' resurrection. To rationalize or mythologize the resurrection in order to render it more intellectually palatable is to reduce it to merely human dimensions, to make it something other than a humanly impossible, uniquely divine act. Pursued in this manner,

---

17. Ellul, "Témoignage," 449–50. This analysis is closely allied with Ellul's critique of "propaganda," by which he understands the use of persuasive language that seeks to produce a specific effect among its hearers—not, that is, relying on the power of God to effect spiritual transformation. See further Greenman, Schuchardt, and Toly, *Understanding Jacques Ellul*, 40–46.

discussion of "resurrection" ceases to be true testimony: it is merely the familiar recitation of something we already know to be true.[18] The same observation applies to proclamation of the Christian gospel generally. Preaching as rhetoric, preaching as an instrumental action or technique, preaching as the confession of a personal conviction intended to sway the hearers towards compliance or ethical endeavor—all these are humanly explicable actions. Not one of them requires divine authentication. None of them, indeed, requires God's presence or intervention in any concrete or immediate sense. But preaching that functions as authentic "testimony" bears witness to what Ellul (along with Ricoeur) calls "le Tout Autre," "the Wholly-Other," One who is not subject to human manipulation or technological control.[19] Preaching as testimony waits on God, just as Paul and the disciples in Acts wait on God to countertestify and thereby confirm the words that they have uttered.[20]

This outlook is diametrically opposed to the instinctual models and patterns of leadership that characterize much of Western culture (including the church), according to which leaders are persons of power and authority, distinguished by their duty and ability to bring about change. In the face of such expectations a crucified Messiah, a spiritually powerless preacher, and a message of human weakness together represent an incomprehensible puzzle, a conundrum that does not square with anything else in human experience. By virtue of their equivalent illogic, the preacher and the One who is preached are equally "parabolic," pointing those who receive their testimony toward a reality other than themselves. In practice, then, a parabolic

18. Ellul, "Témoignage," 453–55; cf. 442–43.

19. Ibid., 447–48; cf. 446: "Ainsi le témoignage qui est rendu vain et non nécessaire quand il est relatif à tout ce qui peut être atteint par la technique, devient la condition de vie de celle-ci quand il est relatif au Tout Autre."

20. Similar in some respects to the proposals advanced here (although at a considerably greater level of abstraction) is John McClure's concept of homiletical testimony in the form of "othering," which (borrowing from the work of Jacques Derrida and Emmanuel Levinas) entails a process of personal "identity-erasure" or "ego-martyring" as the basis for ethical preaching (*Other-Wise Preaching*, 20, 152). In this view, responsible preaching consists of having our perspectives and sources of authority (indeed, our very identities) called radically into question by exposure to an endless plurality of other persons and human perspectives. Only in being confronted by the "other" and "otherness," according to McClure, can we "approach the 'glory of the Infinite'" (22, cf. 45; the phrase is from Levinas). But given the primacy within Christian tradition of Jesus as the *ultimate* human "other," there is an important sense in which McClure's argument (radical as it already is) does not go nearly far enough, for the pattern of crucifixion and resurrection challenges us with the prospect of being confronted not simply by the human other, but by the "Wholly-Other," the absolute, transcendent Other who is God.

"God's Field, God's Laborers"   191

and cruciform homiletic has at least three components. First, it embraces the disgraceful and irreligious character of the Christian message, which concerns a shamefully crucified Messiah. Second, at the level of logic and persuasion, it accepts that resurrection is a category wholly outside normal human experience, a reality not accounted for by human means, and certainly not subject to human control. Third, it renounces any pretense of direct rhetorical or spiritual agency, any suggestion that the words of the preacher are themselves able to bring life to their hearers. It is content simply to bear witness to the true source of that life: "All preaching is Easter preaching, dependent upon the truth of Easter to make it work."[21]

For Andrew Purves, the dynamic of Jesus' resurrection indicates a broader theological principle: "*It is not our ministries that make Christ present and possible; it is the present, living Christ who makes our ministries possible.*"[22] This we may take to mean not only that Christ makes our ministries possible in the general sense of being alive and thereby giving us work to do, but in the more precise sense that the church's ministry follows in the wake of the present, life-giving activity of the living Christ. With a forgivable play on words, Purves argues that "Our primary job is to be martyrs," in the sense of giving our lives over to the task of bearing witness to a resurrected and reigning Lord.[23] But before we turn too quickly from the suggestion that Christian testimony may require "martyrdom" in its more lethal modern sense, we should acknowledge that parabolic, cruciform testimony—preaching in particular—implies the paradoxical inutility of the preacher, and in this sense the "death" of the preacher as an effective communicator of the Christian message.

Three scriptural illustrations of this cruciform orientation come immediately to mind: John the Baptist, the disciples on the road to Emmaus, and the healing of the lame man at the temple gate. Even if Jesus places him firmly within a previous dispensation (Matt 11:11 // Luke 7:28), John the Baptist offers a signal illustration of this kind of witness.[24] Long prior to his own martyrdom, prior even to declaring the identity of the Messiah, John bears witness concerning himself:

> This is the testimony [μαρτυρία] given by John when the Jews sent priests and Levites from Jerusalem to ask him, "Who are you?"

21. Willimon, *Undone By Easter*, 29.
22. Purves, *The Resurrection of Ministry*, 79 (emphasis original).
23. Ibid.
24. For Ricoeur's discussion of John the Baptist as witness, see "Hermeneutics of Testimony," 137–39; compare that of Barth, *CD* 4.3.2, 611–12.

> He confessed and did not deny it, but confessed, "I am not the Messiah."
>
> And they asked him, "What then? Are you Elijah?"
>
> He said, "I am not."
>
> "Are you the prophet?"
>
> He answered, "No."
>
> (John 1:19–21; cf. 3:28)

His denials are particularly striking in light of Jesus' testimony that, no matter what he himself may have to say on the question, John is indeed the Elijah of eschatological expectation (Matt 11:14; Mark 9:13 // Matt 17:12–13). Yet whatever others make of him, John himself entertains few illusions—messianic or otherwise—about his importance in the divine scheme of things. If anything, he considers his significance inversely proportional to that of the Christ: "He must increase, but I must decrease" (John 3:30). Much as his role is simply to prepare the way for another, so this negative testimony with regard to his own identity anticipates a more positive confession concerning the identity of Jesus: "Behold, the Lamb of God, who takes away the sin of the world" (John 1:29 RSV). John's task is thus relatively simple: he reports from personal experience what he knows to be true, and how he has come to such knowledge:

> "I myself did not know him; but I came baptizing with water for this reason, that he might be revealed to Israel." And John testified, "I saw the Spirit descending from heaven like a dove, and it remained on him. I myself did not know him, but the one who sent me to baptize with water said to me, 'He on whom you see the Spirit descend and remain is the one who baptizes with the Holy Spirit.' And I myself have seen and have testified that this is the Son of God."
>
> (John 1:31–34)

These two aspects, one negative and the other positive, correspond formally to the kinds of testimony offered by all who subsequently proclaim the death and resurrection of the Son of God. Declaring who and what we are not—we are not prophets or gatekeepers; nor are we holier, closer to, or more favored by God than those to whom we speak—must necessarily precede our confession that all these qualities are true of Christ instead.

From Luke's Gospel comes the story of Cleopas and his companion on the road to Emmaus. It is striking in this account that the testimony of the women and their "vision of angels" has proven singularly ineffective in convincing this pair (or any of the other disciples, for that matter) that Jesus is once more alive (Luke 24:22-24). The Master's strong rebuke—"How foolish you are, and how slow of heart to believe all that the prophets have declared!" (24:25)—implies as much. Only a direct experience of the risen Lord is sufficient to transform them into witnesses. Indeed, following a hasty return to Jerusalem, they are greeted by testimony that is itself dependent upon an encounter with the living Jesus: "The Lord has risen indeed, and has appeared to Simon" (Luke 24:34). Only then do they relate their own experience: "They told what had happened on the road, and how he had been made known to them in the breaking of the bread." Thereupon Jesus himself appears in their midst (24:35-36). The pattern is similar in each case: the words of others prove insufficient and unconvincing; only the presence of Jesus is able to convey the truth of his resurrection. Here again is an indication of how even apostolic testimony to Jesus' resurrection is necessarily cruciform, requiring validation by the Resurrected One himself. This is not to imply that every sermon requires its own postresurrection appearance, for the narrative implies that scriptural testimony (Luke 24:27, 32, 44-45) and the fellowship of the Lord's Supper (24:30-31, 35) will both play a key role in this regard. More to the point, both of these factors are soon overshadowed by the prominence of Lukan pneumatology. In a postascension church, the gift and ministry of the Holy Spirit serve to confirm the message of the gospel in the same manner as did Jesus in the forty days following his resurrection (so Acts 15:7-9). Thus the basic principle still holds: words initially fail, only to be affirmed by the One of whom they speak.

A similar twofold dynamic is evident in the first healing to take place after the day of Pentecost, that of a man at the temple gate who has been lame from birth:

> All the people saw him walking and praising God.... While he clung to Peter and John, all the people ran together to them in the portico called Solomon's Portico, utterly astonished. When Peter saw it, he addressed the people, "You Israelites, why do you wonder at this, or why do you stare at us, as though by our own power or piety we had made him walk? The God of Abraham, the God of Isaac, and the God of Jacob, the God of our ancestors has glorified his servant Jesus, whom you handed over and rejected in the presence of Pilate, though he had decided to release him. But you rejected the Holy and Righteous One and asked to have a murderer given to you, and you killed the Author of life, whom God raised from the dead. To this we are witnesses."
>
> (Acts 3:9-15)

Given that all twelve had earlier abandoned Jesus in his hour of need, Peter had explicitly denied him, and Judas had betrayed him, none of the remaining apostles have any illusions about the quality of their piety or their native ability to do the works of God. Not unlike John the Baptist, Peter and John's initial confession is that they themselves are in no position to take credit for healing the lame man; that clarified, they proceed to testify concerning its true source. Most fitting for our purposes is the fact that they identify Jesus as "the Author of life" (cf. Acts 5:31), the one who by virtue of resurrection leads his followers into new life. They then conclude by reiterating the precise character of their own role: "To this we are witnesses." While this is the most informal and extemporaneous of sermons, its rhetorical and theological dimensions are nonetheless both cruciform and parabolic, renouncing any claim to spiritual agency in favor of the "Author of life."

What then of the preacher? This approach to preaching is more a question of character than of technique. Yielding our own words to the Living Word will require, first, deep courage, for the simple reason that we find it so threatening to be confronted by anything we cannot control. In theory we confess our trust in the love of God, but often, deep down, this may not alleviate our innermost fear. Yielding to the One whom Ellul calls "Wholly-Other," in an encounter that will reveal our profound frailty and human insignificance, calls for utmost bravery. This is perhaps less a personality trait than a gift from God, the kind of spiritual boldness for which even Paul asks the saints to pray on his behalf (Eph 6:20). Yielding will likewise require deep humility and patience, above all the patience to cease from our frantic efforts to please God and make ourselves indispensable to the work of the kingdom. We will need to renounce all claims to instrumentality, including the unspoken assumption that, as preachers, we have the right to set the terms and conditions of our hearers' encounter with God. Listening for the voice of the Spirit, or waiting for the leading of the Shepherd, will require of us both silence and stillness, which tend to be the very first casualties of a busy pastoral life. We have much to learn in this regard from Jesus, who made it a priority to spend time alone with God (Mark 1:35, Luke 9:28, etc.). As Thielicke explains, this was the key to Jesus' spiritual authority:

> Why was it that he spoke with authority, as the scribes and Pharisees did not? Because he was rhetorically gifted, because he was dynamic? No; he spoke with such power because he had first spoken with the Father, because always he came out of silence. . . . He lived in communion with God; that's why his speech . . . becomes an event of judgment and grace which none can escape.

> Jesus' powerful speech derives from the power of his prayer life.[25]

The opposite of such an approach is for us to proceed on the assumption that spiritual transformation is primarily a consequence of human exertion, or, in the case of preaching, what Thielicke too calls "propaganda":

> The propaganda of men, even when it masquerades as a kind of evangelism and becomes an enterprise of the church, is always based on the accursed notion that success and failure, fruit and harvest are dependent upon our human activity, upon our imagination, energy, and intelligence. Therefore the church too must guard against becoming merely a busy enterprise and pastors must beware of becoming religious administrators devoid of power and dried up as far as spiritual substance is concerned.[26]

Perhaps failure will be our most significant asset in this regard, for the great blessing of failure (whatever its precise dimensions in any particular case) is that it causes us to question our own abilities, to acknowledge our limitations, and (unless wisdom is lacking) to turn elsewhere for help. If nothing else, this will consist of our inability to save or sanctify ourselves, our unsuitability as role models for the people of God, and our wholesale failure to establish God's kingdom. For those called to ministry, and particularly for those of us who preach, the idolatry of our own self-importance will stand as incontrovertible evidence against us. Because we instinctively seek to justify ourselves before God by means of Christian ministry itself, thereby resisting the conditions of grace, grace will be essential if our ministry is to bear fruit.[27]

Nor should we be in any doubt as to how difficult this will prove in practice, and how desperately we will struggle against it. Still, the promise of his resurrection is that when we are weak, then (and only then) Christ supplies us with divine power (2 Cor 12:9–10); only when we "labor and are heavy laden" does Christ give us rest (Matt 11:28); only once we concede the fact of our own spiritual sterility and fruitlessness will we at last allow the life of Christ to flow through us for the benefit of others (John 15:4–5).

---

25. Thielicke, *The Waiting Father*, 89.

26. Ibid., 89.

27. Cf. Ellul, *The Subversion of Christianity*, 158–63; Ellul acutely observes that, by virtue of our insistence on self-justification, "Grace is odious to us. . . . Grace is intolerable" (159, 172).

"Sweet Fragrance of Resurrection": The Preacher Alive in Christ

Corresponding to the spiritual discipline of turning away from the presumed efficacy of our own preaching with humility, patience, and the fear of God will be a growing awareness of the life and power of Christ at work both in our own lives and in the lives of those whom we serve. Our previous discussion has set Christian preaching generally (exemplified by apostolic preaching of the cross and resurrection) within the context of theological testimony; as one moment within an ongoing, antiphonal exchange between divine and human voices successively initiating, eliciting, acknowledging, and finally affirming the power of divine life at work in creation. But before this dynamic can apply to our own ministries, it will first need to have deep roots in personal experience. How this is so emerges clearly from Paul's Letter to the Philippians.

To all appearances, Paul employs the famous Christ hymn of Philippians 2:6–11 primarily as a basis for moral exhortation:

> Do nothing from selfish ambition or conceit, but in humility regard others as better than yourselves. Let each of you look not to your own interests, but to the interests of others. Let the same mind be in you that was in Christ Jesus . . .
>
> (Phil 2:3–5)

Granted, the subject of verse 5 is disputed: Paul's very compact syntax can refer either to Christ (so NRSV, above; NIV: "Your attitude should be the same as that of Christ Jesus") or to those who are themselves "in Christ" (so RSV: "Have this mind among yourselves, which is yours in Christ Jesus"; NEB: "Let your bearing towards one another arise out of your life in Christ Jesus").[28] But in either case, "The hymn . . . presents Christ as the ultimate model for moral action."[29] As noted earlier, Paul applies only the first half of Christ's example as a pattern for relationships within the church: congregants are to be humble and unselfish, emulating his abasement, but there is no mention of them being either glorified or exalted. Yet when it comes to the inner life of discipleship, both halves of the equation apply. Immediately following the conclusion of the hymn Paul invokes the same model a second time:

> Therefore, my beloved, just as you have always obeyed me, not only in my presence, but much more now in my absence, work out your own salvation with fear and trembling; for it is God

---

28. For a survey of alternatives, see Martin, *Philippians*, 91–93.
29. Hawthorne, *Philippians*, 79.

> who is at work in you, enabling you both to will and to work for his good pleasure.
>
> (Phil 2:12–13)

Corresponding to "crucifixion" in this passage is "fear and trembling," the most likely sense of which is not raw terror in the presence of God but rather due piety and holy awe, "an attitude of 'obedience,' or 'holding oneself in weakness' toward the will of God according to the pattern of Jesus Christ."[30] Likewise corresponding to "resurrection" is the enabling power of God "at work," says the apostle to his readers, "in you." Not least because the personal pronoun here is plural, the phrase can have the sense either of "within you" or "among you." Again, whichever alternative we choose, the underlying principle remains the same: by virtue of our being united with Christ, human obedience and adherence to the will of God no longer represent demands imposed from without but rather are enabled from within by the same divine power that raised Jesus from death.

Paul employs the same key verb for God as the "One who empowers [ὁ ἐνεργῶν]" and for the consequence of this dynamic, which is "to empower [τὸ ἐνεργεῖν]" the believer. His wordplay is important because the language of power is consistently associated in Pauline literature with resurrection on the one hand, and Christian life on the other. Throughout his letters the apostle speaks of Jesus' resurrection as a manifestation of divine "power" (δύναμις, Rom 1:4), of Christian conviction as faith in this "power" (1 Cor 1:18, 6:14d; Col 2:12), and thus of discipleship as being directly enabled by the power that raised Jesus to new life (2 Thess 1:11; Eph 1:19–20). Thus Paul appeals to "the power at work within us" (Eph 3:20; cf. 3:16) and reminds believers that they are "made strong with all the strength that comes from his glorious power" (Col 1:11). Just so, he understands all ministry (including his own) to express this same life-giving, resurrection-producing power, both in the sense that the power of God inspires and sustains the church's ministry (2 Cor 4:7, 6:7; Eph 3:7; Col 1:29) and because ministry in the name of the Resurrected One is attended by manifestations of divine power (Rom 15:19; 1 Cor 2:4–5, 12:10, 28; 2 Cor 12:12, 13:3–4; 1 Thess 1:5). The implication of theological continuity between resurrection, Christian life, and ministry is that such power is available—whether for prospective converts or credentialed preachers—only to the dead, who otherwise would have no need of it. Conversion, discipleship, and ministry thus reflect the resurrection not in the sense that they endeavor to imitate or repeat it, but

---

30. Ibid., 100.

in that they are equally enabled and made possible by the same God-given vitality that raises the dead and brings forth a new creation.

For preachers, this is more than a matter of intellectual conviction: it requires intimacy and personal knowledge of the One of whom we speak. Again, as the Puritan Richard Baxter explains, this is not knowledge *about* God, as though God were merely the object of our scrutiny, but rather a kind of experiential authenticity that shines through our words to lend them spiritual depth and authority:

> The more of God appeareth in our duties, the more authority they will have with men. . . . I know not what it doth by others; but the most Reverent Preacher, that speaks as if he saw the face of God, doth more affect my heart, though with common words, then an unreverent man with the most exquisite preparations. Yea, if he bawl it out with never so much seeming earnestness, if Reverence be not answerable to fervency, it worketh but little.[31]

To borrow the distinction Paul makes in Galatians 4:9, this is less a matter of knowing God and more one of knowing that we are known by God, of knowing ourselves to be in the very presence of God even as we speak. Instead of seeking to amuse or delight our hearers, writes Baxter,

> We should as it were suppose we saw the Throne of God, and the millions of Glorious Angels attending him, that we may be awed with his Majesty, when we draw near him in holy things, lest we profane them, and take his name in vain.[32]

Describing his own ministry of proclamation, Paul makes the same point in 2 Corinthians 2:17: "We are not peddlers of God's word like so many; but in Christ we speak as persons of sincerity, as persons sent from God and standing in his presence."[33] Thus as preachers from Augustine (notwithstanding his love of Cicero) to today's African American tradition (with its delight in rhetorical flourish) all acknowledge, faithful preaching is ultimately less a matter of skillful technique than it is a product and expression of deep spirituality.

Knowledge and awareness of God call for discernment regarding the responsibilities of pastoral ministry, discernment that is a necessary, if indirect, consequence of the resurrection.[34] For resurrection is not simply a

---

31. Baxter, *Gildas Salvianus*, 128. For a brief introduction to Baxter and *The Reformed Pastor*, see Purves, *Pastoral Theology*, 98–114.

32. Baxter, *Gildas Salvianus*, 128.

33. See further Knowles, *We Preach Not Ourselves*, 94–111, esp. 102–4.

34. The following discussion is informed by the work of Purves, especially *The*

"God's Field, God's Laborers" 199

past event in the life history of Jesus: it implies the present, active reign of the living Lord. Recognition of this fact prompts a radical redefinition of ministry itself that now, as Stephen Seamands points out,

> is not so much asking Christ to join us in our ministry as we offer him to others; ministry is participating with Christ in his ongoing ministry as he offers himself to others through us.[35]

Christ's living and active reign consists of bringing to fulfillment the same human transformation indicated by his death and resurrection; it is a reign of reconciliation, healing, and new life for all who will receive Jesus' gift of himself. We are free, of course, to pursue our ministries as though he were long since risen and gone, as if we were the only ones left to carry on his mission. But the Gospel narratives do not encourage so optimistic a view of human potential. If Jesus' earthly ministry consisted solely of entering into the work of his heavenly Father, and his disciples could accomplish nothing apart from him, then the operative question for pastoral ministry today is not the often-cited slogan, "What Would Jesus Do?" but rather, "What is the living Lord doing, here and now, and how can I join him in it?"[36] Soteriologically, ministry concerns not only the present (or future) *consequences* of Jesus' death and resurrection, but also the present, ongoing *activity* of Christ in his continuing intercession before the Father and in the sending of the Holy Spirit as the agent of enablement for our lives and ministries. In this context, discernment consists of the ability to see the signs of his handiwork, both in ourselves and in others. This is a matter of learning to discern the voice of the Shepherd:

> He calls his own sheep by name and leads them out. When he has brought out all his own, he goes ahead of them, and the sheep follow him because they know his voice. They will not follow a stranger, but they will run from him because they do not know the voice of strangers.... My sheep hear my voice. I know them, and they follow me.
>
> (John 10:3–5, 27)

Resurrection of Ministry, 44–58. Purves speaks in particular of "testing the spirits" (57), discerning the difference between what is of Christ or not by appeal to Scripture and Christian tradition as the norms by which to evaluate our own experience and that of others.

35. Seamands, *Ministry in the Image of God*, 20.

36. So Anderson, *The Shape of Practical Theology*, 56. Similarly Purves, *Crucifixion of Ministry*, 51–59.

After all, "pastoral" ministry consists of caring for the Lord's flock; faithfulness in this task requires that we be able to discern where the "Chief Shepherd" (1 Pet 5:4) is leading us.

This is of critical importance because it implies that spiritual discernment of any and all matters involving others is first and foremost a matter of discernment and obedience on our own part. Eugene Peterson describes in detail what this will consist of for the practice of pastoral ministry:

> There is a text for this work in St. Mark's Gospel: "He has risen, . . . he is going before you to Galilee; there you will see him, just as he told you" (16: 6–7). In every visit, every meeting I attend, every appointment I keep, I have been anticipated. The risen Christ got there ahead of me. The risen Christ is in that room already. What is he doing? What is he saying? What is going on?[37]

The same is surely true for preaching: the implication of his ongoing reign is that Jesus bears witness to his resurrection not as an abstract principle or an event independent of himself, but by the fact of his presence and self-offering even in the moment of preaching:

> Jesus is not only the subject of proclamation (the one about whom we preach), but he is himself the proclaimer of every act of proclamation (the one who proclaims himself through the event of preaching).[38]

For this reason, sermon preparation is akin to prayer: it begins with silence that bespeaks our theological inability to do the Lord's work for him, and with a willingness to listen for the voice of the Shepherd in order to know what to say.[39] Yet it proceeds in the assurance that just as he has made himself known in the past, so Jesus will continue to do so in the present. "For where man's strength ends," declares Luther, "God's strength begins, provided faith is present and waits on him."[40] A parabolic and cruciform homiletic thus not only renounces all degrees of instrumentality (from coercion at one extreme, to the desire to be God's gatekeeper, however charitably, at the other), it also remains fundamentally oriented toward inspiration and divine initiative, such that the external process of utter reliance on God to "make good"

---

37. Peterson, *Under the Unpredictable Plant*, 127. Similarly Purves, *Crucifixion of Ministry*, 56–58.

38. Anderson, *The Shape of Practical Theology*, 56.

39. Seamands (*Ministry in the Image of God*, 22–23) offers a practical illustration from personal experience.

40. *Luther's Works* 21:340, cited in Prenter, *Luther's Theology of the Cross*, 16.

on his word corresponds to an internal process of prayer, meditation, reflection, and waiting that gives rise to the sermon in the first place.

This observation adds a final nuance to the earlier discussion of preaching as testimony, or rather it subsumes testimony more fully within a cruciform and Trinitarian understanding of ministry as a whole. Preachers who set out to bear witness to the life-giving power of God as it has been manifested in the history of Israel and the experience of Jesus are not, as it were, left to their own devices in doing so, as if their own words were responsible for conveying the full reality of God. Such is the power of divine self-testimony that it provides not only the prior content and subsequent affirmation of Christian proclamation, but also the means of preaching itself. Just as the gift and gifts of God's Spirit confirmed apostolic preaching in the experience of the hearers, so the empowerment of the Holy Spirit makes proclamation possible in the experience of the preacher today. Whether the linguistic phenomena of Pentecost—specifically, xenoglossia—are repeatable is a matter of debate. But the underlying theological principle is not in dispute: the apostles were able to speak only "as the Spirit gave them ability" (Acts 2:4). Just so, preaching emerges (in most cases much less spectacularly) out of quiet waiting and the willingness to be dependent on God, as those unsure of their ability or worthiness find themselves given words and confidence to speak of the One who sustains them even as they mount the pulpit steps.

Attentiveness to Jesus' present ministry, discernment of his voice, and reliance on his strength will give rise to a lively sense of hope and expectation on the part of the preacher. Some would call this "faith," but I think of it more precisely as an attitude of expectation that Christ himself will remain faithful. Just as God in Christ has spoken the first, definitive word that gives me something worth talking about, indeed a living Word to which my words bear witness, so I expect that faithful testimony to God's life-giving power will be met with new evidence of Christ continuing to accomplish the same thing in the lives of my hearers, as well as in my own life. The church's ministry of preaching is always sustained by the ministry of Christ that precedes, accompanies, and confirms it. This is not confidence in our own abilities, or even hope that our preaching will bear fruit, but expectation that Christ himself will bring life and healing to our hearers in all the ways that we ourselves cannot.

Even so, an important—and subtle—qualification is called for at this point, if our preaching is not to fall into a kind of triumphalism that is altogether inconsistent with cruciform ministry. Faithful, hopeful, theologically sound preaching is sometimes met with stony silence. Or worse: boredom and tired indifference. Long experience indicates that congregational responsiveness (or lack of it!) provides no indication either of the preacher's fidelity or of the true worth of the sermon. Preaching as parable and testimony always bears simultaneous witness in opposite directions: to human weakness and divine power, failure and triumph, crucifixion and resurrection. Sometimes one part of this equation will predominate, sometimes the other. As we have seen, human testimony corresponds to divine testimony past, even as it relies on and awaits divine testimony present, all the while looking forward to the final eschatological testimony that constitutes the whole of our future. But because that initial divine testimony embraces both Good Friday and Easter Sunday (nor one without the other), they *together* represent the circumstances in which Christ invites us to celebrate the grace, power, and life of God. The paradoxical, parabolic character of testimony to cross and resurrection applies not only to preachers and sermons, but to the congregation as well. Accordingly, preaching as testimony to the full dimensions of God's saving work represents the triumph of hope because *it does not consist of or rely on its own testimony alone*. Again, preachers cannot rest on the assumption that God will always "show up" in dramatic fashion every time they enter the pulpit, as if their words had the power to summon divine proof. Preaching as parabolic testimony always occupies a middle ground between the divine word that our words now echo and the confirming word that comes after we fall silent. It is always filled with hope for the same reason that it stops short of presumption: that God, not human voices, will have the last word, especially so should the marks of divine affirmation remain obscure at present. Nor does this observation invalidate the larger principle of divine testimony as the confirmation of preaching; it merely acknowledges what Paul experienced, for example, with his troublesome converts at Corinth, which is that human frailty and divine power coexist for the time being in preachers and congregations alike.

Human testimony to the divine gift of life will always be paradoxical and parabolic precisely *because* it is cruciform: in this, preachers and congregants remain subject to the same conditions of discipleship. Contrary to their deepest human instincts, preachers are not exceptional, or somehow exempt from the struggles and sorrows that characterize the lives of many in their congregations. Rather, they exemplify a cruciform ethos, if only in the course of preaching itself, by acknowledging their own human frailty and turning to God as the source of life. As modeled by the preacher in the very act of preaching, a sermon will invite hearers to turn away from self-reliance and idolatry (that is, insufficient or misleading forms of spiritual sustenance) so as to rely on God instead. Above all, because it testifies to divine life that emerges out of the nullification of human endeavor, such preaching must always be both parabolic and cruciform, for a humanly unimpressive preacher armed with little more than words and a nervous smile will never be mistaken for the source of eternal life.

THE CHURCH AS PARABLE AND COMMUNITY OF GRACE

Neither will a cruciform church be mistaken for the source of life. In a nominally "Christian" culture, people turn up on Sunday for a host of reasons: to meet friends, form community, develop business contacts, find a marriage partner, or enjoy an hour's respite while someone else looks after their children; any or all of these, perhaps, as part of a broader spiritual discipline or quest. But the church's negligible prestige in many segments of post-Christian Western society suggests that considerations of this sort will be pushed increasingly to the periphery (where they belong), and that dwindling congregations with their beleaguered preachers will find reason enough to look once more to Christ as the source of their common life. If the parabolic character of Jesus' death and resurrection establishes the pattern for discipleship generally and Christian ministry in particular, the same will be true for the congregation as a whole. Parabolic, cruciform preaching will both exemplify and call for a cruciform orientation on the part of its hearers, and the same test of authenticity will apply to both:

> Every pragmatic principle of ministry must be subjected to the critical dogmatic test: has it gone through the death and resurrection process? Have we allowed the ministry as such to reveal to us its impossibility before we have assumed its possibility? Does the church understand that it only exists because of Christ's ministry? Does Christ's ministry continue to exist in our ministry as both the presupposition and the goal?[41]

These questions imply three levels or dimensions of theological continuity and coherence. *First*, and most obviously, ministry that waits at the cross assumes an unchanging divine purpose, anticipating that in some measure at present and more fully in future the Father will give life to the dead, even as he once did for his beloved Son. As applied to preaching, this theological premise is well illustrated by Paul Scott Wilson's *Four Pages of the Sermon*, which argues for "trouble" or "sin and brokenness" in the text and "sin and brokenness in our world" being met and matched by "grace in the biblical world" and "grace in our world," respectively.[42] Wilson offers this approach

---

41. Anderson, *The Shape of Practical Theology*, 74.
42. Wilson, *The Four Pages of the Sermon*, 13–27, and passim.

primarily as a method for sermon composition, and is careful to observe that the grace of which he speaks cannot be coerced or controlled by means of any structural device: "Genuine good news comes only from God. If the Holy Spirit does not choose to use our words, there is nothing we can do to make them into good news."[43] Yet the theological genius of his approach is its insistence that God acts in the world today in ways altogether consistent with what we find in the pages of the biblical text.[44] For preachers to bear witness to this principle requires it to be operative in their own experience: otherwise our "testimony" would be false. We cannot proclaim the need to rely on God without relying on God ourselves, especially so in the act of making this proclamation. A cruciform and parabolic homiletic thus calls for consistency, *second*, between our experience of Christ and our words about him.

Finally, *third*, congregants must also reckon with the cruciform nature of grace. Make no mistake: churches look to pastors and preachers for salvation. Not for preachers to announce salvation, but to *provide* it. Many churches entertain the barely concealed hope that with the help of a larger sign out front, a dynamic youth leader, and perhaps new carpeting in the sanctuary, a better qualified or more winsome preacher would finally bring folks from the neighborhood back into church (as well as balancing the annual budget). This implies that the pastor or preacher will be able to do something for them that they are unable to accomplish for themselves. But the true role of the preacher is nothing other than to announce and act out the basic creaturely condition of absolute reliance on the life that God supplies. Acknowledging the cruciform nature of grace will mean that for all members of the church, no matter what their rank or role, the life of Christ will emerge out of weakness and lack. All three dimensions of a parabolic and cruciform orientation are thus interwoven: the word that is preached will take root in the preacher and bear fruit in the hearers as God graciously manifests in present experience the same power of life that raised Jesus from death.

Because it waits on God's supply, the post-Easter church is thus characterized by a continual reorientation from despair to hope, as our focus shifts again and again from retrospective to prospective Christology, from Christ in his earthly ministry to Christ in his eternal reign. The Jerusalem church embodied this orientation by meeting for worship not on the Sabbath but on the first day of the new creation. In the case of Stephen, his imminent death might otherwise have signaled the failure of faith; as it happened, this

---

43. Ibid., 25.

44. Ibid., 201–9, offers a carefully nuanced discussion of this premise.

was the moment when he was able to see—*and testify to*—the reign of Christ at his Father's right hand. So equally with the unexpected conversion of one of his murderers—Saul of Tarsus, who became the church's first and greatest missionary theologian. Whether, then, for the earliest believers or in our own day, every service of worship; every conversion or baptism; and every healing, reconciliation, or restoration celebrates the power of Christ at work amidst his people.

What might such a congregation look like in practice? Perhaps there is no better way of identifying a parabolic, cruciform community that looks to the life of God than to borrow Paul's description of his own ministry:

> genuine, yet regarded as imposters;
> known, yet regarded as unknown;
> dying, and yet we live on;
> beaten, and yet not killed;
> sorrowful, yet always rejoicing;
> poor, yet making many rich;
> having nothing, and yet possessing everything.
>
> (2 Cor 6:9–10 TNIV)

This will be a community well aware of its own weaknesses and shortcomings that nonetheless lives by grace. Neither its pastors nor its congregants will feel the need to be "upwardly mobile"; it may not be regarded as a "prize" appointment or a pulpit worth aspiring to. Yet it will be filled with inexplicably hopeful people, for all their obvious limitations. And the sermons preached in such a church will be worth listening to not for their eloquence, deep learning, or the preacher's native charm, but because they speak of grace, and because it is possible to hear in them the voice of the risen Lord.

Perhaps this is just my imagination (or more likely the work of a gifted narrator), but even though I have never visited it, the church where American essayist Anne Lamott eventually got sober and met Jesus (but not in that order) seems about as fitting an illustration of this principle as any other I am likely to discover. At least as she describes it, St. Andrew Presbyterian Church in Marin City, California is a community of deep faith that embraces the broken but not—as is sometimes the case elsewhere—at the cost of the cross and proclamation of Christ. Lamott is the first to admit (with typical pathos and a quirky sense of humor) that she and her congregation are very far from perfect: precisely for this reason, the reality of Jesus stands out among them.[45] At the same time, I strongly suspect that there are many

---

45. Lamott sketches her journey—and community—of faith in, for example, *Traveling Mercies*; *Plan B*; and *Grace (Eventually)*.

such churches across the ecclesiastical landscape; struggling congregations with harried preachers, united in the realization that few if any of them will ever amount to much in the eyes of society. However discouraging this may seem at times, these are the conditions of the cross, in which Christ declares not only that his grace is sufficient, but that his sustaining power is expressed most perfectly (2 Cor 12:9).

"YOU HAVE THE WORDS OF ETERNAL LIFE": PREACHING AS PARABLE AND TESTIMONY

Our study of preaching concludes as it began, by considering the words of Jesus. In retrospect, our initial discussion of Jesus' parables and the theology that undergirds them seems ironic, perhaps even contradictory, in light of all the other reflections that have ensued. For parables about a sower, or seed growing of its own accord, grains of mustard, wheat amidst weeds, and the like, all concern a natural order brimming over with the vibrant, fecund, life-giving abundance of a generous God. They bespeak a divine vitality, available to saints or sinners in equal measure, which provides the source and sustenance of the life of God's people. Paul's message of the cross, by contrast, appears pessimistic in the extreme, with the apostle fixated on a shameful death that is the very antithesis of God's willingness to grant life. Yet our argument has been that by reason of this arresting contrast, the "word of the cross" and the cruciform vision of the Christian life that it creates are both essentially parabolic. They depict the life of God as it is revealed in paradox and hiddenness, in much the same way as a tiny seed can—despite its modest size and unassuming appearance—spring up to great heights and provide shelter for the birds of the air. We have proposed that preachers and preaching function in much the same manner: we ourselves may be unremarkable and our words unimpressive (or worse), but we nonetheless bear witness to the same divine gift of life that not only makes seeds germinate, but also raised Jesus from death and offers new life to all who join him at the cross. Preaching, we have argued, is likewise parabolic because it is cruciform: it shares all the conditions of human frailty and weakness, but in so doing becomes open to the grace of God and the possibility of transformation.

Preaching is parabolic in the same way that Jesus' life and teaching are themselves parabolic: they testify to an uncontainable, unconstrainable divine power unimaginably greater than their own insufficiency. Without wanting to claim that words from the pulpit represent a special category of specifically *human* discourse (which they do not), the possibility of

Christ and the Holy Spirit bearing witness in relation to the feeble speech of preachers means that proclamation of the Christian gospel represents a subversion of normal patterns of communication. Communication for the purpose of persuasion falls under the category of "rhetoric," yet the strategies first described by Aristotle and expanded by Cicero and Quintilian have changed little in almost twenty-four centuries: the character of the speaker (*ethos*), the logic of the argument (*logos*), and appeal to emotion (*pathos*) are still mainstays of everything from political speechwriting to popular advertising.[46] But much like Jesus' parables, which are sometimes intentionally confusing or outlandish, faithfulness to the basic content of the gospel makes Christian preaching rhetorically subversive and counterintuitive. Not only does it not rely on the classical strategies of rhetorical persuasion, it intentionally reverses and rejects such methods. Paul says as much of his own preaching in a passage that we have examined several times already:

> When I came to you, brothers and sisters, I did not come proclaiming the testimony [μαρτύριον][47] of God to you in lofty words or wisdom. For I decided to know nothing among you except Jesus Christ, and him crucified. And I came to you in weakness and in fear and in much trembling. My speech and my proclamation were not with plausible words of wisdom, but with a demonstration of the Spirit and of power, so that your faith might rest not on human wisdom but on the power of God.
>
> (1 Cor 2:1–5)

To be sure, his letters adopt many stylistic conventions of the day. Yet in so doing, Paul openly confesses the "folly" and "scandal" of the "λόγος of the cross" (1 Cor 1:18, 21–25), and deliberately inverts the typical appeal to a speaker's good character so as to focus instead on the fidelity of God (1 Cor 1:9).[48] Such strategies proceed on the assumption that the ability to persuade rests with God rather than the preacher.

According to Richard Hays, the cross of Jesus represents "the starting point for an epistemological revolution."[49] Just so, Helmut Merklein stresses Paul's point in 1 Cor 1:21 that human wisdom and "the folly of what we

---

46. For an introduction to the history and categories of classical rhetoric, see Resner Jr., *Preacher and Cross*, 17–37.

47. Alternatively, "mystery [μυστήριον]"; see discussion of textual variants in Barrett, *A Commentary on the First Epistle to the Corinthians*, 62–63; Fee, *First Epistle to the Corinthians*, 88 n.1.

48. As argued by Resner Jr., *Preacher and Cross*, 105–14.

49. Hays, *First Corinthians*, 27, quoted in Shi, *Paul's Message*, 96.

preach" stand in opposition to one another, as a result of which the message of the cross cannot be understood except on its own terms. That is to say,

> [The] "word of the cross" forms the basis for its own semantic, and creates its own [linguistic] world. It constitutes a semantic change of paradigm and requires its execution.[50]

This explains why rhetoric and persuasion are insufficient, indeed incapable by themselves of conveying the meaning of the cross, and why testimony is the only category sufficient to explain the act of preaching. The universal import of crucifixion overshadows language itself, as the unwitting wordplay in this quotation—the different senses of "execution"—indicates. Just as the cross itself is a historical scandal, an offense and absurdity in its expression of cruel death, so equally the "word" or "message of the cross" constitutes a "stumbling block," a contradiction of all human wisdom that must be given life by God if it is to prove convincing. Apart from such empowerment it remains semantically irrelevant and inert, a lifeless seed that has yet to germinate.

It is not, as Romano Penna claims, that "revelation is completely dependent on the word, and indeed on the human word," notwithstanding the fact that he quotes as evidence many of the same texts that have informed our study. For Penna, "On this extreme, defenseless fragility of the naked human word depends every prophetic intervention from Elijah to Saint Paul."[51] Yet the parabolic character of the cross and the preaching that concerns it requires that the elements of this formulation be inverted: the "defenseless fragility of the naked human word" itself depends on divine intervention in order for it to assume a prophetic character. To be sure, proclamation remains a human responsibility, for "How are they to believe in him of whom they have never heard? And how are they to hear without a preacher?" (Rom 10:14 RSV). But the historical, theological, and semantic priority in this exchange remains an unconstrainable divine prerogative. According to Penna, "The preacher's mission ... is actually not just to explain the content of the Christian mystery but also, and above all, to bring it about."[52] But this is what a theology of the cross confesses preachers to be incapable of achieving.

If the word that we preach is to be a word of the cross, a word that proceeds by way of the cross, then the only validation we bring to it will be

---

50. Merklein, "Das paulinisches Paradox des Cruzes," 285, quoted in Harrisville, *Fracture*, 104.

51. Penna, *Paul the Apostle*, 2.

52. Ibid., 4.

our theological incapacity, the many ways in which we live out our complicity in the death of Jesus, our trust and reliance on the power of God, and our acknowledgment of the need for God in Christ to bring our words to life. An earlier section of this chapter quoted Seamands with approval:

> Ministry, then, is not so much asking Christ to join us in our ministry as we offer him to others; ministry is participating with Christ in his ongoing ministry as he offers himself to others through us.[53]

In a similar vein was Anderson's identification of Jesus as "the one who proclaims himself through the event of preaching."[54] Purves presses this argument to a logical extreme:

> Through union with Christ we share in his speaking forth the Word of God, for we share in him, in the life of the one Word of God. . . . Accordingly the sermon has personal divine authority. Or, to put it more startlingly: through our union with Christ, whereby we share in the life of Jesus Christ, the sermon becomes a present form of the incarnation, an enfleshment in speech today of the once historical and always eternal and living one Word of God. The sermon *is* the Word of God.[55]

But this is to proceed further than the cross of Christ will allow; or rather, it is to ignore the distinctive character of cross and resurrection, to treat them together as a single undifferentiated principle. In the same way that definitive human failure and glorious divine reversal must be kept distinct—if only, in the case of Jesus, as two sides of the same coin—so also we must keep in mind Ricoeur's distinction between "the word of the cross" and the cross itself, or between the crucified and risen Christ on the one hand, and the testimony that bears witness to him on the other. Ricoeur, we recall, insists that "The kerygma is not first of all the interpretation of a text; it is the announcement of a person. In this sense, the word of God is, not the Bible, but Jesus Christ."[56] This distinction is vital to a proper appreciation of divine and human roles in preaching. Moltmann explains further:

> Although this preaching reveals him to the godless and brings them to faith, when Christ rose, he did not turn into words. The crucified Christ is more than the preaching of the cross. For

---

53. Seamands, *Ministry in the Image of God*, 20.
54. Anderson, *The Shape of Practical Theology*, 56.
55. Purves, *Reconstructing Pastoral Theology*, 156–57.
56. Ricoeur, "Preface to Bultmann," 54; quoted in part by Gross, *If You Cannot Preach*, 62.

> the very reason that this preaching is the only adequate access which the godless have to God who was crucified, this intrinsic distinction must not be removed. Precisely because the person must be apprehended in the word, the word cannot be taken for the person himself. There is a reality in the crucified Christ which cannot be identified with any Logos in such a way that it is replaced.[57]

To speak of preaching in this manner clarifies the respective contributions of its several components and participants. Jesus of Nazareth bears witness to the ever-present life of God in words that confound human expectation and challenge hearers to encounter that reality for themselves. Upon the cross, he illustrates the extent of human folly and the full depth of degradation that results from our rejection of God, only for that death to be reversed in a glorious manifestation of God's power to renew all things. Proclaiming this defeat and victory, Christian preachers are captured by the one so as to be liberated by the other. Even so, that we are incriminated by the first renders us humanly incapable of achieving the second. Preaching the unthinkable death of God's Son and the impossible hope of resurrection means that our words themselves partake of the conditions of the cross: only the risen Christ, himself embodying divinely given life, can effect the transformation to which our words refer. As categories of human speech, parable and testimony together indicate the limits of our own role in proclaiming this gospel, thereby leaving room for Christ to accomplish what we cannot. This is to claim neither too little nor too much for preaching: in fact, it holds out the prospect of a ministry no less shameful and no less glorious than the cross and resurrection that we proclaim. Such ministry will prove an exercise in discovery, an encounter with the risen Lord whereby we experience for ourselves the reality of the gospel, thereby ourselves becoming both parable and testimony to the life of God.

> I don't pass judgments. I said what I thought, and it was not heard. I probably said it badly. But much more important, I may have had the opportunity at times to bear witness to Jesus Christ. Perhaps through my words or my writing, someone met this Saviour, the only one, the unique one, beside whom all human projects are childishness; then, if this has happened, I will be fulfilled, and for that, glory to God alone.
>
> Jacques Ellul[58]

---

57. Moltmann, *The Crucified God*, 75.
58. Ellul, *In Season and Out of Season*, 233.

Glory to God,
whose power, working in us,
can do infinitely more than we can ask or imagine.
Glory to God from generation to generation,
in the Church and in Christ Jesus,
for ever and ever. Amen.[59]

---

59. *The Book of Alternative Services of the Anglican Church of Canada*, 214 (based on Ephesians 3:20–21).

Appendix A

Questions for Preachers

The argument of this study is that Christian discipleship, ministry, and preaching are all rooted in the gift of life whose source is God alone. Coming to full expression in the death and resurrection of Jesus of Nazareth, the dynamic of all-encompassing human insufficiency reversed by all-sufficient divine grace represents the essence of a Christian world view. Even though not all biblical texts appeal to them directly, this decisive set of events provides the basis for human salvation, the essential pattern for Christian discipleship, and therefore also the key to our interpretation of Scripture and all proclamation that arises out of it. The following set of questions can help to orient the various components of sermon preparation so that they reflect this same movement from death to life in the presence of God.

1. In what way does the biblical text speak of the life that God pours out on all creation and humanity, even for the benefit of people like ourselves? What does it say about God's grace in our midst?

2. What does this Scripture say concerning life that is beyond us, about glory that we cannot by ourselves attain? How does the text speak of human insufficiency in God's presence, our own in particular? In what way does it call us to silence and smallness? How does it call us to die, or demonstrate how far we are from God?

3. In what way does the biblical text offer hope, or point to the life-giving power of God? What does God offer that we could not otherwise achieve? How does the biblical text call us to life in the fullness of God's presence?

4. In what way may I as a preacher hear the voice of the text with the ears of my hearers, and see it with their eyes? How does this text speak to us together as those on whom God has mercy, and for whom grace is good news?

5. At what point can I join my voice to the voices of the biblical text—the voice of the Lord, the people, and the circumstances the text describes? In what way can my own words testify concerning God's testimony in the words of this text?

6. If we are to speak, to listen, and to see, to die and live as this text directs us, what must God do in order for such things to occur? How must we be made ready to hear and receive? How should we pray?

7. In what ways do Father, Son, and Holy Spirit bear active witness even now as I seek to join my testimony to the testimony of God?

Appendix B

Sermons

The following sermons illustrate the approach that this study commends. The first two concern Jesus' parables of the Sower, and of the seed that grows of its own accord, respectively, while the third builds on the parable from Luke of the rich man with his abundant crops. Each includes an introductory comment that explains what the sermon seeks to accomplish in relation to the approach advocated above. As might be expected, all three sermons follow the exegesis outlined in previous chapters; of greater significance is the outlook, expectation, and sense of trust that every preacher must bring to the pulpit. That, of course, cannot be reproduced in print.

"WHEN GOD IS THE GARDENER" (MARK 4:1-20)[1]

The following sermon reflects the priorities of this study at two levels. First, as to theological content, it sets out a vision of Christian discipleship in which human inability and failure to do the works of God are normative, so that grace alone is sufficient to sustain us. More importantly, it depicts the preacher as one to whom the same conditions apply. Its primary theme is the priority of divine mercy over human endeavor or moral achievement. Referring to Saint Paul, Timothy Lim explains that

> the preaching of the Gospel is not dependent upon any human techniques of eloquence, but upon the demonstration of the

---

1. This sermon was first preached at Philpott Memorial Church in Hamilton, Ontario, on May 21, 2006; an abbreviated version appeared as "Lessons from the Sower and the Seed," *Sunday Vision* (Kampala, Uganda), December 9, 2006.

> *Spirit and power. This does not mean that devices and strategies of rhetoric are not to be used in preaching, but that they should be confined to their proper limits.*[2]

Thus, second, with respect to rhetoric and style, I include a lame joke (which also appears in chapter 3 above), a bad pun or two, occasional alliteration, and some repetition for emphasis. But I am under no illusion that these by themselves can bear the weight of grace. Rather, as implied by the questions in the previous appendix, the sermon is preached as an exercise in practical dependence on God, relying directly on God's Spirit to bring a word of life to its hearers.

I learned long ago that Protestants normally begin their sermons with a joke. That way if your *sermon* turns out to be a joke, you can console yourself with the thought that they're only laughing at your opening line. So you've heard the one about the pastor and the gardener. This guy is working diligently in his garden the way he does every day, rain or shine: the shrubs are blooming nicely, the flowers are in tidy clumps, the colors all complement one another, all the borders neatly edged, and—best of all—the soil is not only black and damp and rich, but also 99.9 percent weed free! So as the pastor walks past, he says—with all the wisdom that theological education affords him—"Isn't God good to give us gardens like this?" "Oh, yeah?" says the old guy, without even looking up from his work, "You should have seen it when God was the gardener."

Maybe Adam and Eve didn't have to pull weeds, but ever since then they've been a problem. There are weeds in the garden of Eden, and they're hard to get out. There are weeds in my garden that are always healthy, no matter how much I neglect them. Why don't the plants I'm actually trying to grow ever work that way? There are weeds in the wheat field, and Jesus tells us that pulling them out will cause more damage than they're worth. And there's that other parable about weeds, the one about the sower who didn't have the brains to know that you don't cast pearls before swine, or good seed into bad ground, if you want your crops to grow. You begin to wonder whether a carpenter is really the right person to be offering advice on farming!

This is one of Jesus' most famous parables. Perhaps the sower is simply shortsighted: either he doesn't actually see where the seed falls, or he can't think far enough ahead to recognize that hungry birds, solid rock, shallow soil, and thistles in abundance do not make for good growing conditions. Or maybe he's just an unrepentant optimist. However we want to explain it,

---

2. Lim, "'Not in Persuasive Words of Wisdom,'" 148.

he simply flings handfuls of the stuff far and wide—with predictable results. Some seed falls on the path, and the birds eat it; some falls on inch-thick soil, sprouts, and withers in the hot sun; some simply gets choked out by all those wonderfully healthy thistles and thorns that infest the ground. And some, miracle of miracles, actually produces a crop.

Every year at McMaster Divinity College in the course we call "Preparation and Delivery of Sermons," students are each required to, well, prepare and deliver a sermon in front of the rest of the class on a scriptural text of their choosing. Several years ago one particular student chose to preach on the parable of the Sower and the Seed. In his mind, the meaning of the parable was crystal clear. After all, he had read Jesus' explanation of what the parable meant, so he did his best to apply that meaning to his audience: men and women either in preparation for, or already engaged in, Christian ministry.

The seed that falls on the path, the seed that the birds come down and eat, says Jesus, is like what happens when a person hears the word of God, only to have Satan snatch it away, before it can even germinate. The seed that falls on shallow soil, a thin layer of earth that barely covers bedrock: that's like what happens when the word of God takes root in you and me—but not deeply enough. It springs to life, starts out with great promise . . . but as soon as trouble arises, or opposition, it just shrivels up and dies. Faith beats a quick retreat, and that's the end of that. And as for the thorns, they're like the cares of the world, the prospect of getting rich, and the fact that other priorities get in the way of walking in the garden with the Lord, in the cool of the evening. Like Adam and Eve, when the Lord of the estate shows up to settle accounts, you make a beeline for the tree line because you don't want to be exposed. You've been too busy to bother with the things of the Lord. Once more the seed that is the word of God has failed to bear fruit in your life.

But we're not like that, said my student. We don't let anything get in our way. No, we're not like other people—robbers, evildoers, adulterers—or even that tax collector over there. Satan doesn't get to us, opposition doesn't faze us, and like young Simba in *The Lion King*, we laugh in the face of danger. In our ministries, said my student, we look for people who are good soil, people who hear the word of God and accept it, and bear fruit. Our kind of people. Amen?

I can't speak for anyone else who was listening that day, but when I heard that sermon, I felt positively beaten up. It wasn't just that he had set the bar too high for me, refused to allow for error, or even a little slip once in a while. It was the fact that he was so scornful of failure. He had no patience, no charity, no tolerance for anything less than perfect obedience, perfect discipleship. I felt like a failure. And I'm the preaching professor.

But then, isn't that exactly what Jesus says in this parable? "Many are called, but few are chosen"? The seed is sown far and wide, but only the *good* soil brings forth fruit? "Those with *good* ears, let them hear"? And that is what the parable would mean, were it not for a couple of details that derail my former student's train of thought.

If you hang around churches for more than a week or two, you quickly get the idea that it would have been cool to be a disciple of Jesus. Not just any disciple, but one of the Original Twelve. Or let's say the Original Eleven, because Judas didn't quite make the grade. Peter, James, John, Simon and Andrew, Bartholomew, Matthew, Thomas (even if he did have his doubts)—these are the guys who make it into the Bible. What could be better than that? In addition, when Luke recounts the parable of the Sower, he tells us that along with the disciples there were a number of women "who had been cured of evil spirits and infirmities: Mary, called Magdalene . . . and Joanna . . . and Susanna, and many others, who provided for them out of their resources" (Luke 8:2–3). The same women who were the first witnesses to the resurrection. You could be one of them. Or if that's too much to hope for, at least you could have been one of the crowd, the multitude who followed him from town to town and into the wilderness, even if it meant going hungry in the process. What could be better than that?

On the other hand, the disciples themselves aren't exactly perfect. Remember that Jesus is the sower, sowing the word. So in chapter 8, Mark tells us that Jesus "speaks the *word* plainly" about how he is going to suffer many things, then be rejected and crucified. Peter is having none of this, and starts to argue. But Jesus turns to him and says, "Get behind me, *Satan*" (8:32–33). What was that Jesus said about birds picking seeds off the path? In chapter 10, Jesus tells a *rich* man to sell all that he has, give to the poor, and so find treasure in heaven. But the man is shocked by these *words*. So are the disciples when Jesus tells them how hard it will be for those with riches to enter the kingdom of heaven. Exactly what he said earlier about the thorns crowding out the life of the new shoot. Judas is the worst example, handpicked by the Messiah, only to betray him for a handful of silver. But there is good news, says Jesus: "Truly I tell you, there is no one who has left house or brothers or sisters or mother or father or children or fields, for my sake and for the sake of the good news, who will not receive *a hundredfold* now in this age—houses, brothers and sisters, mothers and children, and fields, *with persecutions*—and in the age to come eternal life" (Mark 10:29–30). Do you see the pattern? The "word" Jesus speaks, Satan, riches, persecution, and a hundredfold reward: throughout his Gospel, Mark uses the language of the parable of the Sower and the Seed to describe the disciples, their response to Jesus, and the conditions of discipleship. He applies the parable to *them*.

How do they do, in the end? Remember that at the end of chapter 8, Jesus warns his disciples, "Those who are ashamed of me *and of my words* ... of them the Son of Man will also be ashamed when he comes in the glory of his Father with the holy angels" (Mark 8:38). But Judas betrays him, Peter denies him, and, says Mark, at the moment of his arrest "they *all* deserted him, and fled" (14:50).

So much for the glory of being one of Jesus' first followers, an original disciple, the first to abandon him in his moment of need. So much for the sermon that says we're not like the hard soil, the thin soil, the ground with so many thistles the wheat can't grow. According to Mark's gospel, that's exactly who Jesus chooses to be his closest followers. Even if it doesn't exactly fit the pattern of "victorious Christian living."

So where does that leave us? Back to the parable again. Notice that there's also a pattern to the explanations Jesus provides for each part of the parable. The seed, he says, is sown on four sorts of soil: hard, shallow, thorny, and good. The hard soil, with seed that falls on the pathway for birds to eat, has one explanation: Satan. Shallow soil, in which the seed sprouts only to be shriveled by the sun, gets two explanations: "trouble or persecution." The thorn patch that quickly chokes the life out of any good seed sown there gets three explanations: "the worries of this life, the deceitfulness of wealth, and the desire for other things." That's six, in case you're counting. But this is where the mystery begins, because explanation number seven never appears. Remember, this is a four-part parable, with seed sown in four kinds of soil: one explanation for the first soil, two for the second, three for the third. Then what? "These are the ones," says Jesus, "sown on the good soil: they hear the word and accept it and bear fruit, thirty and sixty and a hundredfold" (Mark 4:20). At least in Mark's gospel, there is no explanation of what, exactly, makes the soil so good. We know all about why the word of God *fails* to germinate, fails to grow, fails to mature and bear fruit—and Jesus' own followers illustrate each point: Satan, persecution, wealth, and the anxieties of life. Case closed.

Yet despite everything, despite their denials, despite their failures, despite the fact that according to the parable of the Sower and the Seed they should by rights have no life left in them because the word of God has failed to bear fruit in them since they have failed to receive it well.... Despite all this, with the sole exception of Judas they are still his disciples at the end of the day, and so are you and I. What gives?

Back to the parable once more. Or more precisely, back to that detail about how good soil produces a crop "some thirty, some sixty, some a hundred times what was sown." I had to do some digging—bad pun—to come up with this information, but it turns out that in the Mediterranean world of Jesus' day, normal crop yields, at least for wheat, were roughly four or five to one. Sow one seed, get back five, on average. In premodern Europe, wheat yields were typically less than that, only 3:1 or 4:1. Chinese wheat farmers in the twelfth century achieved yields of 10:1; whereas the English in the 1700s and American farmers of the 1800s managed only 8:1. In the twentieth and twenty-first centuries, with all of our fertilizers, genetic engineering, and agricultural technology, maximum standard wheat yields are still no more than 20:1. According to one of my students, whose father farmed wheat for years, two bushels of seed produces somewhere between fifty and a hundred bushels of wheat per acre, depending on the weather, which is a yield of between 25:1 and 50:1. But take away the technology and the diesel-powered replacements for backbreaking labor; take away any fertilizer other than what the farm animals leave behind, and a yield of thirty, sixty, or a hundredfold is not only mind-boggling, it's positively miraculous. Or as Paul explains to the church at Corinth, "I planted, Apollos watered, but God gave the growth. So neither the one who plants nor the one who waters is anything, but only God who gives the growth" (1 Cor 3:6–7).

What does all this mean for discipleship? Perhaps you've always wanted to walk with Jesus, but you wonder whether your failures disqualify you. Correction: you're secretly certain that your failures disqualify you. If the person in the pew next to you—not to mention your pastor—only knew the struggles going on in your life, only knew what weighs on your conscience, only knew what God certainly knows . . .

I don't mean to play with emotions or stir up fears. On the contrary. I am convinced—convinced by the example of the disciples and the details of the parable—that failure is both normal and necessary in the life of faithful discipleship. Why? Because without it we wouldn't need a Savior. Salvation is not a need you suddenly outgrow once you get "saved." We are hardhearted, hardheaded, and easily led astray—both before and after we come to Christ. We're like Peter, who insists that should all the others abandon his Master, he alone will be true; only to deny three times, in front of witnesses, swearing and calling *heaven* as his witness, that he doesn't know where Jesus comes from. Never heard of him. We're like the other ten or eleven (if you include Judas) who spend three years, give or take, in discipleship, mission, ministry, and intimate communion with Jesus, only to throw it all away in an instant. We're like Paul, who for the rest of his days confesses that he is the least of all possible apostles because he persecuted the church. His spiritual autobiography reads uncomfortably like a script for *Jackass*: "Five times I have received . . . forty lashes less one. Three times I was beaten with rods. Once I received a stoning. Three times I was shipwrecked; for a night and a day I was adrift at sea . . ." (2 Cor 11:24-25). You get the idea. We're like those two hardworking Christians at ancient Philippi named Euodia and Syntyche who only make it into Scripture because Paul has to write and tell them to stop bickering (Phil 4:2-3).

We've always wanted to know what it would mean to walk with the Messiah, and now we know. It means not measuring up. It means having nothing with which to commend yourself to him, even *while* you follow in his footsteps. No good heart, no clean conscience, no list of assets and accomplishments to outweigh the liabilities. But that's why, miracle of miracles, the disciples are still disciples at the end of Mark's gospel, and so are we at the end of the day. Because Satan has done his worst, persecution and opposition have taken their toll, wealth and worldly cares have cleaned up the leftovers, yet—wonder of wonders—grace still triumphs, the gospel still multiplies, and the seed bears rich fruit, even in people such as ourselves. Because the seed that is God's Word is sown and grows despite our failures; despite, sometimes, our lack of faith or faithfulness. Because the next parable Jesus tells is about a seed that grows "all by itself," even though the sower himself "does not know how" (Mark 4:27-28). Because "unless a grain of wheat falls into the earth and dies, it remains just a single grain; but if it dies, it bears much fruit" (John 12:24). That's how it was with Jesus, who had to die in order to be raised; with Peter, who had to fail in order to know his need for Christ; with the apostles, most of whom disappear into historical obscurity; with Paul who is forever at the end of his own strength; with John who writes while imprisoned for his faith on the island of Patmos.

This is what it means to walk with Jesus the way his first followers walked with him. Some of us are anonymous apostles; our best works go unnoticed, and that's just as well because they're mixed with spectacular failures. Some of us are penitent opponents, and that's just as well because we don't want our histories too widely known. Some of us are simply weary and discouraged, like the two disciples who drag their heels all the way back to Emmaus. Some of us aren't yet walking with Jesus, and some of us have turned aside from the way. Like the Original Twelve, we're poster kids for the parable of the Sower.

Nonetheless, as Paul tells the church at Corinth, notwithstanding the birds, the rocky ground, and the weeds, "You are God's field" (1 Cor 3:9), God's garden. "My father is the gardener," Jesus says in the first verse of John 15. And in John 20, when Mary sees the risen Christ, she mistakes *him* for the gardener (20:15). So I am compelled to disagree with my hardheaded, hardhearted student about the meaning of this parable—even though I'm like him in so many ways. Yes, the birds come down on my garden, and thorns infest the ground. Many times, the word of God falls by the wayside, gets choked out by other interests, and fails to bear fruit in my life. And I'm the professor of preaching.

But God is the gardener, his grace is sufficient, and the seed of the gospel continues to bear fruit . . . even in me. What my own best efforts cannot accomplish, Christ surpasses: thirty, sixty, and even a hundredfold. And I know I'm not the only one.

"BETWEEN SOWING AND REAPING" (MARK 4:26–29)

(A sermon for harvesttime)

Because ministry is such hard work and the results at times so meager, Jesus' story of the lazy peasant comes as a shock. Intended for harvest season, when the parable's metaphors of sowing, growth, and reaping are uppermost in everyone's minds, this sermon addresses laborers in the Lord's vineyard who have grown "weary in well-doing" (Gal 6:9). The farmer is a comic figure, his inactivity bordering on the absurd, yet he illustrates the power and ultimate triumph of divine life. It is this assurance that makes ministry possible.

The kingdom of God, said Jesus, works a lot like this. Like a farmer sowing seeds. No, this isn't the parable you're thinking of, with the hot sun and shallow soil and hungry birds. This is the other little parable that Matthew and Luke both threw out because it seemed too small and unimportant. There at the end of Mark chapter four, and nowhere else. This is a strange little story, because the farmer doesn't seem concerned for any aspect of his task. He doesn't clear away stones, plough the ground, pull up weeds, pray for rain, or pour on water. Jesus says, simply, that the man scatters seed on the ground. Then he goes to bed. What kind of farmer is that?

That's not all. He's not just unconcerned, he's ignorant. Don't blame me for saying so: that's what Jesus says about him. If he was telling this parable to farmers, there might have been a moment of silence at this point, when their eyes narrowed and they began to wonder whether the rabbi was making fun of them. "The kingdom of God," says Jesus, "is as though someone were to scatter seed on the ground, go to sleep and get up day after day, until the seed sprouted and grew, but he himself had no clue how."

We can hardly fault the farmer for his ignorance of biology. Ancient farmers surely knew all about soil and rain and fertilizer, and which animals produced the richest manure. But not about biochemistry or cell division or photosynthesis. So that's not what Jesus has in mind. The clue we need comes from Paul. In chapter 9 of 2 Corinthians, the apostle wants to encourage his converts to be generous in providing for the needs of the saints in Jerusalem. By all accounts Jewish believers in the holy city were suffering from poverty, perhaps compounded by the effects of persecution. "The point is this," says Paul:

> the one who sows sparingly will also reap sparingly, and the one who sows bountifully will also reap bountifully... And God is able to provide you with every blessing in abundance, so that by always having enough of everything, you may share abundantly

> in every good work.... He who supplies seed to the sower and bread for food will supply and multiply your seed for sowing and increase the harvest of your righteousness.
>
> (2 Cor 9:6, 8, 10)

God is able to provide because it is God who supplies seed to the sower and bread for eating, God who gives the gift of life in principle along with the particular gifts that sustain our lives from day to day.

So the farmer's ignorance may be theological. He just throws his seed on the ground and forgets to look up. He doesn't know what every pious farmer should know. Paul was no farmer, but even he knew the true source of life, which is why he explains Christian ministry in much the same terms: "I planted, Apollos watered, but God gave the growth." And just in case his readers haven't grasped the basic principle, the apostle repeats himself: "So neither the one who plants nor the one who waters is anything, but only God who gives the growth" (1 Cor 3:6, 7).

I'm not a farmer either, but I do know that farmers know—even atheist farmers, if there are any—that the end result is not really up to them. They "plough their fields and scatter," as the harvest hymn has it, "the good seed on the land. But it is fed and watered by *God's* almighty hand." And that, I think, is the purpose of the parable. That whether the sower is a saint or a sinner, a careful farmer or a lazy one, ignorant of God's ways or alert to them, the seed grows anyway. It's not really up to the farmer. "The earth produces *of itself*, first the stalk, then the head, then the full grain in the head." Step by step, stage by stage, day by day, the seed sprouts and brings forth fruit until the fields are golden and heavy with grain.

By now, of course, any farmers in the audience really *are* annoyed. Peasant farming in any age is backbreaking, unrelenting labor; day in, day out, with or without the Sabbath to get in the way. Good farming requires unrelenting vigilance, constant care to keep the birds at bay and wildlife out of the field—not to mention the neighbor's sheep. You're forever hoping and praying that there will be enough rain but not too much, warm sun but not too hot; not to mention deliverance from bugs, burrowing animals, black rot, or foreign soldiers, any one of which could produce a long, lean, hungry winter. It's all very well to say that God gives the growth, but God doesn't keep the rabbits and squirrels and deer and raccoons out of the carrot patch that your children have watched and watered all day, every day, for weeks. If the wildlife does get into the garden, then in the direct and unapologetic manner that children often have, they're likely to say something rather uncomplimentary about how God doesn't play fair when it comes to giving growth, then taking it all away again.

Still, according to Jesus, the way the kingdom of God works is like when a farmer, a not too bright or careful farmer, throws seed on the ground then goes to sleep. Gets up and goes back to bed (who knows for how long?), until the seed sprouts and begins to grow, even though he has no idea how any of it happens. All of its own accord the earth pushes up seedlings, then stalks, then clusters of wheat, and finally the full, fat grain in the head. Then and only then, according to this parable, according to the way the kingdom works, it's time for hard work, because the harvest has finally come.

This, I think, is a parable for Christian workers. For laborers in the Lord's vineyard, and all who grow weary in well-doing.

We believe in grace, and are quick to agree that God alone gives the growth. But imagine your outrage were it to transpire that in a congregation just down the road from you—perhaps you know the one I mean—where the pastor neglected his flock, forgot to visit, couldn't remember the names of his congregants, and composed his sermons on the way up the pulpit steps; imagine your outrage if out of all the churches in your local association, that was where revival and renewal were to catch fire. Last-minute prayer is all very good, but even the skinniest church growth manual will tell you that careful organization and strategic management will get you further, faster, nine times out of ten. They don't actually say that, of course. They don't need to.

So what on earth is Jesus talking about? Remember that he's talking to peasant farmers, those who—no offense intended—know better than a carpenter from up north what it takes to make the crops grow. Farmers who know all about exhaustion and disappointment; about abundant harvest one year and devastating crop failure the next. And at least *some* of those listening to him will soon have a hand in sowing the seeds of the New Testament church. Still, because they're tired already, they likely would admit that Jesus has a point. They know best of all they are little more than caretakers of a miracle they have no power to create. They may plant, and someone else may water, but only God gives growth. If life is hidden already deep within the seed—if genetic engineering has so far failed to steal the spark—it springs forth of its own accord as soon as conditions are ripe. You work as hard as you can, but in the end the gift of life is only God's to give.

Christian workers know this. There is plenty of speculation about why Jesus sets out three stages of growth: "first the stalk, then the head, then the full grain in the head." Like others before him, Thomas Aquinas compiled a *Catena Aurea* or "Golden Chain," a running commentary on the Gospels from all the patristic sources he could find. Some of the writers that he cites propose that the seed is the "word of life," sown in the world to bring about knowledge of God; the farmer who sleeps and rises is the resurrected Christ;

the full grain is the growing church, bearing fruit in faith and good works.[3] All very imaginative and interesting, but not especially plausible. Back in the third century, Tertullian thought the parable was about different stages of revelation, from Law to Prophets to Gospel to the gift of the Spirit.[4] But I fail to see any increase of wisdom, grace, or revelation in the parable itself. After all, the farmer is still rolling in and out of bed as the days go by and doesn't have a clue what's going on until it finally dawns on him that the time for harvest has arrived.

You preach or prepare your lessons as best you can; you pray for grace in speaking and grace for those who listen; you sow the seed of the word far and wide. Sometimes you say another prayer just for good measure on the way down the pulpit steps. And you make sure to follow up with first-time visitors so they know they're more than welcome to return next week. You rejoice with those who are joyful and you weep with those who grieve. You do everything in your power to be a good steward of those whom the Lord of the Harvest has committed to your care. Sometimes you grow weary in well-doing. Missionaries sometimes sow and water and weed for years before they see a single convert. Which can be immensely difficult if their mission board or sending agency wants nice fat numbers to post in the annual report. Whether for the farmer, the share cropper, or the far-off shareholders, donor fatigue sets in when there is no return on your investment. Prayer support and dollars soon dry up.

But whether one is a peasant or a pastor, a minister or a missionary, the same truth still holds. There is often a long wait between sowing and reaping. Worry as much as you may, it won't make the seeds come up faster, or the work of grace grow any stronger in the hearts and minds of those who have heard the implanted word. Jesus was speaking of resurrection, but he might as well have been referring to ministry when he said, "Unless a grain of wheat falls into the earth and dies, it remains just a single grain; only if it dies, will it bear much fruit" (John 12:24). The same principle applies in either case: Sunday is a long way from Friday if you're not really sure that Sunday's coming at all.

No one is exempt from the conditions of the kingdom. You write your magnum opus, send it off and wait nine months for the publisher to explain politely how the fruit of your labors doesn't quite meet current requirements. Then you wait another nine months for the next publisher to say the same thing. Week after week, you preach to people who long ago gave

---

3. *Catena Aurea* 3.3, *in loc.*, in Aquinas, *Commentary on the Four Gospels*, Vol. 2. St. Mark, 82–83.

4. *On the Veiling of Virgins* 1, in Oden and Hall, *Mark*, 59–60.

up listening because they already know what you're going to say next. You teach Sunday School for years, praying for each child who comes through your classroom door. Every Friday night at the Drop-In Center, you pour out all the compassion that's in you. You intercede for the prodigal who has wandered off into darkness and doesn't know the way back. Face down on the bedroom floor, you plead and weep for the son or daughter who is away at university, hitchhiking around the world, living nearby but far from home; one way or another still lost in the far country.

However it is for each of us, in whatever circumstances, we share the good news. We sow the seed with trembling hands that have only this to offer. Then we wait. Then we wait some more. Maybe you're still waiting. It's often a long time between sowing and reaping. We live our lives as faithfully as we know how, and do our best to obey. Some things turn out as expected, and others do not. Once in a while we wonder whether it has all been a waste of time and effort, whether we would have been better off like the clueless peasant in the parable simply rolling back into bed once the sowing was done.

A certain brand of hard-line Calvinism might think otherwise, but I don't think Jesus means to encourage either fatalism or lack of due diligence in ministry. On the contrary, this is one of many parables that encourage confidence in small beginnings. Jesus reminds us that even when the farmer is more interested in a soft pillow than hard work, God remains faithful. Because God still brings forth life in our midst, Paul can encourage the saints in Galatia, "Let us not grow weary in well-doing, for in due season we shall reap, if we do not lose heart" (Gal 6:9). No doubt Paul is speaking of discipleship generally, but his words apply just as well to ministry.

If the seed is the Word that bears fruit, then the life that lies hidden in small beginnings will burst forth. God will bring the kingdom to fruition. Even if it takes until dawn on the third day, when the eleven are sure that all is now lost; even if it takes years for the wanderers to return home, for the congregation to catch fire, for the ministry to bear fruit; even if your task is simply to sow and someone else, somewhere else, has the privilege of reaping the fruits of your ministry, God remains faithful in bringing forth new life.

Because that's where the parable ends: "When the grain is ripe, at once he goes in with his sickle, because the harvest has come" (Mark 4:29). The harvest is so certain that, no matter how long it takes, even a clueless slugabed will have work to do. Why? Because the grace of God trumps our best efforts at bringing forth life, and God's goodness is at work even among ministers who haven't the sense to do much more than get out of bed on time. Because in the end the kingdom of heaven is not a monument to human endeavor, but living proof of God's own determination to pour out life and make creation fruitful, no matter how long a wait intervenes between sorrowful sowing and the joy that accompanies harvest.

If you are in Christian ministry, you know full well how imperfect your own efforts are. You already know how difficult it can be to give your all, then to wait for a return on your investment, your sacrifice, your labor. You can understand how simple peasant farmers—hands creased and faces lined with the good earth God gave to Abraham—might have felt with a carpenter telling them how to do their job. How some might have shaken their heads and turned away their gaze. But you also know that in God's land, God's kingdom, God alone gives life. All of its own accord the earth brings forth the shoot, the stalk, then the full head of grain. Even weeds grow without the slightest encouragement on our part. How much more so the good fruit of God's reign. There can be a long wait between sowing and reaping. But in the end, God brings the harvest, so that even lazy farmers and weary, worn-out latecomers like us will rise up together to gather in the grain.

"ABEL, CAIN, AND THE JUDGMENT OF JESUS" (LUKE 12:13-21)[5]

I am deeply convinced that preachers must be the first to receive and live by grace, yet because of our ecclesiastical prominence (however modest) we have greater difficulty in doing so than many of our hearers. In this sermon, I endeavor to explain how the parable of the Rich Fool and his crops applies, first in the world of Jesus' day, but also, second, in my own life. Rather than lecturing or hectoring my hearers, I simply leave room for the Spirit of God to bring insight and conviction where it seems good for God to do so.

I.

There were once two brothers. One was a shepherd, the other a farmer, a tiller of the soil. Both seemed pious, both grateful for all that God had given them. It doesn't actually say that anywhere in the text: I'm simply guessing. But both brought sacrifices, thank offerings: the elder brother the fruit of the earth; the younger brother the firstborn of his flocks, and their fat portions. Two brothers, two offerings, two attempts at worship. But whereas one offering pleased God, the other did not. Whereas the younger brother went away satisfied, the older was angry. Angry with his brother, and angry with God. Murderously angry. So he said to his younger brother, "Brother, why don't we go outside into my wheat fields? Why don't we take a walk together . . . a very *long* walk . . ."

II.

Jesus told a parable: "The land of a rich man produced abundantly. And he thought to himself, 'What should I do, for I have no place to store my crops?'" Jesus tells several parables about brothers, but this one does not—at first sight—seem to be among them. There's the parable of the one brother who said he would obey his father but didn't, and the other who said he wouldn't but eventually did. Or more famously, there's the parable of the prodigal son and *his* elder brother. Even the rich man and Lazarus, who lies and dies at his gate, are both sons of Abraham, and therefore brothers, brothers with very different destinations. This is also a parable about a rich man, a farmer,

---

5. This sermon was preached in Parker Chapel, McMaster Divinity College, on February 2, 2005; an abbreviated version was published as Michael P. Knowles, "Abel, Cain, and the Judgment of Jesus," *Homily Service* 43.3 (April, 2010) 96–99, reprinted by permission of Taylor & Francis LLC, www.tandfonline.com.

a landowner, someone with enough earthly security to know that he can take life easy from here on in. But what makes it a parable about a brother?

The clue is there in the introduction:

> Someone in the crowd said to him, "Teacher, tell my *brother* to divide the family inheritance with me." But he said to him, "Friend, who set me as a judge or arbitrator over you?" And he said to them, "Take care! Be on your guard against all kinds of greed; for one's life does not consist in the abundance of possessions." Then he told them a parable...

Someone in the crowd has a brother, is a brother, and these two brothers are having difficulty dividing the family inheritance. So in reply Jesus not only warns about the dangers of greed, but tells a parable about a brother whose greed did him in.

Understanding the parable in this way requires that we have ears to hear; more specifically, first-century Palestinian Jewish ears. My own hearing has been sharpened by John Byron of Ashland Theological Seminary, who was kind enough to share with me a paper on the subject. John points out that for the Jews of Jesus' day, certain legends had begun to accumulate about a brother by the name of Cain. Cain who claimed not to be his brother's keeper, Cain who was marked for life, a fugitive and a wanderer over the face of the earth. The first son of Adam and Eve who murdered the second son of Adam and Eve because God seemed to be playing favorites. According to tradition, Cain had in fact been fathered by the devil: "We must not be like Cain," says 1 John 3:12, "Who was from the evil one and murdered his brother." According to Josephus, Cain was interested only in accumulating wealth. After all, says Josephus, his name means, "Acquisition." Cain added field to field, property to property, by robbery and by force, urging others to imitate his greed and wickedness (*Antiquities* 1:53–61). In rabbinic tradition, what drove Cain to kill his brother was an argument over who owned the land, the field into which they had both gone out to walk. Were all that not enough, Cain is also credited with the invention of weights and measures, in order to assist him in acquiring wealth. He was also the first to set boundary lines, so as to distinguish his own property from that of others. Worst of all, according to Philo, is that fact that Cain fails to recognize the true source of all his wealth: he thinks that the fields in which he works belong to him, not God, and that everything they produce is the result of his own endeavors. He is the ultimate self-made man.

> And he thought to himself, "What should I do, for I have no place to store my crops?" Then he said, "I will do this: I will pull down my barns and build larger ones, and there I will store all

my grain and my goods. And I will say to my soul, Soul, you have ample goods laid up for many years; relax, eat, drink, be merry."

In one of the Aramaic paraphrases of Scripture, Targum Neofiti, Cain even denies the existence of God: "There is no judgment," says Cain, "and there is no judge and there is no other world; and there is no giving of good reward to the just nor is retribution exacted of the wicked."

> But God said to him, "You fool! This very night your life is being demanded of you. And the things you have prepared, whose will they be?" So it is [says Jesus] with those who store up treasures *for themselves* but are not rich toward God.

Abel, according to the same, broad set of traditions, is the very opposite of his older brother: he is the archetype of the righteous servant. "By faith," says the writer to the Hebrews, "Abel offered to God a more acceptable sacrifice than Cain's. Through this he received approval as righteous, God himself giving approval to his gifts" (Heb 11:4). And Abel is the first to be killed just because he is righteous. Which is why Jesus himself can appeal to "all the righteous blood shed on earth, from the blood of righteous Abel to the blood of Zechariah" (Matt 23:35). One more thing: whereas Cain claims there is no justice, no judgment, no judge, Abel says the very opposite. So in the *Testament of Abraham*, a Jewish apocryphal work from around 100 AD, Abel himself has been appointed judge of all creation; it is Abel who examines the righteous and the wicked and sends them to their appointed fates.

Remember how the passage from Luke's gospel began:

> Someone in the crowd said to him, "Teacher, tell my brother to divide the family inheritance with me." But he said to him, "Friend, who set me to be a judge or arbitrator over you?"

"Shall I play Abel," asks Jesus, "To your Cain? If you have set your heart on an abundance of possessions, shall I be the one to declare you just?"

III.

I've tried to hear the parable with Palestinian Jewish ears, hear it as if I had been one of Jesus' first hearers. Which, of course, I'm not. This isn't first-century Judea, we're not in an argument about dividing the inheritance, and even if we were it might be wiser to ask a lawyer for help. And my real audience consists of pastors—past, present, and future—most of you students with enormous debt loads that you will probably still be repaying in ten years' time. On a pastor's salary. One of the things that often worried me when I was chair of the college's Student Financial Aid Committee was how many students whose applications I assessed might have to declare personal bankruptcy. So Jesus' warning about the dangers of greed, and how life does not consist in the abundance of possessions, might seem a little out of place. A bit like lecturing on the dangers of drowning—in the middle of the Sahara Desert. Or preaching about the wickedness of drink to the Woman's Christian Temperance Union. Wrong time. Wrong place. Wrong crowd. They're not the ones who most need to hear the message.

IV.

So instead, on the assumption that preachers preach first to themselves, and because Jesus used the parable to warn against "*all kinds* of greed," I want to ask what Cain and the rich farmer might mean to someone such as myself. I'll just muse aloud for a while and invite you to listen in as I do so.

Few academics ever get rich, and seminary professors are not often among them. At most, we aspire to larger libraries, more books, the latest edition of some important work. You can see in my own office proof that I have already succumbed to that temptation. But that's not the real danger. That's not what I hear in Jesus' parable when I listen with my own ears.

Someone has said that academics argue so bitterly because the stakes are so small. I'm not sure I agree: in fact, we are caught up in a system that rewards the brightest and the best. Higher grades: more prizes and scholarships; more books, and more articles in more prestigious journals: faster promotion and greater honor. If we are not very careful, we will soon come to the conclusion that grades are the only thing that counts, or else the length and wealth of one's resume. We might conclude that scholarship is success, and that rank and reputation amongst one's peers are the truest indicators of personal worth. Not Christian character. Not unnoticed acts of compassion. Not kindness, or courage in the face of adversity, trust in Christ amidst otherwise overwhelming circumstances. Faith despite all odds. Caught up in this way of thinking, we might forget what really matters in the presence of Christ and the sight of God. We might even conclude, as students and scholars in a system of academic endeavor and intellectual accomplishment, that we have reached these goals by virtue of our own aptitudes and abilities; that we have gotten ahead by the work of our own hands and the acuity of our minds. We might even pray for success.

We might be like that man, standing in front of Jesus, begging for help to get ahead in life, all the while failing to recognize the one he is looking at.

I tell my students that every sermon must point to grace, or else it can't be called a truly Christian sermon. Grace for the rich farmer, grace for the brother who wants his share of the inheritance, grace for Abel and Cain, grace for you and me is standing right in front of us if only we have eyes to see and ears to hear.

I worry that I might study Jesus, examine his life, debate his teaching, explore the effect he has had on others, and all the while fail to heed the one who is speaking. I worry that I will try to build my library, fatten my résumé, preach a better sermon, go looking for a better pulpit to preach it from, or a more prestigious institution at which to teach others how to do the same thing, only to forget the One who called me in the first place, taught me the only things worth knowing, gave me words to speak, and brought me here to say them. "And I will say to my soul, 'Soul, you have ample goods laid up for many years; relax, eat, drink, be merry.'" And all these goods that I have spent my life accumulating, whose will they be?

Feel free to fill in your own equivalents.

At least in Greek, Jesus doesn't actually call the man his "friend." What he says, sounding very contemporary, is "*Man*, who set me as judge or divider, one who settles property disputes, over you?" Yet in the last analysis, on the last day, Christ *is* the judge, the divider of sheep from goats, the one at the right hand of glory, the Lamb on the throne. Not Abel, but Jesus. And he *will* judge us, not by the glory we have sought for ourselves, but by the glory we have given to him. Not by the work of our own hands, but by the work he accomplished for us. Not by our own successes, academic or otherwise. Not even by our failures. But by whether we are, in his own words, "rich toward God." Rich by grace. Rich by Christ's own gift.

One day two brothers came to Jesus (or maybe it was their mother), and said, "Master, we'd like to get ahead, both in this life and the next: do you mind if we take those two seats on either side of your throne?" (Matt 20:21). There he was, and they couldn't really see him. In fact, the twelve whom *Jesus* called "brothers" were forever arguing about which of them was the greatest in the kingdom. If it could happen to them, it will surely happen to us.

So back to Cain, in closing. Cain is angry that God seems to have rejected the fruit of his labors, the work of his hands. God says to him—I'm paraphrasing, of course—"I have nothing against you, but I'm not interested in all your hard work. If you do well, will you not be acceptable in my sight? I want you, not your work."

May we have ears to hear what Cain could not.

Bibliography

Adar, Zvi. *The Biblical Narrative*. Translated by Misha Louvish. Jerusalem: Department of Education and Culture of the World Zionist Organization, 1959.
Althaus, Paul. *The Theology of Martin Luther*. Translated by Robert C. Schultz. Philadelphia: Fortress, 1966.
Anderson, A. A. *The Book of Psalms*. 2 vols. New Century Bible Commentary. London: Marshall, Morgan, and Scott, 1972.
Anderson, Ray S. *The Shape of Practical Theology: Empowering Ministry with Theological Praxis*. Downers Grove, IL: IVP Academic, 2001.
Anselm. *Basic Writings*. Edited and translated by Thomas Williams. Indianapolis, IN: Hackett, 2007.
Arida, Robert M. "Hearing, Receiving and Entering ΤΟ ΜΥΣΤΗΡΙΟΝ/ΤΑ ΜΥΣΤΗΡΙΑ: Patristic Insights Unveiling the Crux Interpretum (Isaiah 6:9-10) of the Sower Parable." *St. Vladimir's Theological Quarterly* 38, no. 2 (1994) 211–34.
Augustine. *Of True Religion*. Translated by J. H. S. Burleigh. Chicago: Henry Regnery, 1959.
———. *On Christian Doctrine*. Translated by D. W. Robertson. Library of Liberal Arts 80. Indianapolis, IN: Bobbs-Merrill, 1958.
———. *The Teacher. The Free Choice of the Will. Grace and Free Will*. Translated by Robert P. Russell. Fathers of the Church 59. Washington: Catholic University of America Press, 1968.
Aune, David E. *Revelation 1–5*. Word Biblical Commentary 52A. Dallas: Thomas Nelson, 1997.
Barrett, C. K. *Essays on Paul*. London: SPCK, 1982.
———. *The Gospel According to St. John: An Introduction with Commentary and Notes on the Greek Text*. London: SPCK, 1972.
———. *A Commentary on the First Epistle to the Corinthians*. 2nd ed. Black's New Testament Commentaries. London: Adam and Charles Black, 1971.
———. *A Commentary on the Second Epistle to the Corinthians*. Black's New Testament Commentaries. London: Adam and Charles Black, 1973.
Barth, Karl. *Homiletics*. Translated by Geoffrey W. Bromiley and Donald E. Daniels. Louisville: Westminster John Knox, 1991.
———. *Church Dogmatics*. 14 vols. Translated by G. W. Bromiley. Edinburgh: T & T Clark, 1956–1981.
Bauckham, Richard. *Bible and Mission: Christian Mission in a Postmodern World*. Carlisle: Paternoster; Grand Rapids: Baker, 2003.

Baxter, Richard. *Gildas Salvianus: The Reformed Pastor. Shewing the Nature of the Pastoral Work; Especially in Private Instruction and Catechizing with an Open Confession of Our Too Open Sins*. London: Nevil Simmons, 1656.

———. *Poetical Fragments: Heart-Imployment with God and It Self: The Concordant Discord of a Broken-Healed Heart. Sorrowing-rejoycing, Fearing-hoping, Dying-living*. London: B. Simmons, 1681.

Beasley-Murray, George R. *John*. Word Biblical Commentary 36. Dallas: Word, 1991.

Black, C. Clifton. "Four Stations En Route to a Parabolic Homiletic." *Interpretation* 54 (2000) 386–97.

———. "Preaching from the Gospels and Acts." *Catalyst* 37, vol. 4 (2011) 4–6.

Blomberg, Craig. *Preaching the Parables: From Responsible Interpretation to Powerful Proclamation*. Grand Rapids: Baker Academic, 2004.

Bonner, Gerald. "Augustine as Biblical Scholar." In *The Cambridge History of the Bible. Volume 1: From the Beginnings to Jerome*, edited by Peter R. Ackroyd and Craig F. Evans, 541–63. Cambridge: Cambridge University Press, 1970.

Borg, Marcus J. *Conflict, Holiness and Politics in the Teachings of Jesus*. Revised edition. Harrisburg, PA: Trinity, 1998.

Bowker, John W. "Mystery and Parable: Mark iv. 1–20." *Journal of Theological Studies* 25, vol. 2 (1974) 300–17.

Brooke, George J. "4Q500 1 and the Use of Scripture in the Parable of the Vineyard." *Dead Sea Discoveries* 2 (1995) 268–94.

Brower, Kent E. "The Holy One and His Disciples: Holiness and Ecclesiology in Mark." In *Holiness and Ecclesiology in the New Testament*, edited by Kent E. Brower and Andy Johnson, 57–75. Grand Rapids: Eerdmans, 2007.

Brown, Raymond E. *The Epistles of John: A New Translation with Introduction and Commentary*. The Anchor Bible 30. Garden City, NY: Doubleday, 1982.

———. *The Gospel According to John I–XII: A New Translation with Introduction and Commentary*. The Anchor Bible 29. Garden City, NY: Doubleday, 1966.

———. *The Gospel According to John XIII–XXI: A New Translation with Introduction and Commentary*. The Anchor Bible 29A. Garden City, NY: Doubleday, 1981.

Brown, Sally A. *Cross Talk: Preaching Redemption Here and Now*. Louisville: Westminster John Knox, 2008.

Bruce, F. F. "Citizenship." In *ABD* 1:1048–49.

Brueggemann, Walter. *Cadences of Home: Preaching Among Exiles*. Louisville: Westminster John Knox, 1997.

———. *Deep Memory, Exuberant Hope: Contested Truth in a Post-Christian World*. Minneapolis: Fortress, 2000.

———. *Finally Comes the Poet: Daring Speech for Proclamation*. Minneapolis: Fortress, 1989.

———. *Theology of the Old Testament: Testimony, Dispute, Advocacy*. Minneapolis: Fortress, 1997.

———. "*Theology of the Old Testament: Testimony, Dispute, Advocacy* Revisited." *Catholic Biblical Quarterly* 74, vol. 1 (2012) 28–38.

Brunner, Emil. *Sowing and Reaping: The Parables of Jesus*. Translated by Thomas Wieser. Richmond: John Knox, 1964.

Buttrick, David. *Speaking Parables: A Homiletic Guide*. Louisville: Westminster John Knox, 2000.

Byron, John. "Living in the Shadow of Cain: Echoes of a Developing Tradition in James 5.1-6." *Novum Testamentum* 48, vol. 3 (2006) 261-74.
Campbell, Charles L. *Preaching Jesus: New Directions for Homiletics in Hans Frei's Postliberal Hermeneutic.* Grand Rapids: Eerdmans, 1997.
———. *The Word Before the Powers: An Ethic of Preaching.* Louisville: Westminster John Knox, 2002.
Carter, Warren. "Matthew's Gospel, Rome's Empire, and the Parable of the Mustard Seed (Matt 13:31-32)." In *Hermeneutik der Gleichnisse Jesu: Methodische Neuansätze zum Verstehen urchristlicher Parabeltexte,* edited by Ruben Zimmerman and Gabi Kern, 181-201. Wissenschaftliche Untersuchungen zum Neuen Testament 1.231. Tübingen: Mohr Siebeck, 2008.
Carter, William G. "Sowing Seeds in Difficult Soil: Preaching to Those Who Won't Listen." *Journal for Preachers* 19, vol. 4 (1996) 20-24.
Castelli, Elizabeth A. *Imitating Paul: A Discourse of Power.* Literary Currents in Biblical Interpretation. Louisville: Westminster John Knox, 1991.
Catchpole, David R. "John the Baptist, Jesus and the Parable of the Tares." *Scottish Journal of Theology* 31, vol. 6 (1978) 557-71.
Chazon, Esther G. "Human and Angelic Prayer in Light of the Dead Sea Scrolls." In *Liturgical Perspectives: Prayer and Poetry in Light of the Dead Sea Scrolls: Proceedings of the Fifth International Symposium of the Orion Center for the Study of the Dead Sea Scrolls and Associated Literature, 19-23 January, 2000,* edited by Esther G. Chazon et al., 35-47. Studies on the Texts of the Desert of Judah 48. Leiden: Brill, 2003.
Colson, F. H., and George H. Whitaker, eds. *Philo.* 10 vols. Loeb Classical Library. London: Heinemann; New York: Putnam, 1929-1962.
Cosgrove, Charles H. *The Cross and the Spirit: A Study in the Argument and Theology of Galatians.* Macon, GA: Mercer University Press, 1988.
Cousar, Charles B. *A Theology of the Cross: The Death of Jesus in the Pauline Letters.* Overtures to Biblical Theology. Minneapolis: Fortress, 1990.
Coward, Howard, and Toby Foshan, eds. *Derrida and Negative Theology.* Albany, NY: State University of New York, 1992.
Craddock, Fred B. *As One Without Authority. Revised and With New Sermons.* St. Louis: Chalice, 2001.
Cranfield, C. E. B. *A Critical and Exegetical Commentary on the Epistle to the Romans.* 2 Vols. International Critical Commentary. Edinburgh: T & T Clark, 1975, 1979.
———. "St. Mark 4:1-34; Part I." *Scottish Journal of Theology* 4, vol. 4 (1951) 398-414.
Crawford, Cory D. "On the Exegetical Function of the Abraham/Ravens Tradition in Jubilees 11." *Harvard Theological Review* 97, vol. 1 (2004) 91-97.
Crossan, John Dominic. "The Seed Parables of Jesus." *Journal of Biblical Literature* 92, vol. 2 (1973) 244-66.
Dahl, Nils A. "The Parables of Growth." *Studia Theologica* 5, vol. 2 (1952) 132-66.
Dale, Ron. "The Sower." *The Expository Times* 116, vol. 9 (2005) 307-309.
Davies, W. D. *The Setting of the Sermon on the Mount.* Cambridge: Cambridge University Press, 1966.
Davies, W. D., and Dale C. Allison. *The Gospel According to Saint Matthew.* 3 vols. International Critical Commentary. Edinburgh: T & T Clark, 1988-1997.
Derrett, J. Duncan M. "The Parable of the Unjust Steward." In *Law in the New Testament,* 48-77. London: Darton, Longman, and Todd, 1970.

Doty, William G. "An Interpretation: Parable of the Weed and Wheat." *Interpretation* 25 (1971) 185–94.

Dreyfus, François. "L'argument scripturaire de Jésus en faveur de la résurrection des morts (Marc, XII, 26–27)." *Revue Biblique* 66, vol. 2 (1959) 213–24.

Drury, John. *The Parables in the Gospels: History and Allegory.* New York: Crossroad, 1985.

Duke, Paul Simpson. *The Parables: A Preaching Commentary.* Nashville: Abingdon, 2005.

Dupont, Jacques. "La parabole de la semence qui pousse toute seul." *Recherches de Science Religieuse* 55 (1967) 367–92.

———. "Encore la parabole de la Semence qui pousse seule." In *Jesus und Paulus: Festschrift für Werner Georg Kummel zum 70. Geburtstag,* edited by E. Earle Ellis and Erich Grosser, 96–108. Göttingen: Vandenhoeck & Ruprecht, 1975.

Edwards, J. Kent. "Deep Preaching." *Journal of the Evangelical Homiletics Society* 10, vol. 1 (2010) 79–111.

Elliott, Mark Adam. *The Survivors of Israel: A Reconsideration of the Theology of Pre-Christian Judaism.* Grand Rapids: Eerdmans, 2000.

Ellul, Jacques. *In Season and Out of Season: An Introduction to the Thought of Jacques Ellul.* Translated by Lani K. Niles. San Francisco: Harper and Row, 1982.

———. "Témoignage et Société Technicienne." In *Le Témoignage; actes du colloque organisé par le Centre international d'études humanistes et par l'Institut d'études philosophiques de Rome, Rome, 5–11 janvier 1972,* edited by Enrico Castelli, 441–55. Paris: Aubier, 1972.

———. *The Subversion of Christianity.* Translated by Geoffrey W. Bromiley. Grand Rapids: Eerdmans, 1986.

———. *The Technological Society.* Translated by John Wilkinson. New York: Knopf, 1964.

Elowsky, Joel C., ed. *John 11–21.* Ancient Christian Commentary on Scripture 4b. Downers Grove, IL: InterVarsity, 2007.

Engberg-Pedersen, Troels. "Proclaiming the Lord's Death: 1 Corinthians 11:17–34 and the Forms of Paul's Theological Argument." In *Pauline Theology Volume II: 1 & 2 Corinthians,* edited by David M. Hay, 103–32. Minneapolis: Fortress, 1993.

Evans, Craig A. "On the Isaianic Background of the Sower Parable." *Catholic Biblical Quarterly* 47, vol. 3 (1985) 464–68.

———. *To See and Not Perceive: Isaiah 6:9–10 in Early Jewish and Christian Interpretation.* Journal for the Study of the Old Testament: Supplement Series 64. Sheffield: JSOT, 1989.

Fee, Gordon D. *The First Epistle to the Corinthians.* New International Commentary on the New Testament. Grand Rapids: Eerdmans, 1987.

Fenton, John C. *The Gospel According To John.* New Clarendon Bible. Oxford: Clarendon, 1970.

Finamore, Stephen. *God, Order, and Chaos: René Girard and the Apocalypse.* Paternoster Biblical Monographs. Eugene, OR: Wipf & Stock, 2009.

Finkel, Asher. "Prayer in Jewish Life of the First Century as Background to Early Christianity." In *Into God's Presence: Prayer in the New Testament,* edited by Richard N. Longenecker, 43–63. McMaster New Testament Studies 5. Grand Rapids: Eerdmans, 2001.

Fish, Stanley E. *Self-Consuming Artifacts: The Experience of Seventeenth-Century Literature*. Berkeley: University of California Press, 1972.
Florence, Anna Carter. *Preaching As Testimony*. Louisville: Westminster John Knox, 2007.
Flusser, David. "Johanan ben Zakkai and Matthew." In *Judaism and the Origins of Christianity*, 490–93. Jerusalem: Magnes, 1988.
Forde, Gerhard O. *On Being a Theologian of the Cross: Reflections on Luther's Heidelberg Disputation, 1518*. Grand Rapids: Eerdmans, 1997.
Freedman, H., and M. Simon, ed. *Midrash Rabbah: Genesis*. London: Soncino, 1983.
Funk, Robert W. "The Looking Glass Tree is for the Birds: Ezekiel 17:22–24; Mark 4:30–32." *Interpretation* 27, vol. 1 (1973) 3–9.
Gerhardsson, Birger. "The Parable of the Sower and its Interpretation." *New Testament Studies* 14, vol. 2 (1968) 165–93.
Glover, Raymond F., ed. *The Hymnal 1982 Companion*, Vol. 3A. New York: Church Hymnal Corporation, 1994.
Goldin, Judah, trans. *The Fathers According to Rabbi Nathan*. Yale Judaica Series 10. New Haven, CT: Yale University Press, 1955.
Gorman, Michael J. *Cruciformity: Paul's Narrative Spirituality of the Cross*. Grand Rapids: Eerdmans, 2001.
———. *Inhabiting the Cruciform God: Kenosis, Justification, and Theosis in Paul's Narrative Soteriology*. Grand Rapids: Eerdmans, 2009.
Greenman, Jeffrey P., Read Mercer Schuchardt, and Noah J. Toly. *Understanding Jacques Ellul*. Eugene, OR: Cascade, 2012.
Greidanus, Sidney. *The Modern Preacher and the Ancient Text: Interpreting and Preaching Biblical Literature*. Grand Rapids: Eerdmans, 1988.
Guthrie, Shirley C., Jr. *Diversity in Faith—Unity in Christ: Orthodoxy, Liberalism, Piety, and Beyond*. Philadelphia: Westminster, 1986.
Gross, Nancy Lammers. *If You Cannot Preach Like Paul . . .* Grand Rapids: Eerdmans, 2002.
Hamel, Gildas. *Poverty and Charity in Roman Palestine, First Three Centuries C.E.* University of California Publications: Near Eastern Studies 23. Berkeley: University of California Press, 1990.
Harrisville, Roy A. *Fracture: The Cross as Irreconcilable in the Language and Thought of the Biblical Writers*. Grand Rapids: Eerdmans, 2006.
Hauerwas, Stanley. *A Cross-Shattered Church: Reclaiming the Theological Heart of Preaching*. Grand Rapids: Brazos, 2009.
Hawthorne, Gerald F. *Philippians*. Word Biblical Commentary 43. Dallas: Word, 1983.
Hayes, Christine. *Gentile Impurities and Jewish Identities: Intermarriage and Conversion from the Bible to the Talmud*. New York: Oxford University Press, 2002.
———. "Intermarriage and Impurity in Ancient Jewish Sources." *Harvard Theological Review* 92, vol. 1 (1999) 3–36.
Hays, Richard B. *First Corinthians*. Interpretation: A Bible Commentary for Teaching and Preaching. Louisville: Westminster John Knox, 1997.
Heil, John Paul. "Reader-Response and the Narrative Context of the Parables about Growing Seed in Mark 4:1–34." *Catholic Biblical Quarterly* 54.2 (1992) 271–86.
Heim, S. Mark. *Saved from Sacrifice: A Theology of the Cross*. Grand Rapids: Eerdmans, 2006.

Hellerman, Joseph H. *Reconstructing Honor in Roman Philippi: Carmen Christi as Cursus Pudorum.* Society for New Testament Studies Monograph Series 132. Cambridge: Cambridge University Press, 2005.

Hengel, Martin. *Crucifixion in the Ancient World and the Folly of the Message of the Cross.* Translated by John Bowden. Philadelphia: Fortress, 1977.

Henry, Matthew. *An Exposition of the Historical Books of the New Testament, viz. St. Matthew, St. Mark, St. Luke, St. John, and the Acts of the Apostles.* London: Clarke and Hett, 1725. Accessed via Gale Eighteenth Century Collections Online: http://galenet.galegroup.com/servlet/ECCO

Himmelfarb, Martha. "Levi, Phinehas, and the Problem of Intermarriage at the Time of the Maccabean Revolt." *Jewish Studies Quarterly* 6, vol. 1 (1999) 1–24.

Hopkins, Jasper, and Herbert Richardson, eds. and trans. *Anselm of Canterbury. Volume Two: Philosophical Fragments; De Grammatico; On Truth; Freedom of Choice; The Fall of the Devil; The Harmony of the Foreknowledge, the Predestination, and the Grace of God with Free Choice.* Toronto: Edwin Mellen, 1976.

Hoskyns, Edwyn Clement. *The Fourth Gospel.* Edited by Francis Noel Davey. London: Faber and Faber, 1947.

Howse, Christopher, ed. *Best Sermons Ever.* London: Continuum, 2001.

Hubbard, Robert L. *The Book of Ruth.* New International Commentary on the Old Testament. Grand Rapids: Eerdmans, 1988.

Hultgren, Arland J. *The Parables of Jesus: A Commentary.* Grand Rapids: Eerdmans, 2002.

Hunzinger, Claus-Hunno. s.v. σίναπι. In *TDNT* 7:287–91.

Instone-Brewer, David. *Prayer and Agriculture.* Traditions of the Rabbis from the Era of the New Testament 1. Grand Rapids: Eerdmans, 2004.

Isaac, Ephraim. "1 (Ethiopic Apocalypse of) Enoch: A New Translation and Introduction." In *Old Testament Pseudepigrapha,* Vol. 1, edited by James H. Charlesworth, 5–89. Garden City, KS: Doubleday, 1983.

Janzen, J. Gerald. "Resurrection and Hermeneutics: On Exodus 3.6 in Mark 12.26." *Journal for the Study of the New Testament* 23 (1985) 43–58.

Jaubert, Anne. "L'image de la Vigne (Jean 15)." In *Oikonomia: Heilsgeschichte als Thema der Theologie. Oscar Cullmann zum 65. Geburtstag,* edited by Felix Christ, 93–99. Hamburg: Herbert Reich, 1967.

Jenkins, Philip. *The Lost History of Christianity: The Thousand-Year Golden Age of the Church in the Middle East, Africa, and Asia—and How It Died.* New York: HarperCollins, 2008.

Jeremias, Joachim. "Palästinakundliches zum Gleichnis vom Säemann (Mark iv.3–8 par.)." *New Testament Studies* 13, vol. 1 (1966) 48–53.

Johnson, Darrell W. *The Glory of Preaching: Participating in God's Transformation of the World.* Downers Grove, IL: IVP Academic, 2009.

Josephus. Translated by H. St. J. Thackeray et al. 10 vols. Loeb Classical Library. Cambridge: Harvard University Press, 1926–1965.

Josephus, Flavius. *Les Antiquités Juives. Introduction et texte, traduction et notes. Livres I à III.* Edited and translated by Étienne Nodet et al. 2 vols. Paris: Cerf, 1990.

Juel, Donald H. "Encountering the Sower: Mark 4:1–20." *Interpretation* 56, vol. 3 (2002) 273–83.

Keegan, Terence J. "The Parable of the Sower and Mark's Jewish Leaders." *Catholic Biblical Quarterly* 56, vol. 3 (1994) 501–18.

Keener, Craig S. *A Commentary on the Gospel of Matthew.* Grand Rapids: Eerdmans, 1999.
Kissinger, Warren S. *The Parables of Jesus: A History of Interpretation and Bibliography.* ATLA Bibliography Series 4. Metuchen, NJ; London: Scarecrow, 1979.
Klauck, H. J. *Allegorie und Allegorese in synoptischen Gleichnistexten.* Neutestamentliche Abhandlungen 13. Münster: Aschendorff, 1978.
Kleinknecht, Karl T. *Der leidende Gerechtfertigte. Die alttestamentlich-jüdische Tradition vom 'leidenden Gerechten' und ihre Rezeption bei Paulus.* Wissenschaftliche Untersuchungen zum Neuen Testament 2.14. Tübingen: Mohr Siebeck, 1984.
Knowles, Michael P. "Abram and the Birds in *Jubilees* 11: A Subtext for the Parable of the Sower?" *New Testament Studies* 41 (1995) 145–51.
———. *Jeremiah in Matthew: The Rejected-Prophet Motif in Matthaean Redaction.* Journal for the Study of the New Testament: Supplement Series 68. Sheffield: JSOT, 1993.
———. "Mark, Matthew, and Mission: Faith, Failure, and the Fidelity of Jesus." In *Christian Mission: Old Testament Foundations and New Testament Developments,* edited by Stanley E. Porter and Cynthia Long Westfall, 64–92. McMaster New Testament Study Series 9. Eugene, OR: Wipf & Stock, 2010.
———. "Reading Matthew: The Gospel as Oral Performance." In *Reading the Gospels Today,* edited by Stanley E. Porter, 56–77. McMaster New Testament Studies 8. Grand Rapids: Eerdmans, 2004.
———. "Sowing Seeds: A Parabolic Homiletic." *Canadian Theological Review* 1 (2012) 52–64.
———. *We Preach Not Ourselves: Paul on Proclamation.* Grand Rapids: Brazos, 2008.
———. "What Was the Victim Wearing? Literary, Economic, and Social Contexts for the Parable of the Good Samaritan." *Biblical Interpretation: A Journal of Contemporary Approaches* 12, vol. 2 (2004) 145–74.
Kugel, James L. *In Potiphar's House: The Interpretive Life of Biblical Texts.* New York: HarperSanFrancisco, 1990.
———. "The Holiness of Israel and the Land in Second Temple Times." In *Texts, Temples, and Traditions: A Tribute to Menahem Haran,* edited by Michael V. Fox, Victor Hurowitz, and Avi Hurvitz, 21–32. Winona Lake, IN: Eisenbrauns, 1996.
Lamott, Anne. *Grace (Eventually): Thoughts on Faith.* New York: Riverhead, 2007.
———. *Plan B: Further Thoughts on Faith.* New York: Riverhead, 2005.
———. *Traveling Mercies: Some Thoughts on Faith.* New York: Pantheon, 1999.
LaRue, Cleophus J. *I Believe I'll Testify: The Art of African American Preaching.* Louisville: Westminster John Knox, 2011.
———, ed. *More Power in the Pulpit: How America's Most Effective Black Preachers Prepare Their Sermons.* Louisville: Westminster John Knox, 2009.
———, ed. *Power in the Pulpit: How America's Most Effective Black Preachers Prepare Their Sermons.* Louisville: Westminster John Knox, 2002.
———. *The Heart of Black Preaching.* Louisville: Westminster John Knox, 2000.
Lathrop, Gordon W. *The Pastor: A Spirituality.* Minneapolis: Fortress, 2006.
Lim, Timothy H. "'Not in Persuasive Words of Wisdom, but in the Demonstration of the Spirit and Power.'" *Novum Testamentum* 29, vol. 2 (1987) 137–49.
Lindars, Barnabas. *The Gospel of John.* New Century Bible Commentary. Grand Rapids: Eerdmans, 1972.

Long, Thomas G. *Preaching and the Literary Forms of the Bible*. Philadelphia: Fortress, 1989.

———. *Testimony: Talking Ourselves into Being Christian*. San Francisco: Jossey-Bass, 2004.

———. *The Witness of Preaching*. 2nd ed. Louisville: Westminster John Knox, 2005.

Longenecker, Bruce W. "Socio-Economic Profiling of the First Urban Christians." In *After the First Urban Christians: The Socio-Historical Study of Pauline Christianity Twenty-Five Years Later*, edited by Todd D. Still and David G. Horrell, 36–59. New York: T & T Clark, 2009.

Longenecker, Richard N. *Acts*. The Expositor's Bible Commentary. Grand Rapids: Zondervan, 1971.

———. *Galatians*. Word Biblical Commentary 41. Dallas: Word, 1990.

———. "The Messianic Secret in the Light of Recent Discoveries." *Evangelical Quarterly* 41, vol. 4 (1969) 207–15.

Lose, David J. *Confessing Jesus Christ: Preaching in a Postmodern World*. Grand Rapids: Eerdmans, 2003.

Lowe, Matthew F. "Death Dismantled: Reading Christological and Soteriological Language in 1 Corinthians 15 in Light of Roman Imperial Ideology." PhD diss., McMaster Divinity College, 2011.

Luccock, Halford E. "The Gospel According to St. Mark: Exposition." *Interpreter's Bible* 7.647–917.

Luther, Martin. *D. Martin Luthers Werke*. 120 vols. Weimar, 1883–2009.

Luz, Ulrich. "Intertexts in the Gospel of Matthew." *Harvard Theological Review* 97, vol. 2 (2004) 119–37.

Matthews, Victor H. "Treading the Winepress: Actual and Metaphorical Viticulture in the Ancient Near East." *Semeia* 86 (1999) 19–32.

Marcus, Joel. "Blanks and Gaps in the Markan Parable of the Sower." *Biblical Interpretation* 5, vol. 3 (1997) 247–62.

———. *Mark 1–8: A New Translation with Introduction and Commentary*. Anchor Bible 27. New York: Doubleday, 2000.

———. *The Mystery of the Kingdom of God*. Society of Biblical Literature Dissertation Series 90. Atlanta: Scholars, 1986.

Marshall, I. Howard. *The Gospel of Luke: A Commentary on the Greek Text*. New International Greek Testament Commentary. Grand Rapids: Eerdmans, 1979.

Martin, Ralph P. *Philippians*. New Century Bible. Grand Rapids: Eerdmans, 1980.

McArthur, Harvey K. "The Parable of the Mustard Seed." *Catholic Biblical Quarterly* 33, vol. 2 (1971) 198–210.

McClure, John S. *Other-Wise Preaching: A Postmodern Ethic for Homiletics*. St. Louis: Chalice, 2001.

McGrath, Alister E. *Luther's Theology of the Cross: Martin Luther's Theological Breakthrough*. Oxford: Blackwell, 1985.

McIver, Robert K. "One Hundred-Fold Yield — Miraculous or Mundane? Matthew 13.8, 23; Mark 4.8, 20; Luke 8.8." *New Testament Studies* 40, vol. 4 (1994) 606–608.

———. "The Parable of the Weeds among the Wheat (Matt 13:24–30, 36–43) and the Relationship Between the Kingdom of God and the Church as Portrayed in the Gospel of Matthew." *Journal of Biblical Literature* 114, vol. 4 (1995) 643–59.

Meeks, Wayne A. *The First Urban Christians: The Social World of the Apostle Paul*. New Haven, CT: Yale University, 1983.

Merklein, Helmut. *Studien zu Jesus und Paulus II.* Wissenschaftliche Untersuchungen zum Neuen Testament 1.105. Tübingen: Mohr Siebeck, 1998.

Metzger, Bruce M. "The Fourth Book of Ezra. With the Four Additional Chapters. A New Translation and Introduction." In *OTP* 1.517–59.

Meyer, Marvin W. "Mystery Religions." In *ABD* 4:941–45.

Miller, Dale, and Patricia Miller. *The Gospel of Mark as Midrash on Earlier Jewish and New Testament Literature.* Studies in the Bible and Early Christianity 21. Lewiston, NY: Mellen, 1990.

Moberly, R. W. L. *At the Mountain of God: Story and Theology in Exodus 32–34.* Journal for the Study of the Old Testament: Supplement Series 22. Sheffield: JSOT, 1983.

Moltmann, Jürgen. *The Crucified God: The Cross of Christ as the Foundation and Criticism of Christian Theology.* Translated by R. A. Wilson and John Bowden. London: SCM, 1974.

Montefiore, C. G., and H. Loewe, eds. *A Rabbinic Anthology, Selected and Arranged with Comments and Introductions.* London: Macmillan, 1938.

Morris, Leon. *The Gospel According to John. Revised Edition.* New International Commentary on the New Testament. Grand Rapids: Eerdmans, 1995.

Mussner, Franz. "1QHodajoth und das Gleichnis vom Senfkorn (Mk. 4, 30–32 par.)." *Biblische Zeitschrift* 4, vol. 1 (1960) 128–30.

Najman, Hindy. "A Written Copy of the Law of Nature: An Unthinkable Paradox?" *Studia Philonica Annual* 15 (2003) 51–56.

———. "Cain and Abel as Character Traits: A Study in the Allegorical Typology of Philo of Alexandria." In *Eve's Children: The Biblical Stories Retold and Interpreted in Jewish and Christian Traditions*, edited by Gerard P. Luttikhuizen, 107–18. Themes in Biblical Narrative 5. Leiden: Brill, 2003.

———. "The Law of Nature and the Authority of Mosaic Law." *Studia Philonica Annual* 11 (1999) 55–73.

Neusner, Jacob, and Richard S. Sarason, eds. *The Tosefta, Translated from the Hebrew. First Division: Zeraim (The Order of Agriculture).* Hoboken, NJ: Ktav, 1986.

Newbigin, Lesslie. *The Gospel in a Pluralist Society.* Grand Rapids: Eerdmans, 1989.

———. *The Light Has Come: An Exposition of the Fourth Gospel.* Grand Rapids: Eerdmans, 1982.

Nicol, George G. "The Narrative Structure and Interpretation of Genesis XXVI 1–33." *Vetus Testamentum* 46, vol. 3 (1996) 339–60.

Nitzan, Bilhah. *Qumran Prayer and Religious Poetry.* Translated by Jonathan Chipman. Studies on the Texts of the Desert of Judah 12. Leiden: Brill, 1994.

Oakman, Douglas E. *Jesus and the Economic Questions of His Day.* Studies in the Bible and Early Christianity 8. Lewiston, NY: Mellen, 1986.

Oden, Thomas C., and Christopher A. Hall, eds. *Mark.* The Ancient Christian Commentary on Scripture 2. Downers Grove, IL: InterVarsity, 1998.

Osborne, Grant R. *Revelation.* Baker Exegetical Commentary on the New Testament. Grand Rapids: Baker, 2002.

Pape, Lance B. *A Ricoeurian Revision of Postliberal Homiletics.* PhD diss., Emory University, 2010.

———. *The Scandal of Having Something to Say: Ricoeur and the Possibility of Postliberal Preaching.* Waco, TX: Baylor University Press, 2013.

Payne, Philip B. "The Authenticity of the Parable of the Sower and its Interpretation." In *Gospel Perspectives: Studies of History and Tradition in the Four Gospels Vol. I*, edited by R. T. France and David Wenham, 163–208. Sheffield: JSOT, 1980.

Pelikan, Jaroslav, and Helmut T. Lehmann, eds. *Luther's Works*. 55 Vols. St. Louis: Concordia; Philadelphia: Fortress, 1955–1986.

Penna, Romano. *Paul the Apostle: A Theological and Exegetical Study. Volume 2: Wisdom and Folly of the Cross*. Translated by Thomas P. Wahl. Collegeville, MN: Michael Glazier, 1996.

Perkins, Pheme. "Mark 4:30–34." *Interpretation* 56, vol. 3 (2002) 311.

Pesch, Rudolf. *Das Markusevangelium. Erster Teil: Einleitung und Kommentar zu Kap. 1,1–8,26*. Herders theologischer Kommentar zum Neuen Testament 2.1. Freiburg: Herder, 1976.

Peterson, Eugene H. *Under the Unpredictable Plant: An Exploration in Vocational Holiness*. Grand Rapids: Eerdmans, 1992.

Pickett, Raymond. *The Cross in Corinth: The Social Significance of the Death of Jesus*. Journal for the Study of the New Testament: Supplement Series 143. Sheffield: Sheffield Academic, 1997.

Porter, Stanley E., and Jason C. Robinson. *Hermeneutics: An Introduction to Interpretive Theory*. Grand Rapids: Eerdmans, 2011.

Porton, Gary G. "Sadducees." In *ABD* 5:892–95.

Postman, Neil. *Technopoly: The Surrender of Culture to Technology*. New York: Knopf, 1992.

Prenter, Regin. *Luther's Theology of the Cross*. Philadelphia: Fortress, 1971.

Purves, Andrew. *Pastoral Theology in the Classical Tradition*. Louisville: Westminster John Knox, 2001.

———. *Reconstructing Pastoral Theology: A Christological Foundation*. Louisville: Westminster John Knox, 2004.

———. *The Crucifixion of Ministry: Surrendering Our Ambitions to the Service of Christ*. Downers Grove, IL: InterVarsity, 2007.

———. *The Resurrection of Ministry: Serving in the Hope of the Risen Lord*. Downers Grove, IL: InterVarsity, 2010.

Quicke, Michael J. *Preaching As Worship: An Integrative Approach to Formation in Your Church*. Grand Rapids: Baker, 2011.

Rashkover, Randi. *Revelation and Theopolitics: Barth, Rosenzweig and the Politics of Praise*. London: T & T Clark, 2005.

Ratzinger, Joseph Cardinal. *Salt of the Earth: The Church at the End of the Millennium. An Interview with Peter Seewald*. Translated by Adrian Walker. San Francisco: Ignatius, 1997.

Rengstorf, Karl Heinrich. s.v. σημεῖον κτλ. In *TDNT* 7:200–69.

———. s.v. τέρας. In *TDNT* 8:113–26.

———. s.v. ἀπόστολος. In *TDNT* 1:419.

Resner, André, Jr. *Preacher and Cross: Person and Message in Theology and Rhetoric*. Grand Rapids: Eerdmans, 1999.

Ricoeur, Paul. *Essays on Biblical Interpretation*. Edited by Lewis S. Mudge. Philadelphia: Fortress, 1980.

———. "L'herméneutique du témoignage," *Archivio di Filosofia (La Testimonianza)* 42, *Le Témoignage; actes du colloque organisé par le Centre international d'études humanistes et par l'Institut d'études philosophiques de Rome, Rome, 5–11 janvier*

1972, edited by Enrico Castelli, 35–61. Paris: Aubier, 1972. Reprinted in *Lectures 3: Aux frontières de la philosophie*, 107–39. Paris: Seuil, 1994.

———. "Listening to the Parables of Jesus." In *The Philosophy of Paul Ricoeur: An Anthology of His Work*. Edited by Charles E. Reagan and David Stewart, 239–45. Boston: Beacon, 1978.

———. "Naming God." In *Figuring the Sacred: Religion, Narrative, and Imagination*, edited by Mark I. Wallace, 217–35. Minneapolis: Fortress, 1995.

———. "Philosophy and Religious Language." *Journal of Religion* 54, vol. 1 (1974) 71–85.

———. "Toward a Hermeneutic of the Idea of Revelation." In *Essays on Biblical Interpretation*, edited by Lewis S. Mudge, 73–117. Philadelphia: Fortress, 1980.

Ringgren, Helmer. *s.v.* ריב. In *TDNT* 13:473–79.

Sabin, Marie. "Reading Mark 4 as Midrash." *Journal for the Study of the New Testament* 45 (1992) 3–26.

Sahlin, Harald. "Zum Verständnis von drei Stellen im Markusevangelium (Mk 4,26–29; 7,18f; 15,34)." *Biblica* 33, vol. 1 (1952) 53–66.

Sandmel, Samuel. *Philo's Place in Judaism: A Study of Conceptions of Abraham in Jewish Literature*. New York: Ktav, 1971.

Savage, Timothy B. *Power Through Weakness: Paul's Understanding of the Christian Ministry in 2 Corinthians*. Society for New Testament Studies Monograph Series 86. Cambridge: Cambridge University Press, 1996.

Schellenberg, Ryan S. "Kingdom as Contaminant? The Role of Repertoire in the Parables of the Mustard Seed and the Leaven." *Catholic Biblical Quarterly* 71, vol. 3 (2009) 527–43.

Schürer, Emil. *The History of the Jewish People in the Age of Jesus Christ (175 B.C.– A.D. 135)*. Vol. 2. Revised by Géza Vermès, Fergus Millar, and Matthew Black. Edinburgh: T & T Clark, 1979.

Schweitzer, Eduard. *The Good News According to Matthew*. Translated by D. E. Green. Atlanta: Knox, 1975.

Scott, Bernard Brandon. *Hear Then the Parable: A Commentary on the Parables of Jesus*. Minneapolis: Augsburg Fortress, 1989.

———. "Parables of Growth Revisited: Notes on the Current State of Parable Research." *Biblical Theology Bulletin* 11.1 (1981) 3–9.

Seamands, Stephen. *Ministry in the Image of God: The Trinitarian Shape of Christian Service*. Downers Grove, IL: InterVarsity, 2005.

Shi, Wenhua. *Paul's Message of the Cross as Body Language*. Wissenschaftliche Untersuchungen zum Neuen Testament 2.254. Tübingen: Mohr Siebeck, 2008.

Simpson, Albert B. *The Gospel of Healing*. New York: Christian Alliance, 1915.

Skehan, Patrick W., and Alexander A. Di Lella. *The Wisdom of Ben Sira: A New Translation with Introduction and Commentary*. Anchor Bible 39. New York: Doubleday, 1987.

Snodgrass, Klyne R. "A Hermeneutic of Hearing Informed by the Parables with Special Reference to Mark 4." *Bulletin for Biblical Research* 14, vol. 1 (2004) 59–79.

———. *Stories with Intent: A Comprehensive Guide to the Parables of Jesus*. Grand Rapids: Eerdmans, 2008.

Soskice, Janet Martin. "The Gift of the Name: Moses and the Burning Bush." *Gregorianum* 79, vol. 2 (1998) 231–46.

Spicq, Ceslas. *L'Épitre aux Hébreux*. Études bibliques. Paris: Lecoffre, 1977.

Steck, Odil Hannes. *Israel und das gewaltsame Geschick der Propheten: Untersuchungen zur Überlieferung des deuteronomistischen Geschichtsbildes im Alten Testament, Spätjudentum und Urchristentum*. Wissenschaftliche Monographien zum Alten und Neuen Testament 23. Neukirchen-Vluyn: Neukirchener, 1967.

Still, Todd D., and David G. Horrell, eds. *After The First Urban Christians: The Socio-Historical Study of Pauline Christianity Twenty-Five Years Later*. New York: T & T Clark, 2009.

Stott, John R. W. *Our Guilty Silence: The Church, the Gospel and the World*. Christian Foundations 22. London: Hodder and Stoughton, 1967.

Strack, Hermann L., and Günter Stemberger. *Introduction to the Talmud and Midrash*. Second edition. Translated and edited by Markus Bockmuehl. Minneapolis: Fortress, 1996.

Straub, S. W. *Crown of Glory: A Choice Collection of New Songs for the Sunday School, Meetings of Praise, Prayer and Conference*. Chicago: Jansen, McClurg, 1876.

Stuhlmann, Rainer. "Beobachtungen und Überlegungen zu Markus iv.26-29." *New Testament Studies* 19, vol. 2 (1972) 153–62.

Tacitus. *The Histories and the Annals*. Translated by C. H. Moore and J. Jackson. 4 vols. Loeb Classical Library. Cambridge: Harvard University Press, 1937.

Taylor, Barbara Brown. "The Gardener in Question." *Christian Century*, August 11, 1999, 82.

Terrien, Samuel. *The Elusive Presence: Toward a New Biblical Theology*. San Francisco: Harper and Row, 1978.

The Book of Alternative Services of the Anglican Church of Canada; with the Revised Common Lectionary. Toronto: Anglican Book Centre, 1985.

Theophrastus. *De Causis Plantarum*. 3 vols. Translated by Benedict Einarson and George K. K. Link. Loeb Classical Library. London: Heinemann; Cambridge, MA: Harvard University Press, 1976–90.

———. *Enquiry into Plants and Minor Works on Odours and Weather Signs* [*De Historia Plantarum*]. 2 vols. Translated by Arthur Hort. Loeb Classical Library. London: Heinemann; New York: Putnam, 1916.

Thielicke, Helmut. *The Waiting Father: Sermons on the Parables of Jesus*. Translated by John W. Doberstein. Cambridge: James Clarke, 1960.

Thomas Aquinas. *Commentary on the Four Gospels, Collected Out of the Works of the Fathers. Vol. 2. St. Mark*. Translated by John Henry Newman. Oxford: Parker; London: Rivington, 1842.

Thrall, Margaret E. *A Critical and Exegetical Commentary on the Second Epistle to the Corinthians*. 2 vols. International Critical Commentary. Edinburgh: T & T Clark, 1994, 2000.

Tolbert, Mary Ann. *Sowing the Gospel: Mark's World in Literary-Historical Perspective*. Minneapolis: Fortress, 1989.

———. "How the Gospel of Mark Builds Character." *Interpretation* 47, vol. 4 (1993) 347–57.

Trites, Allison A. *The New Testament Concept of Witness*. Society for New Testament Studies Monograph Series 31. Cambridge: Cambridge University Press, 1977.

Vanhoozer, Kevin J. *Biblical Narrative in the Philosophy of Paul Ricoeur: A Study in Hermeneutics and Theology*. Cambridge: Cambridge University Press, 1990.

Vermès, Géza. "The Targumic Versions of Genesis 4:3–16." In *Post-Biblical Jewish Studies*, 92–126. Studies in Judaism in Late Antiquity 7. Leiden: Brill, 1975.

von Loewenich, Walther. *Luther's Theology of the Cross*. Translated by Herbert J. A. Bouman. Belfast: Christian Journals, 1976.

Wailes, Stephen L. *Medieval Allegories of Jesus' Parables*. Berkeley: University of California Press, 1987.

Wan, Sze-Kar. *Power in Weakness: Conflict and Rhetoric in Paul's Second Letter to the Corinthians*. The New Testament in Context. Harrisburg, PA: Trinity, 2000.

Webster, John. "Biblical Theology and the Clarity of Scripture." In *Out of Egypt: Biblical Theology and Biblical Interpretation*. Edited by Craig Bartholomew et al., 352–84. Scripture and Hermeneutics 5. Grand Rapids: Zondervan, 2004.

Westendorf, Craig. "The Parable of the Sower (Luke 8:4–15) in the Seventeenth Century." *Lutheran Quarterly* 3, vol. 1 (1989) 49–64.

White, K. D. "The Parable of the Sower." *Journal of Theological Studies* 15, vol. 2 (1964) 300–307.

Wilcox, Max. "The Promise of the 'Seed' in the New Testament and the Targumim." *Journal for the Study of the New Testament* 5 (1979) 2–20.

Williams, Demetrius K. *Enemies of the Cross of Christ: The Terminology of the Cross and Conflict in Philippians*. Journal for the Study of the New Testament: Supplement Series 223. Sheffield: Sheffield Academic, 2002.

Williams, Thomas. "God Who Sows the Seed and Gives the Growth: Anselm's Theology of the Holy Spirit." *Anglican Theological Review* 89, vol. 4 (2007) 611–27.

Willimon, William H. *Undone By Easter: Keeping Preaching Fresh*. Nashville: Abingdon, 2009.

Wilson, Paul Scott. *Setting Words on Fire: Putting God at the Center of the Sermon*. Nashville: Abingdon, 2008.

―――――. *The Four Pages of the Sermon: A Guide to Biblical Preaching*. Nashville: Abingdon, 1999.

Wood, Charles M. *Vision and Discernment: An Orientation in Theological Study*. Studies in Religious and Theological Scholarship. Atlanta: Scholars, 1985.

Wright, N. T. *The New Testament and the People of God. Christian Origins and the Question of God*, Volume 1. Minneapolis: Fortress, 1992.

―――――. *Jesus and the Victory of God. Christian Origins and the Question of God*, Volume 2. Minneapolis: Fortress, 1996.

Yonge, Charles Duke. *The Works of Philo Judæus, the Contemporary of Josephus, Translated from the Greek*. 4 Vols. London: Bohn, 1854–1855.

Ancient Document Index

OLD TESTAMENT/ HEBREW BIBLE

Genesis

1:11–12	22
1:29	23
2:2	91
2:2–3	91
2:8	23
2:15	23
3	62
3:17	61, 62
3:17–19	24, 60, 61, 83
3:19	62
4:3–16	82
4:12	24
8:21–22	24
12:7	30
13:15–16	30
15:3–5, 13, 18	30
17:9	30
18:1–15	12
24:2–4	72
26	53
26:1–11	53
26:12	53
26:3–4, 24	31
26:4	30
26:12–13	31
28:3–4	30
30:22	92
35:12	30

Exodus

3:6	7
3:14	157
15	26
15:17	26
32:13	30
33:1	30
33:19	146
34:5–7	146
34:6	144

Leviticus

19	72
19:18	9
19:19	71, 72
19:23–25	8, 77
25:5, 11	61
25:35–38	8

Numbers

23:10	30
24:5–6	27

Deuteronomy

1:8	30
6:5	9, 51
10:17–18	10
21:18–21	9
22	72
22:9–11	71
26:5b–10b	152
28:4–5, 8–9, 11–12	24
28:12	92

Deuteronomy (continued)

28:38–41	25
34:4	30

Joshua

6:5	61
24:3	30
3:11, 13	13

Ruth

4:12	31
4:17	31

2 Samuel

7:10	27
23:6	51

1 Kings

17:1	25

2 Kings

5:7	91
19:29 (LXX 4 Kgdms)	61

1 Chronicles

17:9	27

2 Chronicles

20:7	30
28:8–15	9

Ezra

9:1–2	31–32, 72

Esther

3:7	10
3:8–11	10

Job

38:12–38	23

Psalms

1:3	27
8:5–7	175
22:24	30
44:2	27
47:2, 7	13
65:9–13	23
65:13	37
66:1	37
78:2	18
80:8–9, 14–15	27
83:18	13
89:2	38
92:12–14	27
95:7	44
97:5	13
104:24	23
104:27–29	23
105:6	30
110:4	175
127	62
127:2	62
128	62
144:12–13, 15	26

Proverbs

3:9–10	24
24:30–31	51

Ecclesiastes

11:4–6	63

Song of Solomon

6:12	62

Isaiah

3:13–14	147
5	27, 79
5:1–10	27
5:2	95
5:7	21
6	56
6:1	51
6:9–10	15, 51
6:13	32
11:1	28

34:4	76	4:21	68
41:8	30		
43:8–10	151	**Hosea**	
43:10	146, 151		
44:7–9	151	2:25	33
45:19	30	4:1	148
53:2	27	9:10	76
55	56	9:13	27
55:10–11	51, 65	10:1	27
60:21	27	14:6–7	27
61:3	27	14:8	26
65:9	30	**Joel**	

Jeremiah

		1:12	76
		2:22	76
1:10	144	4:13	63
2:21	27		
2:3	27	**Amos**	
4:3	51		
8:13	76, 77	4:7–9	23
11:17	27	4:9	76
17:8	27	9:15	27
24:6	27		
31:27–28	27	**Jonah**	
31:33–34	175		
32:41	27	4:6–8	51
33:26	30		
42:10	27	**Micah**	
45:4	27		
51:36	10	4:13	13
		6:1–3	148
Ezekiel		6:9	76
		7:1	76
15:1–8	27	7:4	51
17:3–6	68		
17:5–10	27	**Habakkuk**	
17:22	69		
17:22–23	27, 68	3:17	76
20:5	30		
31:3	68	**Haggai**	
31:5–6	68	1:5–6	25
31:9	69	1:9–11	25
31:11	69	2:17–19	25
37:13	92	2:19	76

Daniel

Zechariah

4:10	68	4:14	13
4:12	68	6:5	13
4:17	69	9:16–17	25–26

APOCRYPHA

Sirach/Ecclesiasticus

11:14, 70–19	82
35:12, 14, 19	10
44:21	30

Tobit

3:7–15	7
4:12	30, 32

Wisdom of Solomon

2:16	71
15:9	71
17:6	61

PSEUDEPIGRAPHA

Ahiqar (Stories of Ahiqar)

8:35	78

1 Enoch

2–5	37
22:6–7	82
62:8	33
65:12	32
80:2–3	26
84:6	32
89:75	72
97:8–10	82

4 Ezra

5:23–27	28–29
8:6	57
8:16	30
8:41	57
9:30	30
9:31–37	57
12:31–38	19
14:44–47	19

Jubilees

11	xxii
11:10–24	51
16:13	32
16:17–18, 26	32
22:11–12	32
22:20–21	33
22:27	32
25:3	32
26:34	33
30:7–10	32
45:3	7

2 Maccabees

7:22	62
7:22–23	91

3 Maccabees

6:3	30

4 Maccabees

6:22	30
18:1	30

Prayer of Manasseh

1	7

Psalms of Solomon

9:9	30
14:3–5	28, 69
18:3	30

Sibylline Oracles

3	53
3:248–60	53
3:263–64	53

2 Baruch

39:7	34, 79
42:4	72

Testament of Abraham

13:3–9	82, 231

Testament of Levi

8:15	30
17–18	32

Testament of Moses

3:9	7

NEW TESTAMENT

Matthew

3:8	77
3:10	77
3:12	33, 74
5:43–45	35
6:25–30	34–35, 84
6:26	61
6:27	44
6:31–33	61
7:9	45
7:16–20	78
9:38	63, 75
10:1	8
10:6	44
10:18	163
10:24	55
11:11	191
11:12	74
11:14	192
11:28	195
12:11	45
12:33	77
13	70
13:3–9	40, 47
13:10–15	15
13:12	16
13:16	16
13:18–23	40, 47
13:23	52
13:25	75
13:29	74
13:29	74
13:24–30	41, 70
13:24–50	19
13:36–43	19, 41
13:31–32	40, 66
13:31–33	4
13:32	68
13:33	67
13:34–35	18
13:36–43	70
13:38	73
13:41, 43	73
13:44	67
13:45–46	67
13:49	74
15:24	44
16:17–19	16
16:23	45
17:12–13	192
17:17	46
17:20	66
17:25	45
18:12	45
18:15–17	75
18:17	45
18:21–35	10
20:1–16	79
20:28	97
21:18–19	77
21:28	45
21:28–31	79
21:33–46	79
21:34	77
22:23–33	7
22:29	7
22:42	45
23:13	16, 46
23:35	231
25:29	16
26:25	45
26:64	45
27:11	45
27:22	106

Mark

1:35	194
1:44	17
2:2	49
2:27	90
3:14–15	50
4	51, 70, 223
4:1–34	57
4:1–20	215
4:2–9	40, 47
4:3–9	13
4:6	51
4:9	48
4:10	18
4:11–12	18

Mark *(continued)*

4:11	40
4:12	51
4:13	47
4:13–20	47
4:14	49, 55, 56, 63
4:15	55
4:14–20	13, 47–48
4:17	50
4:19	50
4:20	50, 219
4:26–29	40, 48, 60, 70, 223
4:27	62
4:27–28	221
4:28	61
4:29	63, 227
4:30–32	40, 48, 66, 70
4:30–34	67, 69
4:30	69
4:31	66
4:32	68
4:33–34	49
5:25–34	75
5:43	17
6:11	163
6:13	50
7:36	17
8:32	49
8:32–33	218
8:33	46, 49, 50
8:35	viii
8:38	50, 219
9:9	17
9:13	192
9:14–29	50
9:19	46
10:22	49
10:23–26	49
10:25	50
10:27	58
10:29–30	49–50, 218
10:30	50
10:45	97
11:12–14	76, 77
11:27–30	17
12:1–12	79
12:2	77
12:18–27	7
12:24	3, 7
12:25	7
12:26	7
12:27	7
12:41–44	50
13:9	163
13:19	50
13:24	50
13:28–29	42
14:11	50
14:13	46
14:14	50
14:50	50, 219
15:2	45
16:6–7	200

Luke

1:55	30
3:9	77
3:17	33
4:17–19	18
6:43–44	78
6:44	77
7:28	191
8:2–3	218
8:4–15	41
8:5–8	40, 47
8:11	56
8:11–15	40, 47
8:15	52
9:2	163
9:4	46
9:5	163
9:23	viii
9:28	194
10:2	75
10:16	59
11:5	45
11:11	45
11:52	16
12:13	12
12:13–21	229
12:14–15	81
12:15–21	12
12:16	81
12:16–21	41, 81
12:18, 24	84
12:22–28	84

12:22–38	35–36	1:45	170
12:25	44	3:3	viii
12:33–34	84	3:5–6	viii
13	78	3:8	62
13:6	76	3:11	171
13:6–9	8, 41, 76, 79	3:28	192
13:7–9	76–77	3:30	ix, 127, 192
13:18–19	40–41, 66	3:32	170
13:19	68	4:35	45
13:20–21	67	4:35–38	96
14:5	45	5:17	90
14:28	45	5:19–21	92
15:4	45	5:30	92–93, 169
15:11–12	81	5:31–34	170
16:1–9	8	5:36–37	170
16:19–31	11	5:39	170
16:29–31	11	5:46	170
17:6	66	6:15	14
17:7–8	45	6:51	94
17:20	64	6:57	94
18:1–8	10	7:28	93
20:9–19	79	8:13	170
20:10	77	8:14	170
20:27–28	7	8:17–18	171
20:38	11	8:28	93
21:13	163	8:58	170
22:70	45	9:39–41	16
22:71	164	10:3–5	199
23:3	45	10:27	199
24:22–24	193	10:14–15	94, 171
24:25	193	10:25	170
24:27	18, 193	12:23	96
24:32	193	12:23–25	95
24:34	193	12:24	viii, 54, 181, 221, 226
24:35–36	193	12:26	122
24:44–45	193	12:41	170
24:30–31, 35	193	12:49	93
24:44–48	163	12:49–50	93
		14:10	93
		14:10–11	93
		14:11	170

John

1:4		14:24	93
1:6	170	14:26	171
1:7–8	170	15:1	79, 221
1:15	170	15:1–6	79
1:19–21	191–192	15:1–8	41, 78
1:29	192	15:4–5	80, 90, 195
1:31–34	192	15:5	179
1:32–34	170		

John (continued)

15:8	80, 94, 96
15:9	80, 94
15:26–27	171
16:13–15	171
17:18	94
19:35	172
19:36	63
20:15	221
20:21	94
21:24	172

Acts

1:1–2	167
1:3	167
1:8	146, 163, 168
1:22	164, 168
2:4	201
2:22	168
2:31–33, 36	164
2:40	166
3:9–15	193
3:12	58
3:15	166
3:25	30
4:33	167
5:30–32	168
5:31	194
6:5	166
6:8	168
6:13	164
7:2–53	166
7:55–56	166–167
7:58	164
8:13	168
8:25	166
10:38	168
10:38–44	164–165
10:39, 41	165
10:40	166
10:42	165
10:43	165, 166
10:44	165
10:45–46	165
10:47	166
11:26	130
12:10	61
13:31	166
14:3	168
14:15–17	34
15:7–8	168
15:7–9	193
15:15	166
18:5	166
18:24–28	85
19:11	168
20:21, 24	166
20:24	166
20:26	164
20:27	128
21:39	126
22:3	126
22:5	164
22:14–15	166
22:18	163
22:20	166
22:25–29	126
23:11	163, 165
26:5	164
26:15–16	167
26:22–23	165
28:23	166
28:24	166

Romans

1:3	34
1:4	197
1:16	114
1:19–20	37
1:20	136
3:23	127
4:13–18	30
4:24–25	97
5:8	107
6:4	viii, 98
6:5	98
6:8	98
8:11	114
8:15–16	174
8:17	118
8:19–22	118
9:1	174
9:7–8	30
10:14	114, 208
10:17	ix, 161, 179

11:1	30	12:10, 28	197
15:5	106	15:12	110
15:16	107	15:15	173–174
15:18–19	113, 173	15:26	110
15:19	197	15:30–31	110
16:25	19	15:36	181
		15:36–38	55
		15:42–44	55

1 Corinthians

1:9	207		
1:17	102		

2 Corinthians

1:18	99, 106, 197, 207	1:3–5, 8–9	104
1:19–25	102	1:8	110, 145
1:21	207	1:9	110, 187
1:21–25	207	1:20	141
1:23	187	1:22	177
1:23–25	100	1:24	101
1:26–30	119	2:7	121
1:28–29	159	2:14–16	100
2:1–5	102, 207	2:14–17	107
2:2	103	2:17	198
2:3	108	3:1	102
2:4	114, 173	3:2–3	112
2:4–5	103, 108, 197	3:3	173
2:6–7	187	3:4–6	108
2:7	121	3:5–6	127
2:7–8	19	3:17–18	112
3:6	85	4:1	187
3:6–7	65, 220, 224	4:1–7	186
3:7	137, 179	4:5	106, 108, 119, 187
3:9	187	4:7	xxiii, 108, 197
4:2	103	4:8–10	111
4:8	119	4:8–11	104
4:9–13	186	4:11	106, 107
4:10	106, 119	4:12	119, 121
4:10–13	104	4:16	111
4:16	105, 127	4:18	112
6:14	197	5:5	177
6:20	163	5:12	102
7:7	105	5:14	107, 108
7:23	163	5:17	116
9:16	186	6:4, 9	117
9:16–17	107, 186	6:4–10	104
9:24–27	109	6:7	197
10:12	58	6:9	186
10:16	101	6:9–10	205
11:1	105, 127	6:14	72
11:26	101	6:17	74
12:8	103	9:6, 8, 10	224

2 Corinthians (continued)

9:8–10	34–35
10:10	102
11:4	188
11:5	102
11:6	85, 102
11:13	102
11:22	30
11:23–27	104
11:24–25	221
12:4	19
12:7–10	104
12:9	115, 121, 206
12:9–10	109, 195
12:10	99, 186
12:11	102
12:10	186
12:12	113, 173, 197
13:3–4	197
13:4	109
13:10	111

Galatians

1:7	188
2:15	45
2:19–20	97, 108, 112
2:20	viii, 116
3:1–5	113
3:2–3	113
3:5	113, 173
3:16	34
3:16–29	30
3:28	115
3:29	34
4:9	198
4:9–10	115
5:16–25	113
6:9	223, 227
6:14–15	115

Ephesians

1:9–10	19
1:14	175
1:19–20	197
3:4–6	19
3:7	197
3:16	197
3:20	197
3:20–21	211
6:20	194

Philippians

1:1	121
1:12–14, 20–21	121
1:27	121
1:28–30	120
2	101, 107, 185
2:3	120
2:3–5	196
2:5	196
2:5–7	ix
2:5–6, 8	120
2:6–8	120
2:6–9	xxii, 185
2:6–11	124, 196
2:8–9	100
2:12–13	196–197
2:30	121
3	185
3:4–6	126
3:4–11	185
3:7	106
3:7–8	126
3:8, 10–11	117
3:10	106
3:11–12	121
3:12	106, 121, 185
3:20	121
4:2–3	221
4:3	72

Colossians

1:11	197
1:24	105, 128
1:26–27	19
1:29	197
2:8	106
2:12	197
2:16–17	115
3:3	108
3:10	120

1 Thessalonians

1:4–5	173

Ancient Document Index

1:5	186, 197
1:6	127
1:7	117
1:10	174
2:13	59

2 Thessalonians

1:11	197

1 Timothy

2:5	161

2 Timothy

1:8	174
2:11	98

Hebrews

1:1–2	175
1:2	174
2:3–4	174
2:4	174–175
2:6–8	175
2:16	30
4:12	65
6:4–8	56
7:17	175
10:10	143
10:14–17	175
11:4	189, 231
12:1	175
12:2	175

James

1:21	49

1 Peter

1:23	viii
1:23–25	56–57
5:4	200

2 Peter

3:11–12	64

1 John

1:3	141
3:12	230
5:6–11	172

Jude

1:12	
1:25	127
12	78

Revelation

1:18	130
14:15	63
21:5	x

DEAD SEA SCROLLS

1Q21 (Aramaic Testament of Levi)

a 17–18	32

1QH^a (Thanksgiving Hymns^a)

14.15–17	28, 69

1QIsa^a

6:13	32

4QMMT

78–81	72
84	32

11Q ApPs^a (Apocryphal Psalms^a)

IV.6	32

RABBINIC SOURCES

Mishnah

Baba Qamma

8:6	30

Baba Meṣiʿa

7:1   30

Kilʾayim

1:1   72
2:8–9   71

Middot

3:8   27

Nazir

1:5   66

Nedarim

3:11   30

Niddah

5:2   66, 75

Pirqe ʾAbot

1:2   38

Ṭeharot

8:8   66

Tosefta

Berakot

6:8   53

Soṭah

10:6   54

Babylonian Talmud

Ketubbot

112a   54

Taʿanit

2a   92

MIDRASHIC, TARGUMIC, HAGGADIC, AND DEVOTIONAL TEXTS

ʾAbot de Rabbi Nathan

4   38
7   12
16   77

Genesis Rabbah

13:6   37
59:8   72
73:8   54
86:6   64

Deuteronomy Rabbah

7:7   37

Numbers Rabbah

12:11   54

Pesiqta Rabbati

195b   37

Samaritan Targum

Lev 19:19   72

Shemoneh ʿEsreh

    7, 92

Targum Neofiti

Gen 26:12   53

GRECO-ROMAN AND HELLENISTIC JEWISH TEXTS

Cicero

On the Ends of Good and Evil (De finibus Bonorum et Malorum)

5.27.80	110

Against Gaius Verres (In Verrum)

5.162, 165	105

Columella

Agriculture (De Re Rustica)

11.3.29	70–71

Josephus

Antiquities

1.24	115
1.260	53
1.46	62
1.52–53	82
1.53–61	230
1.54	83
1.60–61	82
15.395	27

Jewish War

5.210	27
7.203	105

Marcus Terentius Varro

Three Books on Agriculture (Rerum Rusticarum Libri Tres)

1.44.1–2	52

Minucius Felix

Octavius

11.9	106

Seneca

Moral Epistles (Epistulae morales)

24.19–20	110
71.26–27	110

Philo

Allegorical Interpretation 1, 2, 3 (Legum Allegoriae)

1 §5	91
1 §6	91
1 §7–8, 16	91

On the Cherubim (De cherubim)

§87	91

On the Change of Names (De mutatione nominum)

268–69	53

Against Flaccus (In Flaccum)

72	105

On the Creation of the World (De opificio mundi)

3	115
40–43	61
80–81	61
167	61

On the Special Laws (De specialibus legibus)

3.46	72
4.203–18	72

Questions and Answers on Genesis (Quaestiones et solutiones in Genesin)

4.189	53

Pliny the Elder

Natural History (Naturalis historia)

18.21.4–5	52, 70

Tacitus

Histories (Historiae)

5.5	27

Theophrastus

Concerning the History of Plants (De Historia Plantarum)

1.163	22
3.1.4	21–22
8.7.4	52

Enquiry into Plants (De Causis Plantarum)

1.1–2	22
1.34	21–22
5.1–2	22

EARLY CHRISTIAN SOURCES

1 Clement

24:5	54

Anselm

On the Harmony of God's Foreknowledge, Predestination, and Grace with Free Choice (De Concordia)

3.1	179

3.6	179, 180

Augustine

Free Will (De Libero Arbitrio)

2.16.43	137

Of True Religion (De Vera Religione)

29.52	136
42.79	136

On Christian Doctrine (De Doctrina Christiana)

1.3	135
1.4	136
3.9.13	137
4.5.7–8	137–138
4.16.33	137

Sermons on New Testament Lessons

73.3	41

Tractates on the Gospel of John

82.1	95
87.1	95

Justin Martyr

First Apology (Apologia i)

13.4	106

Origen

Commentary on the Gospel of Matthew (Commentarium in evangelium Matthaei)

27:22	106

Name Index

Abel (biblical figure), 81–83, 189, 229–33
Abimelech (biblical figure), 31, 53
Abram/Abraham (biblical figure), 7, 11–13, 30, 32–34, 51, 53, 72, 159, 170, 193, 228, 229
Adam (biblical figure), 5, 23, 36, 55–57, 59, 61–62, 216–17, 230
Adar, Zvi, 25
Agrippa, King (biblical figure), 167
Ahab, King (biblical figure), 25
Aland, Kurt, xiii
Alexander, Patrick H., xiii
Allison, Dale, 37, 68, 69, 75
Althaus, Paul, 184
Anaxagoras, 21
Anderson, Albert A., 63
Anderson, Ray S., 199, 209
Andrew (biblical figure), 218
Anselm, Saint, 178–81
Apollos (biblical figure), 65, 85, 120, 220, 224
Arida, Robert M., 16
Aristotle, 21, 207
Augustine, Saint, xx, 5, 41, 95, 135–38, 140, 142, 148, 160, 167, 176, 198
Aune, David E., 92

Barnabas (biblical figure), 34, 168
Barrett, C. K., 72, 91–93, 95, 103, 115, 205
Barth, Karl, xiii, 140–43, 146, 149, 156, 160, 167, 176, 191
Bartholomew (biblical figure), 218
Bartow, Charles L., x

Bauckham, Richard, 131
Baxter, Richard, 108, 198
Beasley-Murray, George, 27, 93, 95, 170
Benjamin (biblical figure), 126
Betz, Hans Dieter, 103
Black, C. Clifton 85, 180–81
Blomberg, Craig, 73
Boaz (biblical figure), 31
Boda, Mark, 31
Bonner, Gerald, 136
Boreland, Dustin, xi
Borg, Marcus J., 33
Botterweck, G. Johannes, xiv
Bowker, John W., 16, 51, 55–56
Boyarin, Daniel, 12
Bozarth, Alla Renée, ix–x
Bromiley, Geoffrey W., xiv
Brooke, George J., 28
Brower, Kent E., 33, 75
Brown, Adam, xi
Brown, Raymond E., 27, 91, 93, 96, 170–72
Brown, Sally A., 123–25
Bruce, F. F., 126
Brueggemann, Walter, xx, 140, 143–47, 149, 176
Brunner, Emil, 63, 75, 99
Bullinger, Heinrich, 59
Bultmann, Rudolf, 95, 161–62, 209
Burleigh, J. H. S., 136
Buttrick, David, 82, 83, 182–83
Byron, John, 12, 82, 83, 230

Name Index

Cain (biblical figure), 12, 24, 81–83, 229–33
Calvin, John, 184
Campbell, Charles L., 128–30
Campbell, Jane Montgomery, 64
Carter, Warren, 68
Carter, William G., 48
Castelli, Elizabeth A., 105
Catchpole, David R., 73
Charlesworth, James H., xiv
Chazon, Esther G., 116
Chrysostom, John, 16, 67
Cicero, Marcus Tullius, xv, xvi, 105, 110, 198, 207
Claudius, Matthias, 64
Cleopas (biblical figure), 192
Clidemus, 22
Columella, 70–71
Cosgrove, Charles H., 105, 113–17
Courey, David, xi, 184
Cousar, Charles B., 1907, 112, 117, 118, 128
Coward, Howard, 148
Craddock, Fred B., 109
Cranfield, C. E. B., 57–58, 114
Crawford, Cory D., 51
Crossan, John Dominic, 43
Cyril of Alexandria, 16

Dahl, Nils A., 42–43, 53, 67, 74
Dale, Ron, 58
Daniel (biblical figure), 68
David, King (biblical figure), 31, 33–34, 164
Davies, W. D., 37, 38, 75
Derrett, J. Duncan M., 8
Derrida, Jacques, 148, 190
Di Lella, Alexander A., 82
Diogenes, 21
Doty, William, 75
Dreyfus, François, 7
Drury, John, 49
Duke, Paul Simpson, 65–66, 73, 183
Dupont, Jacques, 64

Edwards, J. Kent, 184
Einstein, Albert, vii
Elijah (biblical figure), 25, 192, 208

Elliger, Karl, xiii
Elliott, Mark Adam, 22, 28, 29, 32, 51
Ellul, Jacques, xx, 188–90, 194–95, 210
Elowsky, Joel C., 95
Engberg-Pedersen, Troels, 101
Epaphroditus (biblical figure), 121
Esau (biblical figure), 33
Euodia (biblical figure), 221
Evans, Craig A., 51, 56
Eve (biblical figure), 23, 36, 59, 216–17, 230
Ezekiel (biblical figure), 68–69, 181
Ezra (biblical figure), 19, 31

Fee, Gordon D., 187, 207
Fenton, John C., 95
Finamore, Stephen, 163
Finkel, Asher, 38
Fish, Stanley E., xxi, 136, 138
Fishbane, Michael, 12
Florence, Anna Carter, 140, 149, 151, 155, 159
Flusser, David, 18, 37
Forde, Gerhard O., 124
Foshan, Toby, 148
Freedman, H., 54
Freedman, David Noel, xiii
Frei, Hans, 128–29
Friedrich, Gerhard, xiv
Frye, Northrop, 185
Funk, Robert W., 5, 68–69

Gerhardsson, Birger, 51, 66
Gerrard, Aaron, xi
Glover, Raymond F., 64
Goldin, Judah, 38
Gorman, Michael J., 98–99, 105, 106, 114–17, 121, 124
Greenman, Jeffrey P., 189
Greidanus, Sidney 59
Gross, Nancy Lammers, 122, 153, 160–62, 209

Haggai (biblical figure), 25
Hall, Christopher A., 226
Hamel, Gildas, 52
Harrisville, Roy A., 110, 185, 208
Hauerwas, Stanley, 129

Hawthorne, Gerald F., 196
Hayes, Christine, 32, 72
Hays, Richard B., 207
Heidegger, Martin, 98
Heil, John Paul, 49
Heim, S. Mark, 125
Hellerman, Joseph H., 120-21
Hengel, Martin, 105-6
Henry, Matthew, 95
Himmelfarb, Martha, 32
Hopkins, Jasper, 180
Hoskyns, Edwyn Clement, 91
Howse, Christopher, 29
Hubbard, Robert L., 31
Hultgren, Arland J., 53, 77
Hunzinger, Claus-Hunno, 66

Instone-Brewer, David, 73, 77
Isaac, Ephraim, 33
Isaac (biblical figure), 7, 30-33, 53-54, 72, 193
Isaac, Rabbi, 72
Isaiah (biblical figure), 15-16, 18, 56, 151

Jacob (biblical figure), 7, 30, 33, 193
James (biblical figure), 17
Janzen, J. Gerald, 7
Jaubert, Anne, 79
Jenkins, Philip, 59
Jeremiah (biblical figure), 76
Jeremias, Joachim, 53
Joanna (biblical figure), 218
Johanan bar Nappaha (rabbi), 92
Johanan ben Zakkai (rabbi), 37-38
John (biblical figure), 17, 193-94, 218
John of the Apocalypse, 221
John the Baptist (biblical figure), ix, 17, 33, 74, 77, 80, 127, 153, 169-70, 172, 176, 191-92, 194
Johnson, Darrell W., 172
Joseph (biblical figure),
Josephus, Flavius, xv, xvi, 29, 53, 62, 79, 82-83, 105-6, 115, 230
Joshua ben Nehemiah (rabbi), 37
Judas (biblical figure), 50, 164, 194, 218-20
Juel, Donald H., 48, 55, 60

Jüngel, Eberhard, 5
Justin Martyr, xv, 106

Käsemann, Ernst, 117
Keegan, Terence J., 49
Keener, Craig S., 37, 67
Kissinger, Warren S., 5
Kittel, Gerhard, xiv
Klauck, Hans J., 61
Kleinknecht, Karl Theodor, 125
Knowles, Michael P., vii-x, xxii, 9, 18-19, 51, 107, 112, 127-28, 147, 198, 229
Kugel, James L., 12, 32, 72

Lamott, Anne, 205
LaRue, Cleophus J., 139
Lathrop, Gordon W., 98
Lazarus (biblical figure), 11-13, 229
Lehmann, Helmut T., 123
Levinas, Emmanuel, 190
Lim, Timothy H., 114, 2215-16
Lindars, Barnabas, 95
Loew, J. P., xiii
Loewe, H., 37
Loewenich, Walther von, 122-23
Long, Thomas G., 140, 149, 151, 159
Longenecker, Bruce W., 119
Longenecker, Richard N., 17-18
Lose, David J., 129
Lowe, Matthew F., xi, 110, 162
Luccock, Halford E., 48
Luther, Martin, xx, 5, 98, 122-25, 142, 157, 184, 200
Luz, Ulrich, 12

Marcus, Joel, 52, 57, 61
Marshall, I. Howard, 81
Martin, Ralph P., 196
Mary Magdalene (biblical figure), 218, 221
Matthew (biblical figure), 218
Matthews, Victor H., 26
McArthur, Harvey K., 66
McClure, John S., 190
McGrath, Alister E., 123
McIver, Robert K., 52
Meeks, Wayne A., 105, 119

Meir (rabbi), 53-54
Merklein, Helmut, 207-8
Metzger, Bruce M., 29
Meyer, Marvin W., 19
Miller, Dale, 51
Miller, Patricia, 51
Minucius Felix, xvi, 106
Moberly, R. W. L., 146
Moltmann, Jürgen, 89, 124, 209-10
Montefiore, Claude C., 37
Moore, Henry, 178
Morris, Leon, 95
Moses (biblical figure), 11, 38, 44, 91, 157, 163, 166
Mudge, Lewis L., 152, 155
Mussner, Franz, 69

Najman, Hindy, 106, 115-16
Neusner, Jacob, 54
Newbigin, Lesslie, 8, 172
Nicol, George C., 30
Nida, E. A., xiii
Nitzan, Bilhah, 116
Nodet, Étienne, 53

Oakman, Douglas E., 52-53, 71, 73
Oden, Thomas C., 41, 54, 226
Origen, xv, 5, 106
Osborne, Grant R., 163

Pape, Lance B., 154, 156-57
Payne, Philip B., 52, 53
Pelikan, Jaroslav, 123
Penna, Romano, 208
Perkins, Pheme, 67, 69
Pesch, Rudolf, 51
Peter (biblical figure), 16, 17, 49, 58, 59, 164-65, 168, 193-94, 218-19, 220-21
Peterson, Eugene H., 200
Philip (biblical figure), 93, 168
Philo of Alexandria, xv, xvi, 53, 61, 72, 82-83, 91, 105, 115, 230
Pickett, Raymond, 102, 103, 119
Pilate (biblical figure), 63, 193
Pliny the Elder, xvi, 52
Porter, Stanley E., xi, 156
Porton, Gary G., 7

Postman, Neil, 188
Prenter, Regin, 200
Pseudo-Dionysius, 148
Purves, Andrew, xxiii-xxiv, 96, 101-2, 109, 128, 191, 198-99, 200, 209

Quicke, Michael J., 126-27, 178
Quintilian, 207

Rahlfs, Alfred, xiii
Rashkover, Randi, 141-42
Ratzinger, Joseph Cardinal, 69-70
Reagan, Charles, 153
Rebekah (biblical figure), 31
Rengstorf, Karl Heinrich, 92, 174
Resner, Jr., André, 207
Richardson, Herbert, 180
Ricoeur, Paul, xx, 3-5, 140, 143, 149-62, 167, 176, 189-91, 209
Ringgren, Helmer, xiv, 148
Robinson, Jason C., 156
Rohrbaugh, Richard, 5
Ruth (biblical figure), 31

Sabin, Marie, 12-13, 51, 63, 69
Sahlin, Harald, 62
Sandmel, Samuel, 30
Sarason, Richard S., 54
Saul of Tarsus (biblical figure), 205
Savage, Timothy B., 102, 104, 106, 117, 120
Schellenberg, Ryan S., 66, 71
Schuchardt, Read Mercer, 189
Schürer, Emil, 92
Schweitzer, Eduard , 28
Scott, Bernard Brandon, 12, 42, 54, 61, 71, 73-74, 77, 82, 83
Seamands, Stephen, 199-200
Seneca the Younger, 110
Shi, Wenhua, 105, 108, 110, 114, 119, 126, 207
Simeon ben Yoḥai (rabbi), 54
Simeon the Just (rabbi), 37-38
Simon (biblical figure), 218
Simon, Maurice, 54
Simon ben Kosiba, 239
Simpson, Albert B., 105

Skehan, Patrick W., 82
Smith, Sandra K., xi
Snodgrass, Klyne R., 5, 16, 18, 51, 67-68, 84-85
Soskice, Janet Martin, 148
Spicq, Ceslas, 174
Steck, Odil Hannes, 127
Stemberger, Günter, 37, 38
Stephen (biblical figure), 166-68, 204
Stern, David, 12
Stewart, David, 153
Stewart, Patrick, 160
Stott, John R. W., 162
Strack, Hermann L., 37, 38
Straub, Maria, 36
Stuhlmann, Rainer, 61, 62
Susanna (biblical figure), 218
Syntyche (biblical figure), 221

Tacitus, xv, 29
Taylor, Barbara Brown, 75
Terrien, Samuel, 144-45
Thackeray, Henry St. John, 106
Theophilus (biblical figure), 167
Theophrastus, xv, 22, 52
Thielicke, Helmut 41-42, 65, 194-95
Thomas (biblical figure), 218
Thomas Aquinas, 225-26
Thrall, Margaret E., 72, 115
Tolbert, Mary Ann, 5, 49
Toly, Noah J., 189

Trites, Allison A., 169, 175
Tsui, Tommy, xi

Vanhoozer, Kevin J., 154-55
Varro, Marcus Terentius, xvi, 52
Vermès, Géza, 82
Victor of Antioch, 16

Wailes, Stephen L., 41
Wan, Sze-Kar, 102-3, 107, 109
Webster, John, 158
Westendorf, Craig, 41
White, K. D., 54
Wilcox, Max, 30, 33
Williams, Demetrius, 102, 117, 120, 121, 123
Williams, Thomas, 178, 180
Willimon, William H., 161, 191
Wilson, Paul Scott, v, vii-x, 98, 114, 138, 142, 203-4
Wood, Charles M., 142
Wright, N. T., 5, 14, 59

Xerxes, King (biblical figure), 10

Yonge, C. D., 91

Zechariah (biblical figure), 25
Zechariah [ben Berechiah] (biblical figure), 231

www.ingramcontent.com/pod-product-compliance
Lightning Source LLC
Chambersburg PA
CBHW022000220426
43663CB00007B/903